BUSINESS CHINESE 101

www.royalcollins.com

BUSINESS CHINESE 101

GUAN DAOXIONG

Books Beyond Boundaries

ROYAL COLLINS

Business Chinese 101

Guan Daoxiong

First published in 2021 by Royal Collins Publishing Group Inc.
Groupe Publication Royal Collins Inc.
BKM Royalcollins Publishers Private Limited

Headquarters: 550-555 boul. René-Lévesque O Montréal (Québec) H2Z1B1 Canada
India office: 805 Hemkunt House, 8th Floor, Rajendra Place, New Delhi 110008

ISBN: 978-1-4878-0855-6

To find out more about our publications, please visit www.royalcollins.com.

Preface

Chinese 101 is a series of handbooks of conversational Chinese designed for non-native speakers of Chinese who study or work in China as well as primary and intermediate learners of Chinese. The content is reasonably simple with a clear aim. It is developed to enable users to learn, imitate, and master useful vocabulary and sentences in a meaningful context so that they can quickly improve Chinese skills and easily adapt to Chinese culture in the short term.

Chinese 101 is composed of *Survival Chinese 101*, *Business Chinese 101* and *Travel Chinese 101*. Each book in the series is divided into thematic units that cover major aspects of living, doing business or traveling in China. Thematic units are subdivided into 101 situational topics or chapters, hence the title of the series. And each unit starts with a key sentence followed by short and practical dialogues.

Business Chinese 101 is composed of 10 thematic units, including "Business Social Intercourse," "Business Communication," "On a Business Trip," "Business Negotiation," "Around the Office,"

"Having a Meeting," "Human Resources," "Marketing," "Freight Transport Service," and "Investigation and Investment." Each thematic unit includes 9 to 11 topics. The content of topics under the same thematic unit is interrelated while each is also a unique and complete chapter. Each topic chapter includes the following 6 components:

Key Sentence: A sentence that represents the core of the chapter. For example, the key sentence in the chapter of "General Inquiry" is "I would like to inquire about this product's price" while in the chapter of "Advertisement Planning" is "This time our advertisement should give prominence to brand image."

Substitution: Generally, three to six substitution phrases are provided for learners. For example, the phrase "brand image" in the key sentence "This time our advertisement should give prominence to brand image" can be substituted with "special feature of the product," "fashion trend," "casual style" or "environment-friendly motif," extending the flexibility of the key sentence and the scope of application.

Extension: Four sentences that relate to the topic of the chapter are provided for readers to choose to use in relevant situations. For example, in the chapter of "General Inquiry," extension sentences like "Do you want to know the retail price of this product?" "This is our products' catalogue and price list" and "We do not currently have this service yet" are listed.

Dialogue: A situational dialogue is presented through which users can learn how Chinese people express themselves in this context and their logic of speaking. It is suggested that learners recite the dialogue in order to express their opinions and understand Chinese culture.

Related Words: A list of words closely related to the topic is provided for readers to choose from in practical applications. Words that have already appeared in Key Sentence, Substitution, Extension, and Dialogue are generally not included in Related Words to avoid redundancy.

Cultural Navigation: This is one of the most unique aspects of the *Chinese 101* series. In *Business Chinese 101*, this section covers social and cultural phenomena related to business activities, management, and work environment in today's China, as well as situations where confusion or misunderstandings can arise due to differences in language, traditions and cultural backgrounds. The section aims to provide a clear and engaging explanation of these issues to help the readers navigate the Chinese business world.

For the convenience of the users, each book also provides a list of sentences in the appendix that may be used in emergency contexts in China. Besides, the appendix of *Business Chinese 101* includes a list of 30 notable Chinese companies as well as a curriculum vitae template for the convenience of the user's reference.

With English translation and CDs, this series of handbooks should be a useful companion and reference book for foreign people living in China. The series can also be used as a textbook for primary and intermediate students' conversational Chinese as well as for self-study.

During the process of material collection, textual preparation and editorial revision, I received constant guidance, support and assistance from Ms. Li Caixia, Senior Editor of Chinese Division at the Foreign Language Teaching and Research Press. I am deeply indebted to her. I would like to thank Editor Meng Jiawen for her contributions to the book. I will appreciate all the suggestions.

Guan Daoxiong
Santa Barbara, California

Contents

Business Communication

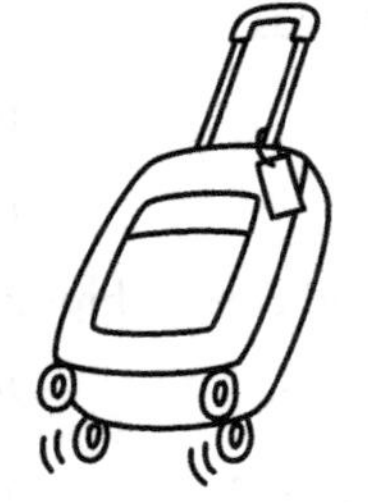

On a Business Trip

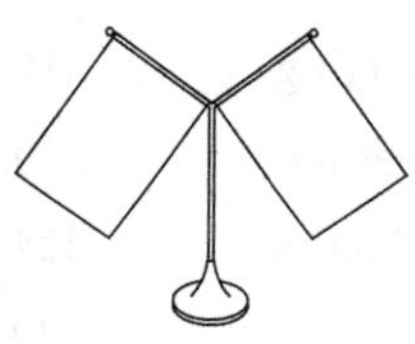

Business Negotiation

Around the Office

Having a Meeting

Human Resources

Marketing

Freight Transport Services

Investigation and Investment

Business Social Intercourse

1 Names and Forms of Address

Key Sentence

Qǐngwèn, nínguìxìng?
请问，您贵姓?
May I ask your last name?

Substitution

nǐmen liǎngwèi
你们两位
two of you

nǐmen jīnglǐ
你们经理
your manager

nǐmen lǎozǒng
你们老总
your boss

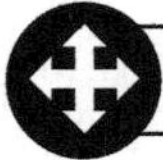

Extension

1. Wǒ xìng Wáng, jiào Wáng Zhìyuǎn.
   我姓王，叫王志远。
   My last name is Wang, and my name is Wang Zhiyuan.

2. Wǒ de Zhōngwén míngzi jiào Shǐ Qiángshēng.
   我的中文名字叫史强生。
   My Chinese name is Shi Qiangsheng.

3. Nǐ zhīdào nà wèi nǚshì jiàoshénme míngzi ma?
   你知道那位女士叫什么名字吗?
   Do you know that lady's name?

4. Tā shì wǒmen de shìchǎngbù jīnglǐ.
他是我们的市场部经理。
He is our Marketing Department Manager.

A: Qǐngwèn nín guìxìng?
请问您贵姓?
May I ask your last name?

B: Wǒ xìng Zhāng, jiào Zhāng Rényuǎn. Nín ne?
我姓张，叫张仁远。您呢?
My last name is Zhang, and my name is Zhang Renyuan. And you?

A: Wǒ jiào Johnson Smith, wǒ de Zhōngwén míngzi jiào Shǐ Qiángshēng.
我叫Johnson Smith，我的中文名字叫史强生。
My name is Johnson Smith and my Chinese name is Shi Qiangsheng.

B: Nǐ hǎo, Shǐ xiānsheng!
你好，史先生!
Hello, Mr. Shi!

A: Nǐ hǎo! Jiào wǒ Johnson jiù xíng le! Nǐ zhīdào nà wèi xiānsheng jiào shénme míngzi ma?
你好！叫我Johnson就行了！你知道那位先生叫什么名字吗?
Hello! Just call me Johnson! Do you know that gentleman's name?

B: Tā shì wǒmen de shìchǎngbù jīnglǐ, jiào Huáng Zhìqiáng.
他是我们的市场部经理，叫黄志强。
He is our Marketing Department Manager, and his name is Huang Zhiqiang.

A: Wǒ yīnggāi zěnme chēnghu tā cái héshì
我应该怎么称呼他才合适?
What is the proper way for me to address him?

B: Jiào tā Huáng jīnglǐ jiù xíng le.
叫他黄经理就行了。
Just call him Manager Huang.

Related Words

1	guìxìng 贵姓	last name; surname (polite form)	7	fūrén 夫人	Mrs.; lady; madam
2	míng míngzi 名/名字	first name; given name	8	nǚshì 女士	Ms.; (educated) woman
3	xìngmíng 姓名	full name (literally: surname and given name)	9	xiǎojiě 小姐	Miss; young lady
4	chēnghu 称呼	to address; to call; form of address	10	lǐmào 礼貌	courtesy; politeness; manners
5	wèi 位	a measure word for person (polite form)	11	zūnjìng 尊敬	respect; to respect
6	xiānsheng 先生	sir; Mr.; gentleman			

Cultural Navigation

When Chinese exchange greetings, they often address people by using one's family name with the title. It is a way to show respect to others. In everyday life, Chinese generally call each other by their full names. Only among family members or close friends will Chinese call each other by their first names. If your Chinese coworkers, friends or business partners address you in this way, it is a sign that they have considered you as a good friend or "one of them."

2 Introducing Each Other

Key Sentence

Wǒ lái jièshào yíxià, zhèwèi shì wǒmen gōngsī de
我来介绍一下，这位是我们公司的
Wáng zǒng jīnglǐ.
王 总（经理）。

Let me introduce! This is our company's General Manager Wang.

Substitution

wǒmen de zhòngyào kèhù
我们的重要客户
our important client

wǒmen de yèwù hézuòrén
我们的业务合作人
our business partner

wǒ de tóngshì
我的同事
my colleague

1. Zhè wèi shì Měiguó lái de xiānsheng.
这位是美国来的Johnson Smith先生。
This is Mr. Johnson Smith who is from the USA.

2. Tā shì wǒmen de zhòngyào kèhù.
他是我们的重要客户。
He is our important client.

3. Ràng wǒ lái zìwǒ jièshào yíxià.
（让）我来自我介绍一下。
Allow me to introduce myself.

4. Nín jiànguo wǒmen shìchǎngbù de Lǐ jīnglǐ le ma?
您见过我们市场部的李经理了吗?
Have you met Manager Li from our Marketing Department?

Dialogue

A: Wǒ lái jièshào yíxià, zhèwèi shì wǒmen gōngsī de Wáng zǒngjīnglǐ.
我来介绍一下，这位是我们公司的王总经理。
Let me introduce! This is our company's General Manager Wang.

Wáng zǒng, zhè wèi shì Měiguó lái de Johnson Smith xiānsheng,
王总，这位是美国来的Johnson Smith先生，
wǒmen de zhòngyào kèhù.
我们的重要客户。
General Manager Wang, this is Mr. Johnson Smith from the USA. He is our important client.

B: Ràng wǒ lái zìwǒ jièshào yíxià. Wǒ de Zhōngwén míngzi jiào Shǐ Qiángshēng.
（让）我来自我介绍一下。我的中文名字叫史强生。
Allow me to introduce myself. My Chinese name is Shi Qiangsheng.

C: Hěn gāoxìng rènshi nín!
很高兴认识您!
Very happy to know you!

B: Rènshi nín wǒ yě hěn gāoxìng!
认识您我也很高兴!
I am very happy to know you too!

C: Nín jiànguo wǒmen shìchǎngbù de Lǐ jīnglǐ le ma?
您见过我们市场部的李经理了吗?
Have you met Manager Li from our Marketing Department?

B: Hái méiyǒu. Nín kěyǐ jièshàowǒ hé tā rènshi yíxià ma?
还没有。您可以介绍我和他认识一下吗?
Not yet. Could you introduce me to him?

Related Words

1	zhǔguǎn 主管	person in charge; to be responsible for; to be in charge	6	xiāoshòu dàibiǎo 销售代表	sales representative
2	zhùlǐ 助理	assistant	7	fǎrén dàibiǎo 法人代表	legal representative
3	kèhù 客户	client	8	xìnghuì 幸会	to be honored to meet sb.
4	yèwù hézuòrén/ shāngwù huǒbàn 业务合作人/商务伙伴	business partner/ associate	9	jiǔyǎng 久仰	a short form of "久仰大名," which means "I have heard of your illustrious name for a long time."
5	dàilǐshāng 代理商	agent			

Cultural Navigation

There is one special title used broadly in today's Chinese business world, which is "zǒng." In this content, "zǒng" means "chief" or "head." It is a short form for general manager, chief director, CEO, CFO, president of a company, chairman of the board, etc. It is used right after one's last name. Sometimes, although the person is only in charge of a very small section in the company, he/she would probably still be happy if you address him/her with the title of "zǒng."

3 Exchanging Business Cards

Key Sentence

Wǒmen jiāohuàn yíxià míngpiànba.
我们交换一下名片吧。
Let's exchange our business cards.

Substitution

diànhuà hàomǎ
电话号码
telephone number

shǒujī hàomǎ
手机号码
cell phone number

dìzhǐ
地址
address

diànyóu dìzhǐ
电邮地址
e-mail address

Extension

1. Bù hǎoyìsi, wǒ méi dài míngpiàn.
   不好意思，我没带名片。
   How embarrassing! I didn't bring my business card.

2. Nín néng gěi wǒ liú gè liánxì fāngshì ma?
   您能给我留个联系方式吗?
   Could you give me your contact information?

3. Yǐhòu wǒmen bǎochí liánxì!
   以后我们保持联系!
   Let's keep in touch in the future!

4. Yǐhòu yídìng hái yào xiàng nín qǐngjiào!
   以后一定还要向您请教!
   I'll definitely need to ask for your advice again in the future!

Dialogue

A: Wǒmen jiāohuàn yíxià míngpiàn ba! Zhè shì wǒ de míngpiàn.
我们交换一下名片吧! 这是我的名片。
Let's exchange business cards. Here is my business card.

B: Xièxie! Zhēn bù hǎoyìsi, wǒ méi dài míngpiàn.
谢谢! 真不好意思，我没带名片。
Thanks! How embarrassing! I didn't bring my business card.

A: Méi guānxi. Fāngbiàn dehuà, nín néng liú gè liánxì fāngshì ma?
没关系。方便的话，您能留个联系方式吗?
It's OK. If it's convenient, could you give me your contact information?

B: Dāngrán, dāngrán! Zhè shì wǒ de shǒujī hàomǎ hé diànzǐ yóuxiāng.
当然，当然！这是我的手机号码和电子邮箱。
Of course! Here are my cell phone number and e-mail address.

A: Xíng! Yǐhòu wǒmen bǎochí liánxì!
行！以后我们保持联系！
Good! We'll keep in touch in the future!

B: Yídìng, yídìng. Zài yèwù shang, yǐhòu yídìng háiyào xiàng nín qǐngjiào!
一定，一定。在业务上，以后一定还要向您请教！
Definitely! In terms of business, I'll definitely need to ask for your advice again in the future!

Related Words

1	diànzǐ yóujiàn 电子邮件	e-mail	6	chuánzhēn 传真	fax
2	diànzǐ yóuxiāng 电子邮箱	e-mail box; e-mail address	7	yóubiān 邮编	zip code
3	wǎngzhǐ 网址	website	8	qūhào 区号	area code
4	bàngōngshì diànhuà 办公室电话	office phone	9	liánxì/liánluò fāngshì 联系/联络方式	ways to contact; contact information
5	gōngsī diànhuà 公司电话	company phone	10	yèwù 业务	professional work; business

Cultural Navigation

Many Chinese professionals, including business people, tend to exchange business cards when they first meet each other. When you hand out or receive a business card, you should use both hands as an expression of courtesy. Business cards can help you remember the person's name, get to know his or her background, and also make it easy for people to get in touch with each other later. Some people like to list a lot of official titles on their business cards. It is enough to just remember the first title on the card. Generally speaking, the title listed first is often the most important one.

4 Everyday Greetings

Key Sentence

Nínhǎo, Wáng jīnglǐ!
您好，王经理！
Hello, Manager Wang!

Substitution

Nín zǎo.
您早。
Good morning.

Zǎoshang hǎo.
早上好。
Good morning.

zhǔrèn
主任
director

chǎngzhǎng
厂长
factory director

dǒngshìzhǎng
董事长
chairman of the board

xiānsheng
先生
Mr.

1. Nín zhè shì qù nǎr a?
您（这是）去哪儿啊？
Where are you going?

2. Wǒ chūqu bàn diǎnr shìr.
我出去办点儿事儿。
I'm going out to run some errands.

3. Nín zài máng shénme ne?
您在忙什么呢？
What are you busy doing?

4. Quán dōu tǐng hǎo de.
全都挺好的。
Everything is going quite well.

A: Nín hǎo, Wáng jīnglǐ! Nín zhè shì qù nǎr a?
您好，王经理！您这是去哪儿啊？
Hello, Manager Wang! Where are you going?

B: Nín hǎo, Lǐ zhǔrèn! Wǒ chūqu bàn diǎnr shìr.
您好，李主任！我出去办点儿事儿。
Hello, Director Li! I'm going out to run some errands.

Nín zài máng shénme ne? Zuìjìn yíqiè dōu hǎo ba?
您在忙什么呢？最近（一切）都好吧？
What are you busy doing? Is everything going well with you recently?

A: Lǎo yàngzi. Nín zuìjìn zěnmeyàng?
老样子。您最近怎么样？
Same old same old. How are you doing recently?

B: Quán dōu tǐng hǎode, xièxie!
（全）都挺好的，谢谢！
Everything is going quite well. Thank you!

Wǒděizǒu le, huítóu jiàn!
我得走了，回头见！
I have to go. See you later!

Related Words

1	Zhōumòyúkuài! 周末愉快！	Have a nice weekend!	6	hái hǎo 还好	still OK; just fine
2	Xīnnián hǎo 新年好/ Guònián hǎo! 过年好！	Happy New Year!	7	mǎmǎhūhū 马马虎虎	fair; so-so
3	Jiérì kuàilè! 节日快乐！	Happy holiday!	8	duō xiè 多谢	many thanks
4	dàiwǒxiàng... 代我向…… wènhǎo 问好	to give my regards to …; to say hello for me to…	9	Xièxieguānxīn! 谢谢关心！	Thanks for your concern/care!
5	tǐng hǎo 挺好	quite good			

Cultural Navigation

In daily or informal occasions, questions like "Where are you going?" "What are you going to do?" "What are you busy doing?" and even "Have you eaten?" are often used as a way to say hello among Chinese coworkers, friends or acquaintances. However, foreigners often feel hesitant about how to respond to these kinds of questions. Actually, the intention behind these questions is that your Chinese coworker wants to show that you two are familiar and close. They do not really want to know where you are going or what you are going to do. Therefore, a vague answer such as "I'm going to run some errands" will be enough unless you are willing to give a specific answer.

5 Showing Concern

Key Sentence

Zuìjìn gōngsī de yèwù zěnmeyàng?
最近公司的业务怎么样?

How is the company's business recently?

Substitution

shēngyi
生 意
business (semiformal/colloquial speech)

xiāoshòu
销 售
sales

gōngzuò
工 作
work

qíngkuàng
情 况
situation

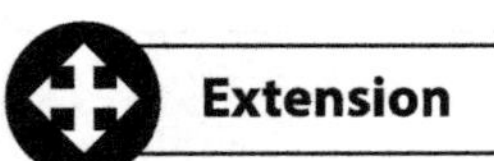

Zuìjìn nǐ shēngyi máng ma?
1. 最近（你）生意 忙 吗?

Has your business kept you busy recently?

Jīnnián de shìchǎng yǒu qǐsè.
2. 今年的市 场 有起色。

This year's market has picked up.

3. Xiāoshòu mǎmǎhūhū ba.
销 售 马马虎虎吧。
Sales are just so-so.

4. Yào zhùyì shēntǐ ò.
要注意身体哦。
Please pay attention to your health.

Dialogue

A: Zuìjìn shēngyi máng ma?
最近生意 忙 吗？
Has your business kept you busy recently?

B: Bǐjiào máng. Nínne? Zuìjìn gōngsī de yèwù zěnmeyàng?
比较忙。您呢？最近公司的业务怎么样？
Quite busy. How about you? How is the company's business recently?

A: Hái xíng. Jīnnián de shìchǎng yǒu qǐsè.
还行。今年的 市 场 有起色。
It's OK. This year's market has picked up.

Wǒ tīngshuō nǐmen zhègeyuè de xiāoshòu hěn búcuò a!
（我） 听 说 你们这个月的 销 售 很不错啊！
I heard that your sales this month were really not bad!

B: Mǎmǎhūhū ba!
马马虎虎吧！
Just so-so!

A: Gōngzuò máng, yào zhùyì shēntǐ ò!
工 作 忙，要注意身体哦！
Your work keeps you busy. Please pay attention to (your) health!

Related Words

1	yèwù 业务	business (formal)	7	hái guòdeqù 还过得去	all right; passable
2	háixíng 还行	it's OK; not bad (neutral)	8	hái kěyǐ 还可以	not too bad; passable
3	búcuò 不错	not bad (relatively positive)	9	hái còuhe 还凑合	barely passable; not too bad
4	yìbān 一般	nothing special; ordinary	10	yōuzhe diǎnr 悠着点儿	not to work too hard; to relax a little bit
5	yǒu qǐsè 有起色	to have picked up	11	bǎozhòng 保重	to take care of oneself
6	shùnlì 顺利	smooth; smoothly			

Cultural Navigation

"...zěnmeyàng" (How is...) is considered a common form of greeting among colleagues and friends in casual or informal occasions. For example, you may often hear the greetings such as "Shēngyi zěnmeyàng?" (How is your business?) or "Gōngsī zěnmeyàng?" (How is the company?) in an office building's hallway or at a gathering at your company. To respond to these question-like greetings, Chinese often use modest words, such as "hái xíng (it's OK)," "búcuò (not bad)," "mămă-hūhū (just so-so)" or "hái kěyĭ (not too bad)," in order to show a humble attitude. Traditionally, Chinese believe that even if one has some great achievements, he still shouldn't be arrogant and show off all around.

6 Promoting Goodwill and Friendship

Key Sentence

Zhǎo shíjiān wǒmen jù yí jù!
找 时间我们聚一聚!
Let's find a time to get together!

Substitution

gǎitiān
改天
some other day

jīntiān wǎnshang
今天 晚 上
tonight

zhège zhōumò
这个周 末
this weekend

huìyì wán le
会议完了
after the meeting

shìr bànwán le
事儿办 完 了
after finishing the business

yǒukòng
有 空
have free time

Extension

1. Hǎojiǔ bú jiàn.
好久不见。
We haven't seen each other for a long time.

2. Nín shì dàmángrén!
您是大忙人！
You are the busy man!

3. Wǒ hái méi láidejí xiè nín ne!
我还没来得及谢您呢！
I haven't been able to express my appreciation yet!

4. Wǒmen shì lǎopéngyou le, yīnggāi de!
我们是老朋友了，应该的！
We are old friends. That's the way it's supposed to be.

Dialogue

A: Wáng zǒng, hǎojiǔ bú jiàn a!
王总，好久不见（啊）！
Hello, General Manager Wang. We haven't seen each other for quite a while.

B: Shì a, Lǐ zǒng, nín shì dàmángrén a!
是啊，李总，您是大忙人啊！
Yes, General Manager Li. You are the busy man!

A: Nǎlǐ nǎlǐ, dàjiā dōu máng. Zhèyàng ba, zhǎo shíjiān wǒmen jù yí jù?
哪里哪里，大家都忙。这样吧，找时间(我们)聚一聚？
That's not true. Everyone is busy. How about finding a time to get together?

B: Hǎo a. Zhè cì wǒ qǐngkè.
好啊。这次我请客。

Sounds good. This time will be my treat.

Shàng cì nín bāngle wǒ dà máng, wǒ hái méi láidejí xiè nín ne!
上次您帮了我大忙，我还没来得及谢您呢！

Last time you helped me a lot, and I haven't been able to express my appreciation yet!

A: Zhè shì nǎr de huà, nín tài kèqi le. Lǎopéngyou le, yīnggāi de!
这是哪儿的话，您太客气了。老朋友了，应该的！

What are you talking about? You are too polite! We are old friends. That is the way it's supposed to be.

Related Words

1	jùhuì 聚会	gathering; reunion; party	6	dáxiè 答谢	to express appreciation (for sb.'s kindness)
2	qǐngkè 请客	to invite sb. to lunch or dinner; to entertain guests	7	chóuxiè 酬谢	to thank sb. with a gift
3	qǐng... chīfàn 请……吃饭	to invite sb. to lunch or dinner	8	Bié kèqi. 别客气。	You are welcome; Please don't be so polite.
4	bāngmáng 帮忙	help; to help; to lend a hand	9	Méi guānxi. 没关系。	It's OK; It doesn't matter.
5	qǐng... bāngmáng 请……帮忙	to ask sb. for a favor			

Cultural Navigation

As the old saying goes, "Zàijiā kào fùmǔ, chūmén kào péngyou" (When you are at home, you rely on your parents; when you are away from home, you rely on your friends); "Duō gè péngyou duō tiáo lù" (You will get more help and opportunities when you have more friends). It is easy to see how important interpersonal relationships are in Chinese society and culture. Therefore, almost every foreigner who has ever worked or lived in China knows the word "guānxi" and understands the necessity of building up interpersonal relationships (namely "guānxi"). However, "guānxi" is definitely not a magic key. It may not only bring some unnecessary troubles, but sometimes also put you in a position against the law if you abuse your "guānxi."

7 Sending Out an Invitation

Key Sentence

Chén zǒng xiǎng qǐng nín Zhōuliù wǎnshang yìqǐ
陈总想请您周六晚上一起
chī gè fàn.
吃（个）饭。

General Manager Chen would like to invite you to dinner on Saturday night.

Substitution

míngtiān zhōngwǔ
明天中午
tomorrow noon

jīntiān xiàwǔ
今天下午
this afternoon

xià gè zhōumò
下个周末
next weekend

pǐnchá
品茶
have a tea party

hē kāfēi
喝咖啡
have a cup of coffee

cānjiā yí gè zhāodàihuì
参加（一个）招待会
attend a reception

cānjiā jiǔhuì
参加酒会
attend a cocktail party

cānjiā wǎnyàn
参加晚宴
attend an evening banquet

1. Xià gè Xīngqī'èr nǐ yǒukòng ma?
   下个星期二你有空吗?
   Do you have time next Tuesday?

2. Mùqián hái méiyǒu rènhé ānpái.
   目前还没有任何安排。
   Right now I don't have any plans yet.

3. Xīngqīrì wǎnshang wǒ gēn jǐ wèi kèhù yǒu yí gè yìngchou.
   星期日晚上我跟几位客户有一个应酬。
   On Sunday night I'll have a social appointment with several clients.

4. Wǒ yídìng zhǔnshí cānjiā.
   我一定准时参加。
   I'll definitely be there on time.

A: Wēiliánsī xiānsheng, Chén zǒng xiǎng qǐng nín Zhōuliù wǎnshang yìqǐ chī gè fàn.
威廉斯先生，陈总想请您周六晚上一起吃(个)饭。
Mr. Williams, General Manager Chen would like to invite you to dinner on Saturday night.

B: Zhēn bù qiǎo! Xīngqīliù wǎnshang wǒ gēn jǐ wèi kèhù yǒu yí gè yìngchou. Duìbuqǐ!
真不巧！星期六晚上我跟几位客户有一个应酬。对不起！
It's really a pity! On Saturday night I'll have a social appointment with several clients. I'm sorry!

Méi guānxi. Nà, xià gè Xīngqī'èr nínyǒukòng ma?
A: 没关系。那，下个星期二您有空吗？
It's OK. Well then, do you have time next Tuesday?

Mùqián hái méiyǒu rènhé ānpái.
B: 目前还没有任何安排。
Right now I don't have any plans yet.

Wǒmen gōngsī xiǎng yāoqǐng nín hé nín de fūrén zuòwéi guìbīn chūxí kāimùshì.
A: 我们公司想邀请您和您的夫人作为贵宾出席开幕式。
Our company would like to invite you and your wife as honored guests to attend the opening ceremony.

Qǐngnín wùbì guānglín!
请您务必光临！
Please make sure to attend!

Xièxie! Wǒ yídìng zhǔnshí cānjiā.
B: 谢谢！我一定准时参加。
Thanks! I'll definitely be there on time.

Related Words

1	kèrén 客人	guest	4	chūxí 出席	to attend; to be present
2	guìbīn 贵宾	honored guest; distinguished guest	5	guānglín 光临	to be present; to be patronized (polite form)
3	cānjiā 参加	to attend; to participate	6	shǎngguāng 赏光	to honor me with your presence

(Continued)

7	kāimùshì 开幕式	opening ceremony	9	ānpái 安排	to arrange; arrangement; plan
8	huódòng 活动	activity; event	10	yìngchou 应酬	to have social intercourse with; social appointment/ engagement; dinner party

Cultural Navigation

Just like the business culture in many other countries, social intercourse, or social engagement in the Chinese business world is indispensable. One of the most common forms of business social activity is to invite your business associates to dinner. Many Chinese businessmen often make business connections by having or attending dinner parties, for instance, getting to know people, making new friends and finding potential business partners or opportunities, etc. Many people are accustomed to taking this opportunity to sound out their business counterparty's intentions, try to resolve certain problems on both sides, or even strike a deal. In short, it is very true that "the banquet table is a part of the business world."

8 Attending a Dinner Engagement

Key Sentence

Nándé néng yǒu zhèyàng de jīhuì, ràng wǒ jìng nín yì bēi!
难得能有这样的机会，（让）我敬您一杯！

It is rare to have such an opportunity, and please allow me to propose a toast to you!

Substitution

hěn gāoxìng
很高兴
very happy

hǎo bù róngyì
好不容易
not easy

Lái, gānbēi!
来，干杯！
Let's drink a toast!

Wǒmen xiān gān yì bēi!
我们先干一杯！
Let's drink a toast first!

Jīntiān dàjiā yídìng yào jìnxìng!
今天（大家）一定要尽兴！
Be sure to have a great time today!

Extension

1. Qǐng zuò zhèr!
请 坐这儿!
Please have a seat here!

2. Nǐ men yě dōu qǐng zuò!
你（们）也（都）请坐!
Please have a seat too!

3. Tāngmǔ bú tài néng hējiǔ.
汤姆不太能喝酒。
Tom isn't very good at drinking.

4. Wèi wǒmen hézuò chénggōng gānbēi!
为我们合作成功干杯!
Let's drink a toast to our successful collaboration.

Dialogue

A: Jiékèxùn xiānsheng, nínqǐng zuò zhèr!
杰克逊先生，您请坐这儿!
Mr. Jackson, please have a seat here!

B: Xièxie. Lǐ jīnglǐ, Zhāng xiānsheng, nǐmen yě dōu qǐng zuò!
谢谢。李经理，张先生，你们也都请坐!
Thank you. Manager Li and Mr. Zhang, please have a seat too!

A: Nándénéng yǒu zhèyàng de jīhuì, ràngwǒjìngnín yì bēi!
难得能有这样的机会，让我敬您一杯!
It is rare to have such an opportunity, and allow me to propose a toast to you!

B: Wǒ bú tài néng hējiǔ, dàjiā yìqǐ gān yì bēiba!
我不太能喝酒，大家一起干一杯吧！
I'm not very good at drinking. Let's drink a toast together!

C: Wèi wǒmen hézuò chénggōng gānbēi!
为我们合作成功干杯！
Let's drink a toast to our successful collaboration.

A: Gèwèi qǐng suíyì.
各位请随意。
Everyone, please help yourselves.

Related Words

1	fànjú 饭局	dinner party; dinner engagement	6	jìngjiǔ 敬酒	to propose a toast
2	yànhuì 宴会	banquet	7	jìnxìng 尽兴	to enjoy oneself to the full
3	zhāodàihuì 招待会	reception	8	hézuò 合作	to cooperate; to work together; cooperation; collaboration
4	jiǔhuì 酒会	cocktail reception	9	shùnlì 顺利	smooth(ly); without a hitch
5	gānbēi 干杯	to drink a toast; bottoms up; cheers	10	suíyì 随意	to do as one pleases

Cultural Navigation

When you are attending a formal dinner party or banquet in China, there are certain customs that you should know. During a banquet, distinguished guests and the host are placed at the seats of honor. Generally speaking, the seats facing the door or entrance are the seats of honor. Of course no banquet is complete without liquor. The meaning of "gān bēi" is to drink up the wine in your glass. If you don't want to become drunk immediately, however, you had better not finish your drink at one go. Chinese are accustomed to drinking and eating various dishes first and then having rice and soup. Therefore, the sequence of serving courses is: first, hors d'oeuvres; then, the fried dishes and the main dishes; and finally, rice, soup and dessert. For a foreigner who is not yet used to the way that Chinese eat and drink during a dinner party, one of the most useful phrases may be "suíyì." It means to eat or drink as one pleases or as one is able to. It can either be said to everyone around table, or it can be used as a good excuse for oneself.

9 Showing Appreciation & Presenting a Gift

Key Sentence

Zhèjiàn xiǎo lǐwù shìsònggěinínde, fēicháng
这件（小）礼物是送给您的，（非常）
gǎnxiè nín de bāngzhù!
感谢您的帮助！

This (small) present is for you. Thank you (so much) for your help!

Substitution

dàlì zhīchí
大力支持
full/great support

zhēnchéng hézuò
真诚合作
sincere cooperation

duōfāng guānzhào
多方关照
care and patronization in many ways

1. Zhè shì wǒmen zhēnchéng hézuò de jiéguǒ.
这是我们真诚合作的结果。
This is the result of our sincere cooperation.

2. Dōushì péngyou le, wǒxīnlǐng le.
都是朋友了，我心领了。
We are friends now. I appreciate your kindness but I can't accept it.

3. Wǒ hái méi láidejí xièxie nínne!
我还没来得及谢谢您呢！
I haven't had a chance to thank you yet!

4. Gōngjìng bùrú cóngmìng.
恭敬不如从命。
It is better to accept than to decline courteously.

Dialogue

A: Zhè cì nénggòu shùnlì qiānyuē quán kào nín de dàlì zhīchí!
这次能够顺利签约全靠您的大力支持！
The fact that we were able to sign the contract without problems this time all depended on your full support!

B: Nǎlǐ nǎlǐ, zhèshì shuāngfāng zhēnchéng hézuò de jiéguǒ.
哪里哪里，这是双方真诚合作的结果。
You flatter me. This is the result of sincere cooperation of both sides.

A: Zhè jiàn xiǎo lǐwù shì sònggěi nín de, zhēnde fēicháng gǎnxiè nín de bāngzhù!
这件小礼物是送给您的，真的非常感谢您的帮助！
This small present is for you and I truly thank you so much for your help!

B: Nín tài kèqi le. Dōu shì péngyou le, wǒ xīnlǐng le. Wǒ hái méi láidejí
您太客气了。都是朋友了，我心领了。我还没来得及
xièxie nín ne!
谢谢您呢！

You are too polite. We are friends now and I appreciate your kindness but I can't accept it. I haven't had a chance to thank you yet!

A: Nín zhè cì yídìng yào shōuxia. Zhè zhǐ shì dàibiǎo wǒ de yìdiǎn xīnyì.
您这次一定要收下。这只是代表我的一点心意。

You have to accept it this time. It is just a small token of my appreciation.

B: Hǎo ba, wǒ xiǎng gōngjìng bùrú cóngmìng. Nà wǒ jiù shōuxia le.
好吧，我想恭敬不如从命。那我就收下了。
Xièxie!
谢谢！

Well, I guess it is better to accept than to decline courteously. I accept it. Thank you!

Related Words

1	guānzhào 关照	to look after; care and help	5	gǎnjī 感激	to feel grateful; to feel indebted (formal)
2	jìniàn 纪念	to commemorate; souvenir	6	xīnlǐng 心领	to appreciate one's kind offer but have to decline gifts
3	jìniànpǐn 纪念品	souvenir; keepsake	7	xīnyì 心意	to thank sb. with a gift
4	zèngsòng 赠送	to present as a gift (formal)	8	xīnyì 心意	feeling; gratitude

(Continued)

9 Gōngjìng bùrú cóngmìng.
恭敬不如从命。

It is better to accept deferentially than to decline courteously (when accepting gifts, etc.).

10 Chīle biérén de zuǐ ruǎn; nále biérén de shǒu duǎn.
吃了别人的嘴软；拿了别人的手短。

Once you accept a favor from other people, you will owe them. (Literally, once people treat you to a meal, your words become soft; once you accept a present, your hands become short.)

Cultural Navigation

Chinese often say: "Lǐ qīng qíngyì zhòng." (The gift is trifling, but the feeling is profound.) Giving gifts to show appreciation is a common practice in Chinese social intercourse. Conventionally, when Chinese are receiving a present from others, most of them tend to decline in a polite manner first. After they have accepted the present and have said "thanks," they usually do not open the present in front of the giver right way. By doing this, one shows politeness as well as conducts oneself with dignity. In business activities in recent years, business gifts have become very popular. During the Spring Festival or on other holidays, giving gifts to those companies and individuals with whom you have business relationships has developed into a means to promote friendships and strengthen relationships. However, you have to distinguish whether it's a gift or bribery. When the present is too valuable, you should be able to make a sagacious judgment and decision. You may tell the other party tactfully that your company has a clear-cut rule of "never accepting any gifts." You may also politely decline the gift by telling the other party that you "don't feel that is proper." As an old saying goes, "Chīle biérén de zuǐ ruǎn, nále biérén de shǒu duǎn." (You owe them once you accept a favor from other people.) A gift with ambiguous and dubious purposes will probably get you into unexpected trouble.

10 Saying Goodbye and Seeing Visitors Out

Key Sentence

Rúguǒ méiyǒu biéde shìdehuà, wǒ jiù xiān gàocí le.
如果没有别的事的话，我就先告辞了。
If there is nothing else, I'll say goodbye.

Substitution

shíjiān bù zǎo le
时间不早了
it's getting late

nín hái yǒu kèrén
您还有客人
you still have another guest

dānwule nín bù shǎo shíjiān
耽误了您不少时间
I have cost you a lot of time

zǒu le
走了
leave

huíqu le
回去了
go back

huí ... qù le
回……去了
go back to…

Extension

1. Shíjiān bù zǎo le, wǒ gāi zǒu le.
时间不早了，我该走了。
It's getting late, and I should be leaving now.

2. Nǐ men nándé lái, zài zuòzuo, zài liáoliao ma.
你（们）难得来，再坐坐、再聊聊嘛。
You rarely come. Let's sit together and chat for another while.

3. Ràng wǒ sòng nín dào ménkǒu.
让我送您到门口。
Allow me to see you out to the doorway.

4. Nín mànzǒu! Yǒukòng cháng lái!
（您）慢走！有空常来！
Watch your step! Come often when you have time!

Dialogue

A: Rúguǒ méiyǒu biéde shì dehuà, wǒ jiù xiān gàocí le.
如果没有别的事的话，我就先告辞了。
If there is nothing else, I will say goodbye.

B: Shì a. Shíjiān bù zǎo le, wǒ yě gāi zǒu le.
是啊。时间不早了，我也该走了。
Right. It's getting late, and I should be leaving now.

C: Nǐmen nándé lái, zài zuòzuo, zài liáoliao ma.
你们难得来，再坐坐、再聊聊嘛。
You rarely come. Let's sit together and chat for another while.

A: Bù le. Nín yídìng háiyǒu hěn duō shìqing xūyào chǔlǐ, xià cì zài lái ba!
不了。您一定还有很多事情需要处理，下次再来吧！
No. You must still have many things to do. We will come again next time!

C: Nàhǎoba, ràngwǒsòngnǐmendàoménkǒu.
那好吧，让我送你们到门口。
Well then, allow me to see you out to the doorway.

B: Búyòng sòng le, bié kèqi!
不用送了，别客气！
There is no need to see us out. Please don't bother!

C: Hǎo, mànzǒu! Yǒukòng chánglái!
好，慢走！有空常来！
OK, watch your step! Come often when you have time!

Related Words

1	gàocí 告辞	to say goodbye; to take one's leave	6	Yíhuìr jiàn! 一会儿见！	See you later; See you in a little while! (The tone is casual.)
2	shīpéi 失陪	please excuse me (when one wants to leave)	7	Huítóu jiàn! 回头见！	See you later! (The tone is casual.)
3	sòngkè 送客	to see a visitor out	8	Gǎitiān jiàn! 改天见！	See you another day!
4	mànzǒu 慢走	to watch your steps (said by the host to a guest at departure)	9	Míngtiān jiàn! 明天见！	See you tomorrow!
5	liúbù 留步	not to bother to see me out (said by the guest to the host at departure)	10	Xià cì jiàn! 下次见！	See you next time!

Cultural Navigation

There are many ways to say goodbye between hosts and guests. "Gàocí" and "shīpéi" are both conventional terms. The term "gàocí" means "I have to say goodbye"; and the original meaning of "shīpéi" is "to excuse me for not being able to accompany you." When the host sees a guest out, he/she will usually say "Ràng wǒ sòngsong nín" (Let me see you out) or "Nín mànzǒu" (Please walk slowly, or watch your step). As a reply, the guest should say something like "Qǐng liúbù" (Please stay inside, or please don't bother to see me out) and so on. As the old saying goes, "Lǐ duō rén bú guài," meaning "Nobody will blame you for being too polite." The usage of courteous language is necessary in social intercourse.

Business Communication

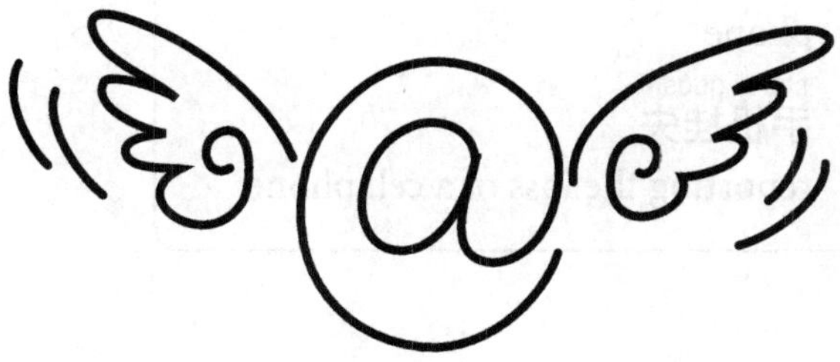

11 Opening a Cell Phone Account

Key Sentence

Zhèr bànlǐ shǒujī kāihù yèwù ma?
这儿办理手机开户业务吗?
Do you handle the business of opening a cell phone account here?

Substitution

wúxiànshàngwǎng
无线 上 网
wireless Internet

shǒujī chōngzhí
手机 充 值
purchasing more air time for a cell phone

shǒujī guàshī
手机挂失
reporting the loss of a cell phone

Extension

1. Nín yào bànlǐ shǒujī kāihù yèwù ma?
   您 要办理手机开户 业务吗?
   Do you want to open a cell phone account?

2. Méiyǒu shǒujī zhēn bù fāngbiàn.
   没有手机真不方便。
   It's really inconvenient without a cell phone.

3. Xiànzài bàn shǒujī kāihù yǒu yōuhuì.
   现在办手机开户有优惠。
   There is a special discount for opening a cell phone account right now.

4. Wǒmen yǒu duō zhǒng tàocān jìhuà.
   我们有多种"套餐"计划。
   We have different kinds of "combo" plans.

Dialogue

A: Qǐngwèn, zhèr bànlǐ shǒujī kāihù yèwù ma?
请问，这儿办理手机开户业务吗?
Excuse me. Do you handle the business of opening a cell phone account here?

B: Méi cuò. Nín yào kāihù ma?
没错。您要开户吗?
Correct. Do you need to open an account?

A: Shì a. Wǒ cháng lái Zhōngguó chūchāi. Zài zhèr méiyǒu shǒujī zhēn bù fāngbiàn.
是啊。我常来中国出差。在这儿没有手机真不方便。
Yes. I often come to China on business trips. It's really inconvenient without a cell phone here.

B: Nín xuǎn yí gè hàomǎ ba.
您选一个号码吧。
Please pick a (phone) number.

A: Xiànzài kāihù yǒu yōuhuì ma?
现在开户有优惠吗?
Is there any special discount for opening an account right now?

B: Bàoqiàn, méiyǒu. Búguò wǒmen yǒu duō zhǒng tàocān jìhuà.
抱歉，没有。不过我们有多种"套餐"计划。
Sorry, we don't have any. However, we have several kinds of "combo" plans.

A: Èng, nǎ zhǒng fúwù jìhuà zuì hǎo?
嗯，哪种服务计划最好？
Uh, which service plan is the best?

B: Nà děi kàn nín de xūyào le.
那得看您的需要了。
Well, that depends on what you need.

Related Words

1	yíngyètīng 营业厅	business hall	7	cǎilíng 彩铃	polyphonic ringtone; customized ringtone
2	huàfèi 话费	expense for air time; phone bill	8	chōngzhí 充值	to add more money to an account; to recharge an account (literally means "to fill up the value")
3	mànyóufèi 漫游费	roaming charge			
4	zīfèi 资费	service charge (on telecommunications or postal service)	9	yōuhuì 优惠	special discount; favorable; preferential
5	tàocān jìhuà 套餐计划	combo plan; service plan	10	dǎzhé 打折	discount
6	cǎixìn 彩信	multimedia messaging service			

Cultural Navigation

China Unicom and China Mobile are the two biggest mobile communication companies in China. In order to use cellular phone service in China, you need to sign a service contract and purchase the calling time. You usually need to use your valid identification, such as a resident ID or passport, to open an account, and then choose the services that you need, for instance, text messaging, Internet access, international call service, etc. Next, you need to sign a contract, make a payment and buy a certain amount of "air time" that you need. Whenever you find that you do not have enough "air time" to make a phone call, you may recharge your account through your cell phone or online at any time. Many banks, post offices and supermarkets offer the service of recharging cell phone accounts too.

12 Contacting the Other Party

Key Sentence

Wǒ zěnme gēn nà jiā gōngsī liánxì?
我怎么跟那家公司联系?
How could I contact that company?

Substitution

nín
您
you (polite form)

zhèwèi kèhù
这位客户
this client

duìfāng
对方
the other side; the other party

Extension

1. Wǒmen dǎ diànhuà liánxì ba.
   我们（打）电话联系吧。
   Let's stay in contact by phone.

2. Wǒ xiǎng xiān fā gè duǎnxìn.
   我想先发个短信。
   I want to send a text message first.

3. Nǐ yǒu nà jiā gōngsī de diànyóu dìzhǐ ma?
   你有那家公司的电邮地址吗?
   Do you have the e-mail address of the company?

4. Nàwèi kèhù de diànhuà hàomǎ shì duōshao?
那位客户的电话号码是多少？
What is that client's phone number?

A: Wǒ zěnme gēn nà jiā gōngsī liánxì ne?
我怎么跟那家公司联系呢？
How could I contact that company?

B: Nǐ dǎ diànhuà liánxì ba, huòzhě xiān fā gè duǎnxìn.
你打电话联系吧，或者先发个短信。
You can make contact by phone, or send a text message first.

A: Nǐ yǒu duìfāng de diànyóu dìzhǐ ma?
你有对方的电邮地址吗？
Do you have the e-mail address of the other party?

B: Nàwèi kèhù méiyǒu liú diànyóu dìzhǐ.
那位客户没有留电邮地址。
That client didn't leave an e-mail address.

A: Nà wèi kèhù de diànhuà hàomǎ shì duōshao?
那位客户的电话（号码）是多少？
What is that client's phone number?

B: Hā, zhǎodào le! Zhè shì nà jiā gōngsī de liánxì fāngshì.
哈，找到了！这是那家公司的联系方式。
Ha, (I've) found it! This is the contact information of that company.

Related Words

1	shǒujī 手机	cell phone	6	diànyóu 电邮	a short form for "e-mail"
2	zuòjī gùdìng diànhuà 座机/固定电话	landline	7	diànyóu dìzhǐ 电邮地址	e-mail address
3	fā duǎnxìn 发短信	to send a text message	8	diànzǐ yóuxiāng 电子邮箱	e-mail box; e-mail account
4	fā chuánzhēn 发传真	to send a fax	9	shàngwǎng 上网	to access the Internet; to go online
5	fā diànzǐ yóujiàn 发电子邮件	to send an e-mail	10	liánxì/liánluò fāngshì 联系/联络方式	contact information

Cultural Navigation

There are many ways to stay in contact with business partners. In addition to the conventional methods of writing letters, making phone calls and faxing, the most commonly used ways today include sending text messages with cell phones, sending e-mails and instant messages, or conducting video conversations over the Internet. Almost everyone in China has a cell phone, and the cost of making a call is getting cheaper too. Smart phones such as iPhone, Samsung and BlackBerry are very popular among businessmen and young people. Broadband Internet and Wi-Fi are also very common. People can not only go online at home or in an office building, but also access the Internet in an Internet bar or café on a street corner. Indeed, today in China, making contacts with clients or business partners all over the world is very convenient.

13 Calling Someone

Key Sentence

Wéi, qǐngwèn shì Dōngfāng Huòyùn Fúwù Gōngsī ma?
喂，请问是东方货运服务公司吗？
Hello, is this the Eastern Cargo Services Company?

Substitution

Běijīng Fàndiàn
北京饭店
the Beijing Hotel

Píng'ān Bǎoxiǎn
平安保险
Ping An Insurance

Wáng jīnglǐ
王经理
Manager Wang

1. Qǐngwèn nín shì nǎ yí wèi?
请问您是哪一位？
May I ask who is speaking?

2. Máfan nín qǐng Zhāng zhǔrèn jiē diànhuà.
麻烦（您）请 张 主任接电话。
May I speak to Director Zhang, please?

3. Nín xū yào liúyán ma?
您（需）要留言吗?
Do you need to leave a message?

4. Máfan nín zhuǎngào Zhāng xiānsheng...
麻烦您 转 告 张 先 生……
Could you please tell Mr. Zhang (that)…?

Dialogue

A: Wéi, qǐngwèn shì Dōngfāng Huòyùn Fúwù Gōngsī ma?
喂，请 问 是 东 方 货 运服务公司 吗?
Hello, is this the Eastern Cargo Services Company?

B: Shì de. Qǐngwèn nín yǒu shénme shìr
是的。请问您有 什 么 事（儿）?
Yes. How can I help you?

A: Máfan qǐng Chén zhǔrèn jiē diànhuà.
麻烦 请 陈 主任接电话。
May I speak to Director Chen, please?

B: Duìbuqǐ, tā xiànzài bú zài.
对不起，他现在不在。
I am sorry. He is not here right now.

A: Nàme, qǐngwèn Wáng zǒng zài ma?
那么，请问 王 总 在吗?
Then, is General Manager Wang available?

B: Qǐngwèn nín shì nǎ yí wèi?
请 问 您是哪一位?
May I ask who is speaking?

A: Wǒshì Chángchéng Kējì de Liú Jūn.
我是长城科技的刘军。
I am Liu Jun from Great Wall Technology.

B: Duìbuqǐ, tā yě bú zài. Nín xūyào liúyán ma?
对不起，他也不在。您需要留言吗？
Sorry, he is not in, either. Do you need to leave a message?

A: Máfan nín zhuǎngào tā, qǐng tā gěi wǒ huí yí gè diànhuà.
麻烦您转告他，请他给我回（一）个电话。
Could you please tell him to give me a call?

Related Words

1	máfan 麻烦	to trouble/bother sb.	6	liúyán 留言	to leave a message
2	jiē diànhuà 接(电话)	to answer (a phone call); to connect	7	zhuǎngào 转告	to transmit (a message); to pass on (a message)
3	guà diànhuà 挂(电话)	to hang up (a phone); to disconnect	8	huí diànhuà 回电话	to call back
4	zhànxiàn 占线	the line (of a telephone) is busy	9	dǎcuò le 打错了	to dial a wrong number
5	xūyào 需要	to need			

Cultural Navigation

Chinese always say "wéi" first when they are making a phone call. Just like saying "Hello" on the phone, it serves as a greeting and draws the attention of the other party. If the person who is answering the phone doesn't know you, he/she usually asks "Nín shì nǎ yí wèi?" (Who are you?) or "Nín zhǎo shéi?" (Who are you looking for?). If you are calling an office phone, the other party would probably first ask you "Nín shì nǎr?" (Where are you calling from?) or "Nín yǒu shénme shì?" (literally: What's the matter? or What kind of business do you have?). Sometimes foreigners are not very used to those kinds of questions. Actually, this is just caused by differences in language and culture. The person who answers your phone call just wants to know whom he/she is talking to and what he/she can do for you.

14 Talking to an Operator

Key Sentence

Nínhǎo, máfan nín bāng wǒ jiē kèfúbù.
您好，麻烦您帮我接客服部。
Hello, would you please connect (me) with the Customer Service Department?

Substitution

jīnglǐ bàngōngshì
经理办公室
the manager's office

301 hào fēnjī
301号分机
extension 301

Extension

1. Qǐng shūrù fēnjīhào.
请输入分机号。
Please enter the extension number.

2. Qǐng shāoděng.
请稍等。
Please hold.

3. Nín bōdǎ de diànhuà zhèngzài tōnghuà zhōng.
您拨打的电话正在通话中。
The number you have dialed is busy.

4. Qǐng shāohòu zài bō.
请稍后再拨。
Please dial again later.

Dialogue

A: yǔyīn tíshì Nǐ hǎo! Zhèli shì Chángchéng Kējì Gōngsī.
(语音提示) 你好！这里是长城科技公司。
(Voice prompt) Hello! This is the Great Wall Technology Company.
Qǐng shūrù fēnjīhào. Cháxún qǐng àn 01.
请输入分机号。查询请按01。
Please enter the extension number. For enquiry, please press 01.

B: àn 01
(按01)
(Presses 01)

C: zǒngjī Nín hǎo!
(总机)：您好！
(Operator): Hello!

B: Nǐ hǎo, máfan nín jiē kèfúbù.
你好，麻烦您接客服部。
Hello! Would you please connect me with the Customer Service Department?

C: zǒngjī Qǐng shāohòu.
(总机)：请稍候。
(Operator): Please hold.

A: (语音提示)对不起，您拨打的电话正在通话中，请稍后再拨。
(yǔyīn tíshì) Duìbuqǐ, nín bōdǎ de diànhuà zhèngzài tōnghuà zhōng, qǐng shāohòu zài bō.

(Voice prompt) Sorry, the number you have dialed is busy. Please try again later.

Related Words

1	总机 zǒngjī	operator	7	拨 bō	to dial
2	分机 fēnjī	(telephone) extension	8	输入 shūrù	to enter (data, such as telephone numbers, a password, etc.)
3	占线 zhànxiàn	the line (of a telephone) is busy	9	稍候/稍等 shāohòu/shāoděng	to hold on
4	接 jiē	to connect; to answer (a phone call)	10	稍后 shāohòu	later
5	转 zhuǎn	to transfer	11	语音信息 yǔyīn xìnxī	voice message
6	按 àn	to press (buttons on the touch pad of a phone)			

Cultural Navigation

Just like in many other countries, you often hear a voice message when you call a company in China. Please don't lose your patience when you come across this kind of situation. If you need help, you may choose "operator" or "enquiry" according to the voice prompts. You may be able to choose different languages for the voice prompt when you call some big companies or organizations.

15 Mailing and Delivery Services

Key Sentence

Zhè fènwénjiàn wǒyào jì tèkuài zhuāndì.
这份文件我要寄特快专递。
I want to send this document by express mail.

Substitution

zhèfēng xìn
这封信
this letter

zhège bāoguǒ
这个包裹
this parcel

zhèxiāng huòyàng
这箱货样
this box of merchandise samples

hángkōng yóujiàn
航空邮件
airmail

guàhào yóujiàn
挂号邮件
registered mail

hángkōng guàhào
航空挂号
registered airmail

Extension

1. Nǐ dǎsuàn jì hángkōng (jiàn) háishi tèkuài zhuāndì (jiàn)?
你打算寄航空（件）还是特快专递（件）?
Do you plan to send it by airmail or express mail?

2. Jì hángkōngjiàn jǐ tiān néng dào Àodàlìyà?
寄航空件几天能到澳大利亚?
How long will it take to get to Australia by airmail?

3. Zhè jiàn bāoguǒ xūyào bǎojià ma?
这件包裹需要保价吗?
Does this parcel need insurance?

4. Yóujiàn kěyǐ suíshí zài wǎngshang gēnzōng cháxún.
邮件可以随时在网上跟踪查询。
The mail can be tracked online anytime.

Dialogue

A: Zhè fèn wénjiàn nǐ dǎsuàn jì hángkōng háishi tèkuài zhuāndì?
这份文件你打算寄航空还是特快专递?
Do you plan to send this document by airmail or express mail?

B: Jì hángkōngjiàn jǐ tiān néng dào Měiguó?
寄航空件几天能到美国?
How long will it take to get to the USA by airmail?

A: Yìbān shuō, dàgài yí gè xīngqī ba.
一般说，大概一个星期吧。
Generally speaking, it's about one week.

B: Yǒudiǎn màn. Zhè fèn wénjiàn wǒ yào jì tèkuài zhuāndì.
有点慢。这份文件我要寄特快专递。
That's a little bit slow. I want to send this document by express mail.

A: Zhèxiē huòyàng nǐ xiǎng zěnme jì?
这些货样你想怎么寄?
How do you want to send these merchandise samples?

B: Wǒmen jiù yòng Liánbāng Kuàidì jì ba. Kěyǐ suíshí zài wǎngshang gēnzōng cháxún.
我们就用联邦快递寄吧。可以随时在网上跟踪查询。
Let's use FedEx. They can be tracked online anytime.

A: Zhè jiàn bāoguǒ xūyào bǎojià ma?
(这件)包裹需要保价吗?
Does this parcel need insurance?

B: Búyòng le.
不用了。
No need.

Related Words

1	píngxìn 平信	ordinary mail; surface mail	6	guójì 国际	international
2	míngxìnpiàn 明信片	postcard	7	yóupiào 邮票	stamp
3	bāoguǒ 包裹	parcel	8	bǎojià 保价 yóujiàn 邮件	insured mail
4	chāozhòng 超重	overweight	9	gēnzōng 跟踪 cháxún 查询	to track (mails parcels, etc.)
5	guónèi 国内	domestic	10	wúfǎ 无法 tóudì 投递	undeliverable

Cultural Navigation

In China, the postal service and express delivery service are very quick and convenient. China Post provides domestic and international delivery service for all kinds of mails, such as letters, documents, monetary instruments and merchandise samples. EMS is China Post's worldwide express mail service, which reaches more than 200 countries and regions in the world as well as almost 2,000 cities domestically. In addition, the express services provided by privately-run enterprises, such as SF Express and Shentong Express, are very popular too. Some world-famous express delivery companies as FedEx, UPS and DHL, have established their business in several hundred cities of China. Today, China's postal service and express delivery service have become completely connected to the whole world.

16 Sending E-mails

Key Sentence

Wǒ gāng gěi nǐ fāle yì fēng diànzǐ yóujiàn.
我刚给你发了一封电子邮件。
I have just sent you an e-mail.

Substitution

zuótiān
昨天
yesterday

yì xiǎoshíqián
一小时前
one hour ago

chuánzhēn
传真
fax

kuàijiàn
快件
express mail

jíjiàn
急件
urgent document

Extension

1. Wǒ yòng diàn zǐ yóu jiàn bǎ chǎnpǐn zīliào fāgěi nǐ le.
我用电（子）邮（件）把产品资料发给你了。
I have sent you the product information by e-mail.

2. Xiángxì nèiróng zài fùjiàn li.
详细内容在附件里。
The details are in the attachment.

3. Wǒ fāgěi nà jiā gōngsī de diànyóu bèi tuì huilai le.
我发给那家公司的电邮被退回来了。
The e-mail that I sent to that company bounced.

4. Kèhù de diànyóu dìzhǐ hǎoxiàng bú duì.
客户的电邮地址好像不对。
The e-mail address of the client seems incorrect.

Dialogue

A: Wǒ gāng gěi nǐ fāle yì fēng diànyóu.
我刚给你发了一封电邮。
I have just sent you an e-mail.

B: Shōudào le. Wǒ yǐjīng yòng diànyóu bǎ chǎnpǐn zīliào fāgěi nǐ le, xiángxì nèiróng zài fùjiàn li.
收到了。我已经用电邮把产品资料发给你了，详细内容在附件里。
I have received it. I have already sent you the product information by e-mail. The details are in the attachment.

A: Hǎo. Nǐ kěyǐ bǎ tā chāosòng Wáng jīnglǐ yí fèn ma?
好。你可以把它抄送王经理一份吗?
Good. Could you send a copy to Manager Wang?

B: Chāosòng le, kěshì wǒ fāgěi Wáng jīnglǐ de diànyóu bèi tuì huilai le.
抄送了，可是我发给王经理的电邮被退回来了。
I did, but the e-mail that I send to Manager Wang bounced.

A: Wèi shénme?
为什么?
Why?

B: Tā de diànyóu dìzhǐ hǎoxiàng bú duì.
他的电邮地址好像不对。
His e-mail address seems incorrect.

Related Words

No.	Word	Meaning	No.	Word	Meaning
1	diànyóu 电邮/ diànzǐ yóujiàn 电子邮件	e-mail	7	huífù 回复	to reply
2	yóujiàn 邮件	mail (either regular mail or e-mail)	8	shānchú 删除	to delete
3	zhuǎnfā 转发	to forward (an e-mail)	9	fùjiàn 附件	attachment
4	qúnfā 群发	to send to a group of recipients	10	bǎocún 保存	to save; to keep
5	chóngfā 重发	to resend	11	luànmǎ 乱码	unrecognizable characters; error codes
6	chāosòng 抄送	cc (i.e. "courtesy copy" or "carbon copy" of an e-mail message)			

Cultural Navigation

In today's business communication, e-mail has already become the most commonly used tool. However, when you receive an e-mail written in Chinese, you might sometimes encounter a bunch of unrecognizable characters. This is probably because your computer's default language is not Chinese. One solution to this problem is that you ask the other party to send that Chinese letter as an attachment to you to prevent problems.

17 Replying to a Letter

Key Sentence

Nǐ gěi nà jiā gōngsī huí gè diànzǐ yóujiàn jiěshì yíxià ba.
你给那家公司回个（电子）邮件，解释一下吧。

Could you reply to that company by e-mail and explain (to them)?

Substitution

huí gè chuánzhēn
回个传真
reply by fax

huí fēng xìn
回封信
reply by letter

huí gè diànhuà
回个电话
reply by phone

gōutōng
沟通
communicate with

zīxún
咨询
consult with

gǎnxiè
感谢
thank

quèrèn
确认
confirm with

1. Wǒ gāngcái shōudào gōnghuòshāng de diànyóu.
   我刚才收到供货商的电邮。
   I have just received an e-mail from the supplier.

2. Wǒ yǐjīng gěi tāmen huíxìn le.
   我已经给他们回信了。
   I have already replied to their letter.

3. Wǒmen yuē gè shíjiān dāngmiàn tán yì tán.
   我们约个时间当面谈一谈。
   Let's arrange a time for a face-to-face talk.

4. Nín qīnzì gěi tāmen huí gè diànhuà ba.
   您亲自给他们回个电话吧。
   Could you return a phone call to them personally?

A: Wǒ gāngcái shōudào gōnghuòshāng de diànyóu.
我刚才收到供货商的电邮。
I have just received an e-mail from the supplier again.

B: Zhè shì tāmen dì-sān fēng láixìn le.
这是他们第三封来信了。
This is the third letter from them.

A: Nǐ gěi tāmen huí gè yóujiàn, jiěshì yíxià ba.
你给他们回个邮件，解释一下吧。
Could you reply to them by e-mail and explain (to them)?

B: Shàng xīngqī wǒ yǐjīng gěi tāmen huíxìn le.
上星期我已经给他们回信了。
I replied to their letter last week.

Zhè cì wǒ gāi zěnme dáfù tāmen ne?
这次我该怎么答复他们呢?

How should I reply to them this time?

Gēn tāmen yuē gè shíjiān dāngmiàn tán yì tán ba.
A: 跟他们约个时间当面谈一谈吧。

Let's arrange a time for a face-to-face talk with them.

Yàobù nín qīnzì gěi tāmen huí gè diànhuà ba?
B: 要不您亲自给他们回个电话吧?

Could you please return a phone call to them personally?

Related Words

No.	Word	Meaning	No.	Word	Meaning
1	láixìn 来信	an incoming letter	7	huífù 回复	to reply (mostly used in written language)
2	huíxìn 回信	a letter in reply; to write back	8	dáfù 答复	to reply; to respond (with an answer)
3	shuōmíng 说明	to make clear; to explain	9	yuē yí gè shíjiān 约(一)个时间	to set up a time
4	jiěshì 解释	to explain; explanation	10	dāngmiàn tán 当面谈	to speak to sb. face to face
5	jiāoliú 交流	to communicate; to exchange (information)	11	yàobù 要不	in another way; otherwise; what about
6	gōutōng 沟通	to communicate; to link up			

Cultural Navigation

We all know that communication skills are very important in business correspondence. Although both "jiāoliú" and "gōutōng" refer to "communicate" in Chinese, their usages are different. "Jiāoliú" is to exchange information in general, while "gōutōng" is a well-intentioned interaction that tends to eliminate misunderstandings and solve existing problems between two parties. There is a Chinese old saying, "Shēnshǒu bù dǎ xiàoliǎnrén." (You can't slap someone's face when he smiles at you.) Even if there is unpleasantness and misunderstanding, we should still respect others and treat them politely. Only in this way can solutions to problems be found.

18 Instant Messaging

Key Sentence

Wǒ yòng jíshí tōngxìn gēn shāngyè huǒbàn bǎochí liánxì.
我用即时通信跟商业伙伴保持联系。

I keep in contact with business partners by using instant messenger.

Substitution

diànzǐ yóujiàn
电子邮件
e-mail

wǎngluò diànhuà
网络电话
Internet phone

wǎngluò shìpín
网络视频
Internet video

kèhù
客户
client

chǎngjiā
厂家
manufacturer

dàilǐshāng
代理商
agent

chéngbāoshāng
承包商
contractor

gōnghuòshāng
供货商
supplier

Extension

1. Nǐ zěnme gēn dàilǐshāng suíshí liánxì?
你怎么跟代理商随时联系?
How do you keep in contact with the agent at any time?

2. Yǒu shíhou tāmen yě yòng shìpín liánxì.
有时候他们也用视频（联系）。
Sometimes they also use Internet video (to keep in touch).

3. Nǐ yòng nǎ zhǒng jíshí tōngxìn ruǎnjiàn?
你用哪种即时通信软件?
Which instant messenger do you use?

4. Wǒ yìbān yòng
我一般用MSN。
I usually use MSN.

Dialogue

A: Nǐ zěnme gēn dàilǐshāng suíshí liánxì?
你怎么跟代理商随时联系?
How do you keep in contact with the agent at any time?

B: Wǒ yòng jíshí tōngxìn gēn shāngyè huǒbàn bǎochí liánxì.
我用即时通信跟商业伙伴保持联系。
I keep in contact with business partners by using instant messenger.

Yǒu shíhou wǒmen yě yòng shìpín liánxì.
有时候我们也用视频（联系）。
Sometimes we also use Internet video (to keep in touch).

A: Nǐ cháng yòng nǎ zhǒng jíshí tōngxìn ruǎnjiàn?
你常用哪种即时通信软件?
Which instant messenger do you often use?

B: Wǒ yìbān yòng
我一般用QQ。
I usually use QQ.

A: Kěyǐ bǎ wǒ jiājìn nǐ de liánxìrén míngdān ma?
可以把我加进你的联系人名单吗?
Could you add me to your contact list?

B: Hǎo a, dāngrán xíng!
好啊，当然行!
Sure, of course!

Related Words

1	liánxì liánluò 联系/联络	to contact	5	jíshí 即时	immediate(ly); instant(ly)
2	liánxìrén 联系人	contact person	6	suíshí 随时	at any time
3	míngdān 名单	name list	7	wēibó 微博	twitter; weibo
4	tōngxìnlù 通信录	address book			

Cultural Navigation

Cyber interaction has already become one of the main communication methods in business activities today. In China, many people are using e-mail services provided by Microsoft, Yahoo and Google. IM (instant messaging) is also very popular among the white-collar class and young people. The instant messaging service with the most Chinese users is QQ. It is a free instant messaging software developed by a Chinese information technology company named Tencent. Currently, it has an estimated user base of over 800 million. In recent years, Tencent has developed a mobile text and voice messaging communication service WeChat, which has an enormous number of users too.

19 Company Websites

Key Sentence

Wǒmen de wǎngzhàn nèiróng xūyào gēngxīn le.
我们的网站（内容）需要更新了。

Our website (contents) needs to be updated.

Substitution

zhǔyè 主页 homepage	wǎngyè 网页 webpage
bókè 博客 blog	liǎnshū 脸书 facebook

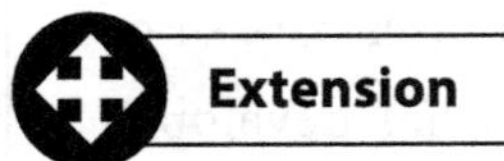

1. Wǎngyè shang hěn duō xìnxī yǐjīng guòshí le.
   网页上很多信息已经过时了。
   A lot of information on the webpage has already gone out of date.

2. Qǐng nǐ bǎ zhè jǐ zhāng túpiàn shàngchuán shangqu.
   请（你）把这几张图片上传上去。
   Please upload these pictures.

3. Jiù de xìnxī xūyào shānchú ma?
旧的信息需要删除吗?
Does the old information need to be deleted?

4. Zhèxiē nèiróng zànshí bǎoliú ba.
这些内容暂时保留吧。
Let's keep these contents for a while.

Dialogue

A: Wǒmen gōngsī de wǎngzhàn xūyào gēngxīn le.
我们公司的网站需要更新了。
Our company's website needs to be updated.

B: Shì a, hěn duō xìnxī yǐjīng guòshí le.
是啊，很多信息已经过时了。
Yes, a lot of information has already gone out of date.

A: Kèhù fǎnyìng zàixiàn kèfú de gōngnéng yě yǒu yìxiē wèntí.
客户反映在线客服的功能也有一些问题。
Customers report that the online customer service function has some problems too.

B: Shìma? Ràng wǒ lái jiǎnchá yíxià.
是吗? 让我来检查一下。
Is that true? Let me check it.

A: Jīnglǐ yào nǐ bǎ zhè jǐ zhāng túpiàn shàngchuán shangqu.
经理要你把这几张图片上传上去。
The manager wants you to upload these pictures.

B: Hǎo de. Jiù de xūyào shānchú ma?
好的。旧的需要删除吗?
OK. Do the old ones need to be deleted?

A: Zànshí bǎoliú ba.
暂时保留吧。
Let's keep them for a while.

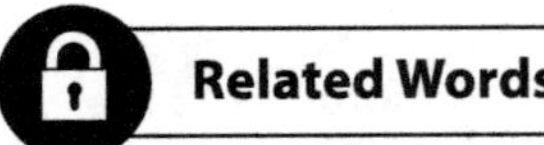

Related Words

1	shàngchuán 上传	to upload	7	bǎocún 保存	to save
2	xiàzǎi 下载	to download	8	bǎoliú 保留	to keep
3	shānchú 删除	to delete	9	zīliào 资料	data; information; material
4	gēngxīn 更新	to update	10	ruǎnjiàn 软件	software
5	shēngjí 升级	to upgrade	11	gōngnéng 功能	function
6	tìhuàn 替换	to replace	12	nèibùwǎng 内部网/ nèiliánwǎng 内联网	intranet

Cultural Navigation

Most Chinese companies and enterprises have their own websites. These companies' websites not only provide information on their products and services, but also offer related online services. In addition, e-commerce has also been developing rapidly in China. The famous Alibaba Group is currently the largest Internet-based e-commerce enterprise in China. In 2012, two of Alibaba's portals, Taobao.com and Tmall.com, had a total sales volume of US $170 billion, which is more than their competitors Amazon.com and eBay combined. However, except for some big companies' websites that have multi-language versions to choose from, many websites are written in Chinese only. Therefore, in China, Chinese should be learnt if you do business here.

20 Online Chatting

Key Sentence

Zuìjìn zài wǎngshang méi kànjiàn nǐ.
最近在网上没看见你。
I haven't seen you online recently.

Substitution

xiànshàng 线上 online; on the Internet	lùntán 论坛 forum
liáotiānshì 聊天室 chatting room	qún QQ群 QQ group

Extension

1. Wǒ de diànnǎo zhòng bìngdú le.
   我的电脑中病毒了。
   My computer has a virus.
2. Wǒ yǐwéi nǐ bǎ wǒ de xìnxī "lánjié" le.
   我以为你把我的信息"拦截"了。
   I thought that you "blocked" my message.
3. Shàngbān shíjiān bù zhǔn zài wǎngshang liáotiān.
   上班时间不准在网上聊天。
   Online chatting is not allowed during working hours.

4. Děng huìr zài liáo!
等会儿再聊!
I'll talk to you later!

A: Nǐ hǎo! Zuìjìn zài wǎngshang méi kànjiàn nǐ.
你好!最近在网上没看见你。
Hi! I haven't seen you online recently.

B: Shàng xīngqī wǒ de diànnǎo zhòng bìngdú le, méi fǎ yòng.
上星期我的电脑中病毒了,没法用。
Last week my computer was infected by a virus, and it didn't work.

A: Wǒ yǐwéi nǐ bǎ wǒ de xìnxī lánjié le.
我以为你把我的信息"拦截"了。
I thought that you "blocked" my message.

B: Děng huìr zài gēn nǐ liáo.
等会儿再(跟你)聊。
I'll talk to you later.

A: Zěnme le?
怎么了?
What's wrong?

B: Zuìjìn gōngsī yǒu xīn guīdìng, shàngbān shíjiān bù zhǔn zài wǎngshang liáotiān.
最近公司有新规定,上班时间不准在网上聊天。
The company has a new rule that online chatting is not allowed during working hours.

A: Nǐmen gōngsī guǎn de zhēn yán!
你们公司管得真严!
Your company is really strict!

B: Shì a. Nà wǒ kāishǐ gōngzuò le, zàijiàn.
是啊。那我开始工作了，再见。
Yes. Then I'll start my work. Bye.

A: Hǎo ba, wǒ yě děi xiàxiàn le.
好吧，我也得下线了。
OK, I have to log off too.

Related Words

1	shàngwǎng 上网	to go online; to surf the Internet	7	lánjié 拦截	to block
2	xiàxiàn 下线	to log off; to go offline	8	guīdìng 规定	rule; regulation; to regulate
3	dēngrù 登入	to log in	9	yán gé 严(格)	strict; rigorous
4	tuìchū 退出	to log out	10	kāijī 开机	to turn on a computer
5	zhùcè 注册	to register	11	guānjī 关机	to turn off a computer
6	liáotiān 聊天	to chat			

Cultural Navigation

Having an understanding of popular Internet language is both interesting and practical. In today's Internet era, young Chinese like to borrow existing Chinese phrases to express totally different meanings. Once this new usage is accepted by many Internet users, it will quickly become very popular, and even influence mainstream media and everyday conversation. For instance, the original meaning of "fā tiězi" is "to send out a note" or "to send out an invitation," but its new meaning is "to post a message on the Internet." "Pāi zhuān" originally means "to strike with a brick," but now it means to express disagreement or criticize others' opinions posted online. The original meaning of "fān qiáng (to climb over the wall)" is quite straightforward, but in Internet language it means to bypass a firewall and visit a blocked website by using technological means. Without doubt, new Internet language is bringing new energy into the old Chinese language.

On a Business Trip

21 Planning an Itinerary

Key Sentence

Gōngsī pài wǒ xià gè xīngqī qù Shànghǎi chūchāi.
公司派我下个星期去上海出差。
The company has assigned me to Shanghai on a business trip next week.

Substitution

jīnglǐ
经理
manager

lǎobǎn
老板
boss

zǒngbù
总部
headquarters

dānwèi
单位
work unit

hòutiān
后天
the day after tomorrow

xià gè yuè
下个月
next month

Shēnzhèn
深圳
Shenzhen

Ōuzhōu
欧洲
Europe

Extension

1. Nǐ de xíngchéng ānpái hǎo le ma?
你的 行 程 安排好了吗?
Have you arranged your itinerary?

2. Wǒ dǎsuàn xiān fēidào Běijīng.
我 打算 先 飞到 北京。
I plan to fly to Beijing first.

3. Cóng Hángzhōu zuò huǒchē dào Nánjīng yào duō cháng shíjiān?
从 杭 州 坐 火车 到 南京 要 多 长 时间?
How long does it take to go from Hangzhou to Nanjing by train?

4. Rúguǒ zuò gāotiě dehuà, yě hái yào wǔ gè bàn xiǎoshí zuǒyòu.
如果 坐 高铁 的话，也还 要 五个 半 小时 左右。
If you are taking a high-speed train, it will still take about five and a half hours.

Dialogue

A: Gōngsī pài wǒ xià gè xīngqī qù Shànghǎi hé Nánjīng chūchāi.
公司 派我下个星期去 上 海 和南 京 出差。
The company has assigned me to Shanghai and Nanjing on a business trip next week.

B: Nǐ de xíngchéng ānpái hǎo le ma?
(你的) 行 程 安排好了吗?
Have you arranged your itinerary?

A: Wǒ dǎsuàn xiān fēidào Shànghǎi, zài cóng Shànghǎi zuò huǒchē dào Nánjīng.
我 打算 先 飞到 上海，再 从 上 海 坐 火车 到 南 京。
I plan to fly to Shanghai first, and go from Shanghai to Nanjing by train.

B: Cóng Shànghǎi zuò huǒchē dào Nánjīng yào duō cháng shíjiān?
从上海坐火车到南京要多长时间？
How long does it take to go from Shanghai to Nanjing by train?

A: Rúguǒ zuò gāotiě dehuà, zhǐyào yí gè bàn xiǎoshí zuǒyòu.
（如果）坐高铁的话，只要一个半小时左右。
If you are taking a high-speed train, it will only take about one and a half hours.

B: Huílai de shíhou, nǐ xūyào wǒ dào jīchǎng jiē nǐ ma?
回来的时候，（你）需要我到机场接你吗？
When you are back, do you need me to pick you up at the airport?

A: Xièxie, búyòng le. Wǒ zuò jīchǎng dàbā dào shìzhōngxīn, hěn fāngbiàn.
谢谢，不用了。我坐机场大巴到市中心，很方便。
No, thanks. I can take an airport shuttle bus to the downtown area. It's very convenient.

Related Words

1	shāngwù lǚxíng 商务旅行	business trip (formal)	4	dǎsuàn 打算	plan; to plan (relatively casual)
2	chūchāi 出差	business trip (colloquial)	5	gāotiě 高铁	high-speed train
3	jìhuà 计划	plan; to plan (relatively formal)	6	jiē 接	to pick sb. up

(Continued)

7	sòng 送	to see sb. off	9	chūnyùn 春运	the Spring Festival travel period
8	jīchǎng dàbā 机场大巴	airport shuttle bus	10	huángjīnzhōu 黄金周	golden week (such as a weeklong holiday)

Cultural Navigation

China is a big country with a large population and a very busy transportation system. Foreigners traveling in China may not only encounter language barriers, but also run into unforeseen hassles. Therefore, if you plan to go to China, you should plan an itinerary in advance. If possible, you should avoid traveling during holidays, especially during the Spring Festival (the Chinese New Year) and the National Day holiday. During the Spring Festival, most Chinese people go back home to celebrate the New Year, so the passenger transport volume of railways, highways and airways increases sharply. This situation will last for about two weeks. The National Day holiday falls on the first week of October. A lot of Chinese people like to leave home to go vacationing during the week. So it is usually very hard to buy train or airplane tickets, and even hotels will be fully booked.

22 Booking Airplane Tickets

Key Sentence

Wǒ xiǎng dìng yì zhāng qù Shànghǎi de (fēi) jīpiào.
我想订一张去上海的（飞）机票。
I want to book an airplane ticket to Shanghai.

Substitution

Běijīng
北京
Beijing

Luòshānjī
洛杉矶
Los Angeles

dānchéngpiào
单程票
one-way ticket

wǎngfǎnpiào
往返票
round-trip ticket

huǒchēpiào
火车票
train ticket

gāotiě chēpiào
高铁车票
high-speed train ticket

1. Nín yào nǎ tiān de piào?
   您要哪天的票?
   Which day do you need a ticket for?
2. Wǒ xiǎng dìng yì zhāng 17 hào cóng Běijīng dào Nánjīng de jīpiào, jīngjìcāng.
   我想订一张17号从北京到南京的机票，经济舱。
   I'd like to book one flight ticket from Beijing to Nanjing on the 17th. Economy class.
3. Míngtiān de jīpiào màiwán le.
   明天的机票卖完了。
   Tomorrow's flight tickets are sold out.
4. Dānchéng háishi wǎngfǎn?
   单程还是往返?
   Is it one-way or round-trip?

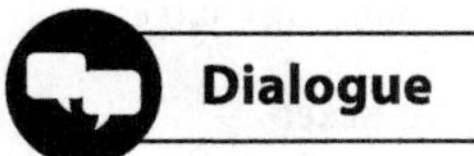

A: Wǒ xiǎng dìng yì zhāng qù Shànghǎi de wǎngfǎn jīpiào.
我想订一张去上海的往返机票。
I want to book a round-trip flight ticket to Shanghai.

B: Nín yào dìng nǎ tiān de piào?
您要（订）哪天的票?
Which day do you need to book a ticket for?

A: Míngtiānde. Huíchéng rìqī shì xià Xīngqī'èr, 6 yuè 25 hào.
明天的。回程（日期）是下星期二，6月25号。
Tomorrow. The return date is next Tuesday, June 25th.

B: Duìbuqǐ, míngtiān fēi Shànghǎi de jīpiào màiwán le.
对不起，明天飞上海的机票卖完了。
I'm sorry. Tomorrow's flight tickets to Shanghai are sold out.

A: Nà jiù dìng hòutiān de ba.
那就订后天的吧。
Then I'll book a ticket for the day after tomorrow.

B: Jīngjìcāng háishi gōngwùcāng?
经济舱还是公务舱？
Economy class or business class?

A: Gōngwùcāng duōshao qián?
公务舱多少钱？
How much is business class?

Related Words

1	tóuděngcāng 头等舱	first class	6	yùdìng 预订	to book in advance
2	ruǎnwò 软卧	soft sleeper	7	dìngpiàofèi 订票费	booking charge
3	yìngwò 硬卧	hard sleeper	8	diànzǐ 电子 (kè 客) piào 票	e-ticket
4	yī děng zuò 一等座	first-class seat (on the train)	9	liánchéngpiào 联程票	connecting ticket for the flight or train; interline ticket
5	èr děng zuò 二等座	second-class seat (on the train)	10	fǎnchéngpiào 返程票/ huíchéngpiào 回程票	return ticket

(Continued)

11 实名制 (shímíngzhì)

a real-name system (i.e. The customer is obliged to present his/her real name and identification when he/she goes through necessary formalities. In China it is used in banking, insurance, traveling, etc.)

Cultural Navigation

There are several different ways to book a ticket when you travel or go on a business trip in China. Most hotels and local travel agencies provide ticket booking service. You can also call a local ticket center to book a ticket. Now it is very convenient to book train or flight tickets online. You can pay through online bank or by credit card and then print the train ticket or the boarding pass at train stations or airports. "Xiéchéng (Ctrip)" and "Yìlóng (eLong)" are both popular travel websites in China, where you can find useful booking and travel information that will bring great convenience to your trips.

23 Picking Up Someone at the Airport

Key Sentence

Nín shì cóng Měiguó lái de Shǐmìsī xiānsheng ma?
您是从美国来的史密斯先生吗?
Are you Mr. Smith from America?

Substitution

Yīngguó
英国
Britain

Rìběn
日本
Japan

Zhōngguó
中国
China

Niǔyuē
纽约
New York

Shǐmìsī fūrén
史密斯夫人
Mrs. Smith

Bùlǎng nǚshì
布朗女士
Ms. Brown

Huáitè xiǎojiě
怀特小姐
Miss White

Wēi'ērsēn zǒngcái
威尔森总裁
CEO/President Wilson

Extension

1. Liú jīnglǐ pài wǒ lái jiē nín.
刘经理派我来接您。
Manager Liu sent me here to pick you up.

2. Huānyíng nín láidào Guǎngzhōu!
欢迎您来到广州！
Welcome to Guangzhou!

3. Ràng wǒ bāng nín ná xíngli ba.
让我帮您拿行李吧。
Let me help you with your luggage.

4. Wǒ zìjǐ néng xíng.
我自己能行。
I can do it myself.

Dialogue

A: Dǎrǎo yíxià, nín shì cóng Měiguó lái de Shǐmìsī xiānsheng ma?
打扰一下，您是从美国来的史密斯先生吗？
Excuse me, are you Mr. Smith from America?

B: Wǒ shì Yuēhànxùn Shǐmìsī. Nín shì...?
我是约翰逊·史密斯。您是……？
I am Johnson Smith. You are…?

A: Wǒ shì Dōngfāng Gōngsī de Lǐ Xìnwén. Gōngsī pài wǒ lái jiē nín.
我是东方公司的李信文。公司派我来接您。
I am Li Xinwen from the Eastern Company. The company sent me here to pick you up.

B: Nín hǎo, Lǐ xiānsheng!
您好，李先生！
How do you do, Mr. Li?

A: Nín hǎo, huānyíng nín láidào Běijīng!
您好，欢迎您来到北京！
How do you do? Welcome to Beijing!

B: Xièxie nín lái jīchǎng jiē wǒ. Gěi nín tiān máfan le.
谢谢您来机场接我。给您添麻烦了。
Thank you for picking me up at the airport. (I'm) sorry for troubling you.

A: Bú kèqi. Nín yí lù xīnkǔ le! Ràng wǒ bāng nín ná xíngli ba.
不客气。您一路辛苦了！让我帮您拿行李吧。
You are welcome. You must be tired after the trip. Let me help you with your luggage.

B: Xièxie, xièxie. Wǒ zìjǐ néng xíng!
谢谢，谢谢。我自己能行！
Thanks. But I can do it myself!

Related Words

1	jiē rén 接人	to pick sb. up	7	dàodá 到达	to arrive
2	děng rén 等人	to wait for sb.	8	wǎndiǎn 晚点	to be late; to delay
3	rèncuò rén 认错人	to mistake sb. for another person	9	zhǔndiǎn 准点	on time
4	lǚxíngxiāng 旅行箱	traveling suitcase/case	10	hángzhàn-lóu 航站楼	terminal
5	shǒutuīchē 手推车	handcart	11	chūkǒu 出口	exit
6	dàogǎng 到港	to land (at the airport)			

Cultural Navigation

In China, when people pick up a guest at the airport or train station, they often use a sentence like "Yí lù xīnkǔ le" (You must be exhausted after the trip) to convey greetings to the traveler, or say something like "Lùshang yíqiè shùnlì ma?" (Was everything fine during the trip?) to express their care. Confucius once said, "Yǒu péng zì yuǎnfāng lái, bú yì lè hū?" (Isn't it a joy to have friends coming from afar?) To pick up a guest from afar will not only provide convenience to the visitor, but also show your eager expectation and respect for him/her. It will make a guest "feel at home" at the first moment of his/her arrival. This is often the first step to establish a harmonious cooperative relationship in business activities.

24 Hotel Check-in

Key Sentence

Wǒ yù dìngle yì jiānbiāo zhǔn jiān.
我（预）订了一间标（准）间。
I have booked a standard room.

Substitution

dān rén jiān
单（人）间
single room

dàchuángfáng
大床房
king-bed room

tàofáng
套房
suite

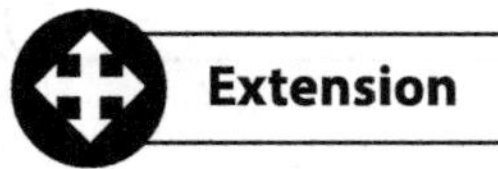

1. Nín yù dìng de shì sān gè wǎnshang de biāozhǔnjiān.
   您（预）订的是三个晚上的标准间。
   You have reserved a standard room for 3 nights.

2. Qǐng chūshì yíxià nín de hùzhào.
   请出示一下您的护照。
   Please show me your passport.

3. Nín jiāo xiànjīn háishi shuā xìnyòngkǎ?
   您交现金还是刷信用卡?
   Will you pay by cash or credit card?

4. Nín de fángjiān shì 2018.
您的房间是2018。
Your room is 2018.

A: Nǐ hǎo. Wǒ dìngle yì jiān biāozhǔnjiān.
你好。我订了一间标准间。
Hello, I have booked a standard room.

B: Qǐngwèn nín guìxìng?
请问您贵姓?
May I ask your last name?

A: Wǒ xìng Shǐmìsī, wǒ jiào Yuēhàn Shǐmìsī.
我姓史密斯，我叫约翰·史密斯。
My last name is Smith, and I'm Johnson Smith.

B: Nín dìng de shì sān gè wǎnshang de biāozhǔnjiān.
您订的是三个晚上的标准间。
You have reserved a standard room for 3 nights.

Qǐngchūshì yíxià nín de zhèngjiàn.
请出示一下您的证件。
Please show me your ID.

A: Hǎode. Zhè shì wǒ de hùzhào.
好的。这是我的护照。
Sure. This is my passport.

B: Nín jiāo xiànjīn háishi shuā xìnyòngkǎ?
您交现金还是刷信用卡?
Will you pay by cash or credit card?

A: Wǒ yòng xìnyòngkǎ ba.
我用信用卡吧。
I will use my credit card.

B: Xièxie! Nín de fángjiān shì 907. Zhè shì nín de fángkǎ.
谢谢！您的房间是907。这是您的房卡。
Thanks! Your room is 907. This is your room card.

Related Words

1	rùzhù dēngjì (入住)登记	check in (for staying at a hotel)	7	hùzhào 护照	passport
2	qiántái/fúwùtái 前台/服务台	front desk (of a hotel); service desk	8	shēnfènzhèng 身份证	identity card
3	fúwùyuán 服务员	attendant; waiter	9	yājīn 押金	deposit
4	dàtīng 大厅	(hotel) lobby	10	fángkǎ 房卡	room card
5	zhíbān jīnglǐ 值班经理	manager on duty	11	qiānmíng 签名	signature; to sign one's name
6	zhèngjiàn 证件	ID; certificate			

Cultural Navigation

In Chinese, a hotel is called "lǚguǎn," "bīnguǎn," "fàndiàn" or "jiǔdiàn." You can make a hotel reservation through travel agencies or on the Internet by yourself. When you check in at a hotel, you need to show an ID. You also need to pay the deposit by cash or credit card. When you check out, the front desk personnel will notify the attendant to check the room, a procedure called "cháfáng," to make sure that nothing is damaged or lost in the room. If a problem is discovered, the hotel staff and the guest can determine who should be responsible in the presence of both sides.

25 Hotel Services

Key Sentence

Nǐmen lǚguǎn yǒu zūchē fúwù ma?
你们旅馆有租车服务吗?
Does your hotel have car rental service?

Substitution

jiàoxǐng fúwù
叫醒服务
wake-up call service

xǐyī fúwù
洗衣服务
laundry service

piàowù fúwù
票务服务
ticket service

yóujì fúwù
邮寄服务
postal service

kèfáng sòngcān fúwù
(客房) 送餐服务
room service

wàibì duìhuàn fúwù
外币兑换服务
foreign exchange service

Extension

1. Qǐng nín chéng diàntī shàng èr lóu, dào kèfú zhōngxīn.
   请您乘电梯上二楼，到客服中心。
   Please take the elevator to the second floor and go to the Customer Service Center.

2. Zài nàr kěyǐ dìng jīpiào ma?
   在那儿可以订机票吗?
   Can flight tickets be booked there too?

3. Wǎncān shì jǐ diǎn?
   晚餐是几点?
   What time is dinner?

4. Nín xūyào jiàoxǐng fúwù ma?
   您需要叫醒服务吗?
   Do you need a wake-up call service?

Dialogue

A: Qǐngwèn, nǐmen yǒu zūchē fúwù ma?
请问，你们有租车服务吗?
Excuse me, do you have car rental service?

B: Yǒu. Qǐng nín chéng diàntī shàng èr lóu dào shāngwù zhōngxīn.
有。请您乘电梯上二楼到商务中心。
Yes. Please take the elevator to the second floor and go to the Business Center.

A: Zài nàr yě kěyǐ dìngpiào ma?
在那儿也可以订票吗?
Can tickets be booked there too?

B: Shìde. Shāngwù zhōngxīn yě tígōng piàowù fúwù.
是的。商务中心也提供票务服务。
Yes. The Business Center also provides ticket service.

A: Zǎocān shì jǐ diǎn?
早餐是几点?
What time is breakfast?

B: Zǎocān shíjiān shì 6 diǎn bàn dào 9 diǎn bàn. Nín xūyào jiàoxǐng fúwù ma?
早餐时间是6点半到9点半。您需要叫醒服务吗?
Breakfast time is from 6:30 to 9:30. Do you need a wake-up call service?

A: Qǐng míngtiān zǎoshang 7 diǎn jiàoxǐng wǒ.
请明天早上7点叫醒我。
Please wake me up at 7:00 tomorrow morning.

Related Words

1	jiànshēnfáng 健身房	gym	8	jiǔbā 酒吧	bar
2	yóuyǒngchí 游泳池	swimming pool	9	kǎlā 卡拉OK	karaoke
3	měiróng 美容	beauty salon	10	huìyìshì 会议室	conference room
4	měifà 美发	hair salon	11	duōgōngnéngtīng 多功能厅	multifunctional hall
5	ànmó 按摩	massage	12	bǎoxiǎnxiāng 保险箱	safe
6	sāngná 桑拿	sauna	13	lǐpǐndiàn 礼品店	gift shop
7	cāntīng 餐厅	restaurant			

Cultural Navigation

Hotels in China have adopted a star-ranking standard. From economy hotels to luxury hotels, hotels are ranked from one to five stars. Three-star hotels or above usually have broadband networks and business centers. At the business center, hotel guests can use some office equipment, such as computers, printers, copiers and fax machines, etc. Many business centers also provide services like car rental, ticket booking, mailing, foreign currency exchange and secretary services. This is very helpful to people who are on a business trip.

26 Taking a Taxi

Key Sentence

Qǐng bāng wǒ jiào yí liàng chūzūchē, wǒ yào qù jīchǎng.
请帮我叫一辆出租车，我要去机场。

Please help me call a taxi. I'll go to the airport.

Substitution

huǒchēzhàn
火车站
train station

dìtiězhàn
地铁站
subway station

Jiàrì Jiǔdiàn
假日酒店
Holiday Inn

Extension

1. Nín qù nǎr?
您去哪儿？
Where do you want to go?

2. Wǒ yào qù zhège dìfang, zhèshì dìzhǐ.
我要去这个地方，这是地址。
I want to go to this place, and here is the address.

3. Qiánmiàn yòu dǔchē le!
前面又堵车了！
There are traffic jams ahead again!

Guòle xià gè hóng-lǜdēng jiù dào le.
4. 过了下个红绿灯就到了。
We'll get there after the next traffic light.

Dialogue

Qǐng bāng wǒ jiào yí liàng chūzūchē.
A: 请帮我叫一辆出租车。
Could you help me call a taxi?

qiántái fúwùyuán Hǎode, nín shāoděng.
B: (前台服务员)：好的，您稍等。
(Front desk clerk): Sure, just one moment.

chūzūchē sījī Nín shàng nǎr?
C: (出租车司机)：您上哪儿?
(Taxi driver): Where do you want to go?

Wǒ yào qù zhège dìfang, zhè shì dìzhǐ.
A: 我要去这个地方，这是地址。
I want to go to this place, and here is the address.

Hǎo lei!
C: 好嘞!
OK!

……

Qiánmiàn yòu dǔchē le!
C: 前面又堵车了!
There are traffic jams ahead again!

Hái yuǎn ma?
A: 还远吗?
Is it still far?

Guòle xià gè hóng-lǜdēng jiù dào le.
C: 过了下个红绿灯就到了。
We'll get there after the next traffic light.

A: Nà wǒ jiù zài zhèr xiàchē ba. Qǐng tíng yíxià!
那我就在这儿下车吧。请停一下！

Then I'll get off the car right here. Please stop.

Wǒ yào fāpiào.
我要发票。

I need a receipt.

Related Words

1	lìjiāoqiáo 立交桥	overpass; flyover; motorway interchange	7	ràodào 绕道	to make a detour
2	chéngqū (城区) gāojiàlù 高架路	(inner-city) elevated motorway	8	jiàochē rèxiàn 叫车热线	taxi hotline
3	gāosù gōnglù 高速公路	expressway	9	hēichē 黑车	unlicensed taxi/vehicle
4	lùkǒu 路口	intersection; crossroads	10	zǎikè 宰客	to rip off passengers; to cheat customers
5	chūkǒu 出口	exit	11	tóusù diànhuà 投诉电话	customer hotline (for reporting unsatisfactory service)
6	dǔchē 堵车	traffic jam			

Cultural Navigation

"Dǎchē" is another way to say "take a taxi" in Chinese. The charge for taking a taxi includes "initial charge" and "mileage charge." Normally, the initial charge covers the first 3 kilometers of the taxi driving. The mileage charge will be added to the bill when the driving distance is over the initial 3 kilometers. You do not need to leave a tip when you take a taxi in China. However, you'd better ask for a receipt when you get off. If you are unsatisfied or have any doubts, you can call the complaint hotline. You can find the taxi that you took and the driver according to the information on the receipt. Please don't take "hēichē (literal: black car)." These unlicensed vehicles usually do not bear the sign of "Taxi" and the drivers often rip off passengers and charge more fare.

27 Asking for Directions

Key Sentence

Nǐ zhīdào qù Shìmào Zhōngxīn zěnme zǒu zuì kuài ma?
你知道去世贸中心怎么走最快吗?
Do you know the fastest way to get to the World Trade Center?

Substitution

jīchǎng
机场
airport

huǒchēzhàn
火车站
train station

Guójì Huìyì Zhōngxīn
国际会议中心
International Conference Center

zuì jìn
最近
shortest

zuì róngyì
最容易
easiest

zuì fāngbiàn
最方便
most convenient

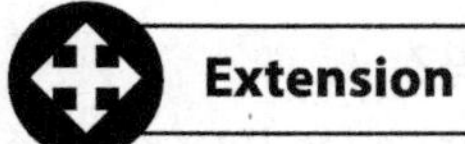

1. Cóng Shànghǎi Lù shàng gāojià wǎng dōng kāi, dào Jiěfàng Lù chūkǒu xià.
   从上海路上高架往东开，到解放路出口下。
   Get on the (inner-city) elevated motorway at Shanghai Road, drive towards the east, then take the exit at Jiefang Road.

2. Cóng gāojià xiàlai jiù shì Shìmào Zhōngxīn.
   从高架下来就是世贸中心。
   The World Trade Center is right there once you get off the elevated motorway.

3. Zài wǎng qián kāi wǔbǎi mǐ jiù dào le.
   再往前开五百米就到了。
   Drive on for another 500 meters and you'll be there.

4. Cóng zhèr dào nàr dàgài duō yuǎn?
   （从这儿到那儿）大概多远？
   How far is it (from here to there) approximately?

A: Nǐ zhīdào qù Shìmào Zhōngxīn zěnme zǒu zuì kuài ma?
你知道去世贸中心怎么走最快吗？
Do you know the fastest way to get to the World Trade Center?

B: Rúguǒ kāichē dehuà, cóng Shànghǎi Lù shàng gāojià wǎng dōng kāi, dào Jiěfàng Lù chūkǒu xià.
(如果)开车的话，从上海路上高架往东开，到解放路出口下。
If driving, you should get on the elevated motorway at Shanghai Road, drive towards the east, then take the exit at Jiefang Road.

A: Cóng gāojià xiàlai jiù shì Shìmào Zhōngxīn ma?
（从高架）下来就是（世贸中心）吗？

The World Trade Center is right there once I get off the elevated motorway?

B: Gāojià xiàlai hòu yòu zhuǎn, kànjiàn dì-yī gè hóng-lǜdēng zài zuǒ zhuǎn, zài wǎng qián kāi sānbǎi mǐ jiù dào le.
高架下来后右转，看见第一个红绿灯再左转，再往前开三百米就到了。

Turn right after you get off the elevated motorway, then turn left at the first traffic light. Drive on for another 300 meters and you'll be there.

A: Cóng zhèr dào nàr dàgài duō yuǎn?
从这儿到那儿大概多远？

How far is it from here to there approximately?

B: Sì-wǔ gōnglǐ ba. Nǐ yě kěyǐ zuò dìtiě qù.
四五公里吧。你也可以坐地铁去。

It's about 4 to 5 kilometers. You may take the subway too.

Related Words

1	wǎng dōng 往东	towards the east	6	wǎng hòu zǒu 往后走	to go back
2	wǎng xī 往西	towards the west	7	wǎng yòu guǎi 往右拐	to turn right
3	wǎng nán 往南	towards the south	8	wǎng zuǒ guǎi 往左拐	to turn left
4	wǎng běi 往北	towards the north	9	dǎohángyí 导航仪	GPS
5	wǎng qián zǒu 往前走	to go straight ahead			

Cultural Navigation

There is a slight difference of giving directions between people in Northern China and in Southern China. For instance, a native resident in Beijing often gives directions using "east, west, south and north," but a local resident in Nanjing will often tell you directions by saying "straight ahead, going back, turning left and turning right." It is not difficult for a person who asks for directions to understand "ahead, back, left and right." However, if you've already lost your way, it will be not that easy to get a clear idea of which direction is east, west, south or north. It is an interesting experience to ask for directions in Chinese. It not only tests your Chinese but also lets you feel a Chinese person's attitude towards a stranger. Generally speaking, most Chinese are quite friendly to foreigners who need help, and are happy to give them a hand.

28 Taking a Bus

Key Sentence

Qù Kējì Zhǎnlǎnguǎn yīnggāi zuò jǐ lù (gōngjiāo) chē?
去科技展览馆应该坐几路（公交）车?
Which bus should I take to the Science and Technology Exhibition Center?

Substitution

chūkǒu shāngpǐn jiāoyìhuì
出口商品交易会
Export Commodities Fair

Shìmào Zhōngxīn
世贸中心
World Trade Center

Shìbó Yuán
世博园
World Expo Park

Wàitān
外滩
the Bund (in Shanghai)

Měiguó Dàshǐguǎn
美国大使馆
USA Embassy

dìtiě jǐ hàoxiàn
地铁几号线
which subway line

qīngguǐ jǐ hào xiàn
轻轨几号线
which light railway

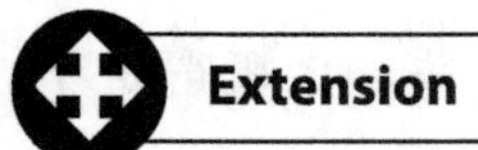

Extension

1. Xiān zuò 103 lù dào Chángjiāng Lù, zài huàn 45 lù.
   先坐103路到长江路，再换45路。
   Take Bus 103 to Changjiang Road first, then transfer to Bus 45.

2. Yǒu dìtiě dào Shìmào Zhōngxīn ma?
   有地铁到世贸中心吗？
   Is there a subway going to the World Trade Center?

3. Dìtiězhàn zài zhè tiáo jiē xī tóu.
   地铁站在这条街西头。
   The subway station is at the west end of the street.

4. Dàgài děi zǒu bàn xiǎoshí.
   大概得走半小时。
   It's about half an hour walk.

Dialogue

A: Cóng zhèr qù Kējì Zhǎnlǎnguǎn yīnggāi zuò jǐ lù chē?
从这儿去科技展览馆应该坐几路车?
Which bus should I take from here to the Science and Technology Exhibition Center?

B: Xiān zuò áěà lù dào Chángjiāng Lù, zài huàn ōó lù. Zuò liǎng zhàn jiù dào le.
先坐103路到长江路，再换45路。坐两站就到了。
Take Bus 103 to Changjiang Road first, then transfer to Bus 45. Get off at the second stop and you'll be there.

A: Yǒu dìtiě dào nàr ma?
有地铁到那儿吗?
Is there a subway going there?

B: Yǒu a. Dìtiězhàn zài (zhè tiáo jiē) dōng tóu. Dàgài děi zǒu shí fēnzhōng.
有啊。地铁站在（这条街）东头。大概得走十分钟。

Yes. The subway station is at the east end (of the street). It's about 10 minutes' walk.

A: Wǒ háishi zuò gōngjiāochē ba.
我还是坐公交车吧。

I guess that I'll take a bus.

B: Wèi shénme bù dǎchē qù?
为什么不打车去?

Why don't you take a taxi?

A: Gāofēng shíjiān, dǎchē tài nán le!
高峰时间，打车太难了!

During the rush hour, it's too hard to get a taxi!

Related Words

1	gōngjiāo 公交/ gōnggòngjiāotōng 公共交通	public transportation	6	shàngchē 上车	to get on (a bus or a train)
2	gōngjiāochē 公交车/ gōnggòng qìchē 公共汽车	bus	7	xiàchē 下车	to get off (a bus or a train)
3	dàozhàn 到站	to arrive at a station	8	huànchē 换车/ zhuǎnchē 转车	to transfer (to another bus or train)
4	jìnzhàn 进站	to enter a station	9	zuòcuò chē 坐错车	on a wrong bus
5	chūzhàn 出站	to leave/exit a station	10	Bié jǐ wǒ! 别挤我!	Don't push me!

Cultural Navigation

In China, public transportation is convenient in many places. Some big cities not only have buses but also have subway and light railway systems. Nonetheless, traffic jams are still very severe during morning and early evening rush hours. During this period of time, the subway and buses become very crowded and getting a taxi is not easy either. If you plan to use public transportation often when you are in China, you might want to buy a local public transportation card (also called IC card). You can use it when you take a bus, the subway or a taxi. It is really convenient.

29 Renting a Vehicle for a Trip

Key Sentence

Wǒyào zū yí liàngchē, yòng sān tiān.
我要租一辆车，用三天。
I want to rent a car for 3 days.

Substitution

jiàochē
轿车
passenger car

yuèyěchē
越野车
SUV(sport utility vehicle)

shāngwùchē
商务车
MPV(multi-purpose vehicle)

xiǎoxíng huòchē
小型货车
minivan

yí gè xīngqī
一个星期
one week

yí gè zhōumò
一个周末
the entire weekend

Extension

1. Nín xūyào nǎ zhǒng chēxíng?
   您需要哪种车型?
   What kind of vehicle do you need?

2. Wǒ xūyào yí wèi yǒu jīngyàn de dàijià (sījī).
   我需要一位有经验的代驾（司机）。
   I need an experienced designated driver.

3. Wǒ míngtiān yòng chē, Xīngqīrì huán chē.
   我明天用车，星期日还车。
   I need the vehicle tomorrow, and will return it on Sunday.

4. Wǒ kěyǐ gěi nín yí liàng Biékè shāngwùchē, dài yí wèi dàijià.
   我可以给您一辆别克商务车，带一位代驾。
   I can give you a Buick MPV with a designated driver.

Dialogue

A: Nín hǎo. Wǒ yào zū yí liàng chē, yòng sān tiān.
您好。我要租一辆车，用三天。
Hello, I want to rent a car for 3 days.

B: Nín xūyào nǎ zhǒng chēxíng?
您需要哪种车型?
What kind of vehicle do you need?

A: Wǒ yào zū yí liàng shāngwùchē. Wǒ yě xūyào yí wèi dàijià.
我要租一辆商务车。我也需要一位代驾。
I need to rent an MPV. I also need a designated driver.

B: Qǐngwèn (nín) nǎ tiān yòng chē?
请问（您）哪天用车?
May I ask when you'll need the vehicle?

A: Míngtiān yòng chē, Xīngqīwǔ huán chē.
明天用车，星期五还（车）。
I need the vehicle tomorrow, and will return it on Friday.

B: Wǒ kěyǐ gěi nín yí liàng Biékè shāngwùchē, dài yí wèi dàijià. Rìzūjīn 750 yuán.
我可以给您一辆别克商务车，带一位代驾。日租金750元。
I can give you a Buick MPV with a designated driver. The daily rental is 750 yuan.

A: Fèiyong bāokuò bǎoxiǎn ma?
费用包括保险吗？
Does this price include insurance?

B: Shìde, bāokuò jīběnxiǎn. Nín shì zìjǐ lái qǔ chē háishi xūyào sòng chē shàngmén?
是的，包括基本险。您是自己来取车还是需要送车上门？
Yes, the basic insurance is included. Will you pick up the vehicle by yourself, or do you need it to be sent to your place?

A: Máfan nín sòng chē shàngmén.
麻烦您送车上门。
Please send it to my place.

Related Words

1	chēxíng 车型	the model of a vehicle	3	dàijià 代驾 (sījī 司机)	a designated driver
2	yìdì huán chē 异地还车	to return a vehicle to a different location	4	jīběnxiǎn 基本险	basic insurance

(Continued)

5	zōnghéxiǎn 综合险	comprehensive insurance	10	wàiguó-rénzài Zhōngguó (外国人在中国) chángqī jūliúzhèng 长期居留证	permanent residence permit (for foreigners in China)
6	shǒuxùfèi 手续费	service fee/charge			
7	chāoshí shōufèi 超时收费	overtime charge			
8	chāolǐchéng shōufèi 超里程收费	extra mileage charge	11	dǎohángyí 导航仪	GPS
9	guòlùfèi 过路费	road toll			

Cultural Navigation

A foreigner has two choices for renting a vehicle in China. One is "dàijià zūchē (renting a car with a designated driver)," which means that when you rent a vehicle, you also "rent" a driver. Another choice is "zìjià zūchē (driving the rented car by yourself)," which means that when you rent a car, you drive it. However, if you plan to do so, you must first go to the local vehicle administration office to apply for a permission by using your home country's driver license or an international driver license along with your identification, and then take a written test of traffic regulations. After passing the test, you can drive a car in China by yourself. It is very convenient to rent a car over the phone or to make a reservation online. In addition to local Chinese car rental companies, world-famous car rental companies including Hertz, Avis and others have also entered China to expand their market.

30 Dealing with an Entrance Guard

Key Sentence

Wǒ zhǎo shìchǎngbù de Zhāng jīnglǐ.
我 找 市场部的 张 经理。
I'm looking for Manager Zhang of the Marketing Department.

Substitution

xiāoshòubù
销售部
Sales Department

yánfābù
研发部
Research & Development Department

rénlì zīyuán bù
人力资源部
Human Resources Department

gōnggòng guānxì bù
公共关系部
Public Relations Department

kèfúbù
客服部
Customer Service Department

Lǐ zhǔrèn
李主任
Director Li

Chén xiānsheng
陈先生
Mr. Chen

Xiè nǚshì
谢女士
Ms. Xie

fùzérén
负责人
person in charge

zhǔguǎn
主管
person in charge

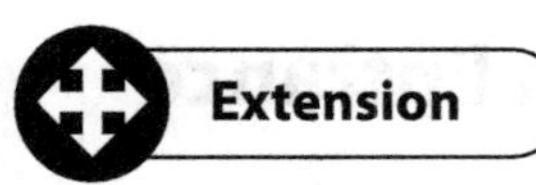

1. Zěnme chēnghu nín?
怎么 称 呼 您?
How should I address you?

2. Wǒ jiào Lǐ Dàwèi, Tōngyòng Qìchē Gōngsī de.
我 叫李大卫，通 用 汽车公司 的。
I'm David Lee from General Motors.

3. Wáng zhǔrèn zhèngzài děng nín.
王 主任 正 在 等 您。
Director Wang is waiting for you.

4. Lǐ jīnglǐ de bàngōngshì shì zài sānlóu ma?
李经理的办 公 室 是 在 三楼 吗?
Is Manager Li's office on the third floor?

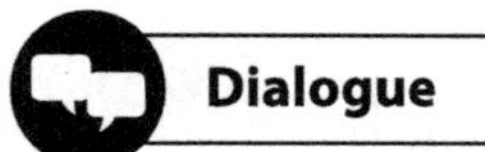

A: Qǐngwèn nín zhǎo nǎ wèi?
请 问 您 找 哪位?
May I ask who you are looking for?

B: Ò, wǒ zhǎo shìchǎngbù de Zhāng jīnglǐ.
哦，我 找 市场部的 张 经理。
Oh, I'm looking for Manager Zhang of the Marketing Department.

A: Zěnme chēnghu nín?
怎么 称 呼 您?
How should I address you?

B: Wǒ jiào Lǐ Dàwèi, Tōngyòng Qìchē Gōngsī de. Wǒ zuótiān dǎ diànhuà yuēhǎo de.
我 叫李大卫，通 用 汽车公司 的。我 昨天打 电 话 约好 的。

I'm David Lee from General Motors. I called yesterday and set up an appointment.

Qǐng shāoděng.
A: 请稍等。

One moment please.

dǎ diànhuà...
(打电话……)

(Making a phone call…)

Tōngyòng Qìchē Gōngsī de Lǐ Dàwèi xiānsheng yàojiàn Zhāng jīnglǐ.
通用汽车公司的李大卫先生要见张经理。

Mr. David Lee from General Motors is here, and he wants to see Manager Zhang.

Hǎo. Nín qǐng jìn. Zhāng jīnglǐ zhèngzài děng nín.
好。您请进。张经理正在等您。

OK. Please come in. Manager Zhang is waiting for you.

Bù hǎoyìsi, Zhāng jīnglǐ de bàngōngshì shì zài èr lóu ma?
B: 不好意思，张经理的办公室是在二楼吗？

Excuse me, is Manager Zhang's office on the second floor?

Related Words

1	dàmén 大门	(front) gate; entrance	5	jiēdàiyuán 接待员	receptionist
2	gēn... 跟…… yuēhǎo le 约好了	to have an appointment with…	6	huìkè 会客	to receive a guest
3	ménwèi 门卫	entrance guard	7	huìkèshì 会客室	reception room
4	bǎo'ān 保安	security guard	8	fǎngkè 访客 dēngjìdān 登记单	visitor registration sheet

Cultural Navigation

Many companies, factories and public institutions in China have an entrance guard or security guard at the front gate or the entrance of the building. However, not all of these places have a front desk receptionist. The entrance guards or security personnel are in charge of inquiring about a visitor's identity. The visitor should state his/her name, identity and the purpose of the visit. Some places and departments may also require visitors to show his/her ID card or fill out a visitor registration sheet.

31 Running into Troubles

Key Sentence

Wǒ de qiánbāo diū le!
我的钱包丢了!
My wallet is lost!

Substitution

hùzhào
护照
passport

jīpiào
机票
airplane ticket

xìnyòngkǎ
信用卡
credit card

lǚxíng zhīpiào
旅行支票
traveler's check

Extension

1. Qiánbāo li yǒu xiànjīn ma?
(钱包里)有现金吗?
Was there any cash (in the wallet)?

2. Qiánbāo li yǒu liǎng zhāng xìnyòngkǎ.
钱包里有两张信用卡。
There were two credit cards in the wallet.

3. Dǎ 110 bàojǐng ba, huòzhě qù pàichūsuǒ bào'àn.
打110报警吧，或者去派出所报案。
Let's call 110 to report to the police, or go to the police station.

4. Qiánbāo yídìng jiù shì nàge rén tōude!
钱包一定就是那个人偷的！
The wallet must be stolen by that man!

A: Bù hǎo, wǒ de qiánbāo diū le!
不好，我的钱包丢了！
Oh no, I lost my wallet!

B: Nǐ shì bú shì wàng zài nǎr le?
（你）是不是忘在哪儿了？
Did you leave it somewhere?

A: Bù kěnéng! Wǒ zǒngshì suíshēn dàizhede.
不可能！我总是随身带着的。
Impossible! I always have it with me.

B: Yǒu xiànjīn ma?
有现金吗?
Was there any cash?

A: Xiànjīn dào bù duō, kěshì yǒu liǎng zhāng xìnyòngkǎ.
现金倒不多，可是有两张信用卡。
Not too much, but there were two credit cards.

B: Dǎ 110 bàojǐng ba, huòzhě qù pàichūsuǒ bào'àn.
打110报警吧，或者去派出所报案。
Let's call 110 to report to the police, or go to the police station.

A: Wǒ xiǎng qilai le! Gāngcái zài dìtiězhàn yǒu gè rén zhuàngle wǒ yíxià.
我想起来了！刚才在地铁站有个人撞了我一下。
Qiánbāo yídìng jiù shì tā tōude!
钱包一定就是他偷的！
I remembered! There was a man who bumped into me at the subway station just now. The wallet must have been stolen by him!

Kàn, jiù shì tā! Zhànzhù, zhuāzhù tā!
看，就是他！站住，抓住他！

Look, it's him! Stop, catch him!

Related Words

1	tōu 偷	to steal	8	sèláng 色狼	lecher
2	qiǎng 抢	to rob	9	jǐngchá 警察	police
3	zhuā 抓	to catch; to get hold of	10	gōng'ānjú 公安局	public security bureau
4	sāorǎo 骚扰	to harass	11	pàichūsuǒ 派出所	local police station
5	xiǎotōu 小偷	thief	12	bàojǐng 报警	to call the police; to report to the police
6	liúmáng 流氓	gangster; hooligan	13	bào'àn 报案	to report a criminal case (to the security authorities)
7	piànzi 骗子	swindler; cheat; cheater	14	Jiùmìng a! 救命啊！	Help! (only used in a life-threatening situation)

Cultural Navigation

A Chinese old saying says, "Zàijiā qiān rì hǎo, chúmén yì shí nán." (A thousand days at home go smoothly; a day away is beset with difficulties.) When you are away from home by yourself, especially when traveling in an unfamiliar place, it is unavoidable that you run into some unpleasant situations. In China, if you encounter a problem that you can't solve by yourself, or if you are facing a risky situation, please remember to call 110 for immediate help. Of course, you may go to a local public security bureau or police station to report a criminal case too.

Business Negotiation

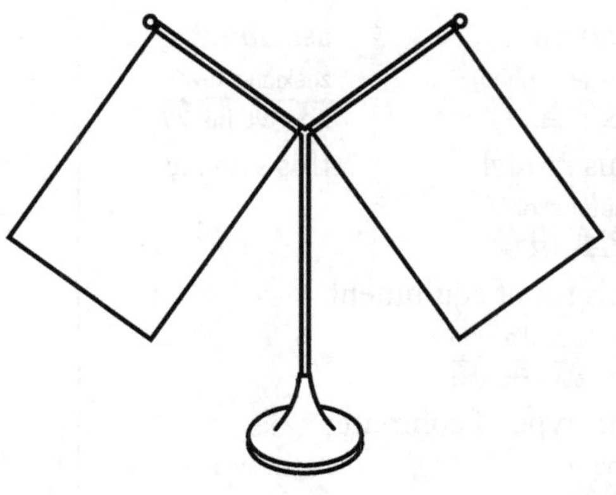

32 General Inquiry

Key Sentence

Wǒ xiǎng xúnwèn yíxià zhè zhǒng chǎnpǐn de jiàgé.
我想询问一下这种产品的价格。
I would like to inquire about this product's price.

Substitution

qǐngwèn
请问
ask

zīxún
咨询
consult

liǎojiě
了解
find out

dǎting
打听
ask about

zhège xínghào
这个型号
this model

zhèxiàng fúwù
这项服务
this service

zhètàoshèbèi
这套设备
this set of equipment

zhè kuǎn diànnǎo
这款电脑
this type of computer

bàojià
报价
quotation; offer

língshòujià
零售价
retail price

pīfājià
批发价
wholesale price

Extension

1. Nín xiǎng zhīdào zhè zhǒng chǎnpǐn de língshòujià shì ma?
您想知道这种产品的零售价是吗?
Do you want to know the retail price of this product?

2. Zhè jǐ zhǒng chǎnpǐn de jiàgé, wǒ dōu xiǎng liǎojiě yíxià.
这几种产品的价格，我都想了解一下。
I would like to find out the prices of these types of products.

3. Zhè shì wǒmen de chǎnpǐn mùlù hé jiàgébiǎo.
这是我们的产品目录和价格表。
This is our products' catalogue and price list.

4. Wǒmen mùqián hái méiyǒu zhèxiàng fúwù.
我们目前还没有这项服务。
We do not currently have this service yet.

Dialogue

A: Nín hǎo wǒ xiǎng xúnwèn yíxià zhè jǐ zhǒng chǎnpǐn de jiàgé.
您好，我想询问一下这几种产品的价格。
Hi, I would like to inquire about the prices of these types of products.

B: Nín xiǎng zhīdào língshòujià háishi pīfājià?
您想知道零售价还是批发价?
Do you want to know the retail prices or the wholesale prices?

A: Wǒ dōu xiǎng liǎojiě yíxià.
我都想了解一下。
I would like to find out both.

B: Zhè shì wǒmen de chǎnpǐn mùlù hé jiàgébiǎo, nín kěyǐ kàn yí kàn.
这是我们的产品目录和价格表，您可以看一看。

This is our products' catalogue and price list. You may take a look.

A: Wǒ kěyǐ zàixiàn xúnjià ma?
我可以在线询价吗?

May I inquire about a quotation online?

B: Bù hǎoyìsi. Wǒmen mùqián hái méiyǒu zhè xiàng fúwù. Búguò, huānyíng nín suíshí dǎ diànhuà huò fā yóujiàn xúnpán.
不好意思。我们目前还没有这项服务。不过，欢迎您随时打电话或发邮件询盘。

I'm sorry. We do not currently have this service yet. But you are welcome to call or e-mail for inquiry at any time.

Related Words

1	xúnwèn 询问	to inquire (formal)	7	cùxiāojià gé 促销价（格）	promotion price; sale price
2	qǐngwèn 请问	to ask (polite form)	8	yōuhuìjià gé 优惠价（格）	discount price; preferential price
3	dǎting 打听	to ask about (colloquial)	9	qīngcāngjià gé 清仓价（格）	clearance price
4	xúnpánxìn/ 询盘信/ xúnjiàxìn 询价信	letter of inquiry	10	shìxiāojià gé 试销价（格）	trial price
5	jiàgé/ 价格/ jiàqián 价钱	price	11	jiànyì 建议 língshòujià gé 零售价（格）	suggested retail price
6	shìchǎngjià gé 市场价（格）	market price			

Cultural Navigation

"Yìbān xúnpán (general inquiry)" does not deal with specific terms of any given business deal. It is only an inquiry about prices of products and may also include requests for a product catalogue or product samples. Therefore, people also call it "xúnjià (price inquiry)" in spoken language. Inquiring about the price is often the first step in a business negotiation. Chinese often say, "Huò bǐ sān jiā bù chīkuī." (Compare the merchandise at three shops, and you won't get the short end). It is a normal practice to ask about the price from different suppliers or manufacturers, then compare their quotations. However, you should inquire about a quotation in a sincere, serious and polite manner. In return, the other party will treat you in the same manner. Even to the same question, people will get a different impression if you use different words. For instance, "Wǒ xiǎng xúnwèn yíxià jiàgé" (I would like to inquire about the price) appears relatively formal; "Wǒ xiǎng wèn yíxià jiàgé" appears more polite; "Wǒ xiǎng dǎting yíxià jiàgé" has a colloquial tone and does not sound formal.

33 Specific Inquiry

Key Sentence

Qǐng gěi wǒ bào yí gè 5000 tái bīngxiāng de Shànghǎi
请给我报一个5000台冰箱(的)上海
gǎng lí'ànjià.
(港)离岸价。

Please quote me an FOB Shanghai (port) for 5,000 refrigerators.

Substitution

10 tái fādiànjī
10台发电机
10 units of generators

5 wàn dá máojīn
5万打毛巾
50,000 dozens of towels

Xiānggǎng
香港
Hong Kong

Niǔyuē
纽约
New York

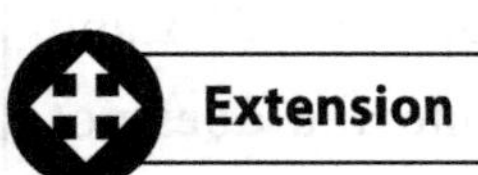

Extension

1. Gòumǎi jiénéng bīngxiāng de nà zhāng dān xūyào xúnpán.
购买节能冰箱的那张单需要询盘。
The deal for purchasing energy-efficient refrigerators needs an inquiry.

2. Nǐ xiàng nà jiā gōngsī (fāchū) xúnpán le ma?
你向那家公司（发出）询盘了吗?
Have you made an inquiry to that company?

3. Wǒmen xūyào chǎngjiā jǐnkuài bàopán.
我们需要厂家尽快报盘。
We need the manufacturer to make an offer as soon as possible.

4. Wǒ mǎshàng gěi chǎngjiā dǎ gè diànhuà xúnpán.
我马上给厂家打个电话询盘。
I'll call the manufacturer for inquiry right away.

Dialogue

A: Gòumǎi jiénéng bīngxiāng de nà zhāng dān xūyào xúnpán. Nǐ xiàng Hǎi'ěr (Gōngsī) xúnpán le ma?
购买节能冰箱的那张单需要询盘。你向海尔(公司)询盘了吗?
The deal for purchasing energy-efficient refrigerators needs an inquiry. Have you made an inquiry to Haier (Company)?

B: Wǒ qǐng tāmen gěi wǒ bào yí gè 5000 tái bīngxiāng de Shànghǎi (gǎng) lí'ànjià.
我请他们给我报一个5000台冰箱的上海（港）离岸价。
I have asked them to quote me an FOB Shanghai (Port) for 5,000 refrigerators.

A: Zhèli háiyǒu yì fēng xúnpánxìn.
这里还有一封询盘信。
There is another inquiry letter.

B: Shì shénme
是什么?
What is it about?

A: Yǒu wèi kèhù xúnwèn 3000 dūn gāngcái Luòshānjī dào'ànjià, xūyào qǐng chǎngjiā jǐnkuài bàopán.
有位客户询问3000吨钢材洛杉矶到岸价，需要请厂家尽快报盘。

There is a client inquiring about CIF Los Angeles for 3,000 tons of steel, and he wants the manufacturer to make an offer as soon as possible.

B: Xíng, wǒ mǎshàng gěi chǎngjiā dǎ gè diànhuà xúnpán.
行，我马上给厂家打个电话询盘。

OK, I'll call the manufacturer for inquiry right away.

Related Words

No.	Word	Meaning	No.	Word	Meaning
1	dān 单	a piece of paper or any given business document that has specific information such as inquiry (of price), quotation, purchasing, etc.			
2	xúnjiàdān 询价单	letter of inquiry; inquiry sheet	7	tiělù jiāohuòjià 铁路交货价	free on rail
3	xúnpán 询盘	inquiry; to make an inquiry	8	cāngkù jiāohuòjià 仓库交货价	ex-warehouse; Ex Works
4	lí'ànjià jiā yòngjīn 离岸价加佣金	free on board and commission; FOB & C	9	chéngběn jiā yùnfèi jià 成本加运费价	cost and freight; CFR
5	dào'ànjià 到岸价	cost, insurance and freight; CIF	10	bàopán 报盘	offer; to make an offer
6	chuánbiān jiāohuò jiàgé 船边交货价格	free alongside ship; FAS			

Cultural Navigation

Different from "general inquiry," "specific inquiry" is to inquire about details of all trade terms. These terms normally include product price, quality, quantity, packing, shipment, payment method, etc. As a business term, the word "xúnpán (inquiry)" is generally used between a manufacturer and a wholesaler or distributor, or between a wholesale dealer and a retailer, which is so-called "B2B" (business-to-business). If you go to a supermarket or a farmers' market for everyday shopping, it is most likely that you will say: "Zhège duōshao qián" (How much is this?) or "Nàge zěnme mài?" (How are you going to sell that?)

34 Quotations and Offers (1)

Key Sentence

Zhè zhǒng chǎnpǐn wǒmen de bàojià shì jiǔbǎi Měiyuán yì xiāng.
这种产品我们的报价是九百美元一箱。
Our quoted price for this product is US $900 per box.

Substitution

jīqì
机器
machine

shèbèi
设备
equipment

yíqì
仪器
instrument

cáiliào
材料
material

pèijiàn
配件
part; accessory

tái
台
unit

tào
套
set; series

jiàn
件
piece; item

dá
打
dozen

gōngjīn
公斤
kilogram

dūn
吨
ton

Extension

1. Nín de bàojià yǒuxiàoqī shì duō jiǔ?
您的报价有效期是多久?
How long is your quoted price valid?

2. Wǒmen de bàojià yí gè yuè nèi yǒuxiào.
我们的报价一个月内有效。
Our quoted price remains valid for one month.

3. Wǒmen kěyǐ àn quánguó shìchǎng jiàgé gěi nín bàojià.
我们可以按全国市场价格给您报价。
We can offer you a quotation based upon the national market price.

4. Qǐng bǎ nín de bàopán yòng yóujiàn fāgěi wǒ.
请把（您的）报盘用邮件发给我。
Please send me your offer by e-mail.

Dialogue

A: Zhè zhǒng chǎnpǐn wǒmen de bàojià shì měi xiāng jiǔbǎi Měiyuán.
这种产品我们的报价是每箱九百美元。
Our quoted price for this product is US $900 per box.

B: Zhège bàojià de yǒuxiàoqī shì duōjiǔ?
这个报价的有效期是多久?
How long is this quoted price valid?

A: Wǒmen de bàojià yì zhōu nèi yǒuxiào
我们的报价一周内有效。
Our quoted price remains valid for one week.

B: Nàzhǒng xínghào de bàojià yě yíyàng ma?
那种型号的报价也一样吗?
Is the quoted price of that model the same?

A: Nà zhǒng xínghào de chǎnpǐn zànshí quēhuò. Rúguǒ nín gǎnxìngqù de huà, wǒmen kěyǐ àn mùqián guójì shìchǎng jiàgé xiān gěi nín bàojià.
那种型号的产品暂时缺货。如果您感兴趣的话，我们可以按目前国际市场价格先给您报价。
Products of that model are temporarily out of stock. If you are interested in that, we can offer you a quotation based upon the international market price.

C: Zhè liǎng zhǒng chǎnpǐn nín gěi wǒmen bào gè zuì yōuhuì shípán ba, yòng yóujiàn fāgěi wǒ.
这两种产品您给（我们）报个最优惠实盘吧，用邮件发给我。
Please try your best to give us the most favorable firm offer of these two products and send it to me by e-mail.

Related Words

1	cānkǎojià gé 参考价（格）	reference price; indicative price	6	tiáozhěng 调整	to adjust
2	zhōngjiānjià gé 中间价（格）	middle price	7	yǒuxiào 有效	valid
3	jūnjià 均价	mean price; average price	8	wúxiào 无效	invalid
4	xiàn xíng jià gé 现（行）价（格）	current price	9	yǒuxiàoqī 有效期	validity period; expiry date
5	guójì shìchǎng jià gé 国际市场价（格）	international market price	10	zuì yōuhuì shípán 最优惠实盘	the most favorable firm offer

Cultural Navigation

In Chinese, the difference between "bàojià (quotation)" and "bàopán (offer)" is similar to the difference between "xúnjià" and "xúnpán." Usually, "bàopán" only illustrates the commodity price while "bàopán" includes the price of the commodity and specific terms of transaction. In other words, "bàojià" is generally a response made by one side to a "general inquiry" or a "price inquiry" made by another side, while "bàopán" replies to a "specific inquiry." Please note that the price provided in "bàojià" is usually an indicative price. Unless this price has been offered specifically with an expiry date, the party who provides the price may change it at any time based on market conditions and their own needs. As an old Chinese saying goes among businessmen: "Suíháng-jiùshì." (The price fluctuates in line with market conditions.)

35 Quotations and Offers (2)

Key Sentence

Zhè shì wǒ fāng de zuì xīn bàopán, qǐng nín guòmù.
这是我方的最新报盘，请您过目。
This is our latest offer. Please take a look.

Substitution

duìfāng
对方
the other side; the other party

Zhōngfāng
中方
Chinese side

Tōngyòng Diànqì Gōngsī
通用电气（公司）
GE (General Electric Corporation)

kàn yí kàn
看一看
take a look

zài kǎolǜ kǎolǜ
再考虑考虑
reconsider it

kànkan shìfǒu héshì
看看是否合适
see if it is suitable

Extension

1. Shénme shíhou néng shōudào nǐmen Niǔyuē dào'ànjià de shípán?
什么时候能收到你们纽约到岸价的实盘?
When can I have your firm CIF New York offer?

2. Qǐng guì gōngsī wùbì zài xià Zhōuyī zhīqián duì wǒ fāng bàopán zuòchū dáfù.
请贵公司务必在下周一之前对我方报盘做出答复。
Please make sure that your company will respond to our offer by next Monday.

3. Wǒmen duì qítā chǎnpǐn de jiàgé yě hěn gǎn xìngqù.
我们对其他产品的价格也很感兴趣。
We are also interested in the prices of other products.

4. Rúguǒ nǐ fāngbiàn dehuà, gěi wǒ yí gè jiǎndān de bàojià jiù xíng le.
(如果)你方便的话,给我一个简单的报价就行了。
If it's convenient for you, just give me a simple price indication.

Dialogue

A: Wáng xiānsheng, shénme shíhou néng shōudào nǐmen dào'ànjià de shípán?
王先生,什么时候能收到你们到岸价的实盘?
Mr. Wang, when can I have your firm CIF offer?

B: Zài zhèr. Zhè shì wǒ fāng de zuì xīn bàopán, qǐng nín guòmù.
在这儿。这是我方的最新报盘,请您过目。
It is right here. This is our latest offer. Please take a look.

A: Xièxie. Bàopán de yǒuxiàoqī shì yí gè xīngqī ma?
谢谢。(报盘的)有效期是一个星期吗?
Thanks. Is this offer valid for one week?

Shìde. Qǐng nín wùbì zài xià Zhōuyī xiàwǔ 5 diǎn yǐqián gěi wǒ dáfù.
B: 是的。请您务必在下周一下午5点以前给我答复。
Yes. Please make sure to respond to me before 5 pm next Monday.

Lìngwài, wǒmen duì guì gōngsī qítā chǎnpǐn de jiàgé yě hěn gǎn xìngqù.
A: 另外，我们对（贵公司）其他产品的价格也很感兴趣。
In addition, we are also interested in the prices of (your company's) other products.

Méi wèntí. Wǒ kěyǐ zài 24 xiǎoshí zhīnèi gěi nín bàopán.
B: 没问题。我可以在24小时之内给您报盘。
No problem. I can have the offer ready for you within 24 hours.

Bù jí, wǒ xiànzài hái bù xūyào nǐmen de bàopán.
A: 不急，我现在还不需要你们的报盘。
No hurry. I don't need you to make an offer right now.

Nǐ fāngbiàn dehuà, gěi wǒ yí gè jiǎndān de bàojià jiù xíng le.
你方便的话，给我一个简单的报价就行了。
If it's convenient for you, just give me a simple price indication.

Related Words

1	fāpán 发盘	selling offer	3	shípán 实盘	firm offer
2	dìpán 递盘	bid; buying offer	5	xūpán 虚盘	non-firm offer

(Continued)

5	jiāoyì tiáojiàn 交易条件	trade terms; commodity terms; conditions of trade	8	dānbǎo 担保	guarantee; to guarantee
6	bǎoliú tiáojiàn 保留条件	terms or conditions with reservations	9	fǎlǜ xiàolì 法律效力	force of law; legally binding
7	chéngnuò 承诺	commitment; to promise	10	yuēshùlì 约束力	binding force

Cultural Navigation

There are two types of "bàopán (offer)." They are "shípán (firm offer)" and "xūpán (non-firm offer)." "Shípán" has a clear-cut and affirmative explanation on quality, quantity, packing, price, shipment, payment and validity without any reserved conditions. Therefore, it is legally binding. "xūpán" is just the opposite. Although "xūpán" also lists the price and related transaction terms, it does not offer any promise or guarantee for the price and other transaction terms. It is an offer without binding force. In addition, if the offer is delivered by a seller initiatively, this offer is also called "fāpán (selling offer)." If the offer is delivered to a seller by a buyer initiatively, the offer is called "dìpán (buying offer or bid)."

36 Counter Offers

Key Sentence

Chúfēi nǐmen jiǎnjià bǎi fēn zhī wǔ, fǒuzé wǒmen wúfǎ jiēshòu bàopán.
除非你们减价百分之五，否则我们无法接受报盘。

Unless you reduce the price by 5%, we can't accept your offer.

Substitution

sì fēn zhī yī
四分之一
one forth

zhìshǎo sānshí yuán
至少三十元
at least 30 yuan

zhǐhǎo fàngqì le
只好放弃了
have to give it up

zhǐhǎo lìng zhǎo huòyuán le
只好另找货源了
have to seek for other sources

Extension

1. Nín de bàojià bǐ wǒmen yùqī de gāole yìxiē.
您的报价比我们预期的高了一些。
Your price is higher than what we expected.

2. Wǒmen de bàojià shì yǐ hélǐ lìrùn wéi yījù de.
我们的报价是以合理利润为依据的。
Our price is based on reasonable profit.

3. Gēn tónglèi chǎnpǐn xiāngbǐ, nín de bàojià gāole bǎifēn zhī èrshí.
跟同类产品相比，您的报价高了百分之二十。
Compared with similar products, your price is 20% higher.

4. Zài mùqián de shìchǎng shang, wǒ rènwéi nín de bàojià méiyǒu jìngzhēngxìng
在目前的市场上，我认为您的报价没有竞争性。
I don't find your price competitive in the current market.

Dialogue

A: Nín de bàojià bǐ wǒmen yùqī de gāole yìxiē.
您的报价比我们预期的高了一些。
Your price is higher than what we expected.

B: Wǒmen de bàojià shì yǐ hélǐ lìrùn wéi yījù de, bú shì màntiān yàojià.
我们的报价是以合理利润为依据的，不是漫天要价。
Our price is based on reasonable profit and not wild speculation.

A: Kěshì, gēn tónglèi chǎnpǐn xiāngbǐ, nín de bàojià jīhū gāole bǎifēn zhī shí.
可是，跟同类产品相比，您的报价几乎高了百分之十。
But compared with similar products, your price is almost 10% higher.

B: Wǒ chéngrèn. Búguò qítā tónglèi chǎnpǐn de zhìliàng shì méi fǎ gēn wǒmen bǐ de.
我承认。不过其他同类产品的质量是没法跟我们比的。

I acknowledge that. But the quality of other similar products can't compare with ours.

A: Wǒ juéde zài mùqián de shìchǎng shang nín de bàojià méiyǒu jìngzhēngxìng
我觉得在目前的市场上您的报价没有竞争性。

I don't find your price competitive in the current market.

B: Nàme, wǒ xiǎng zhīdào guì gōngsī de huánpán shì duōshao.
那么，我想知道贵公司的还盘是多少。

Well then, I would like to know what your company's counter offer is.

A: Chúfēi nǐmen jiǎnjià bǎifēnzhīwǔ, fǒuzé wǒmen wúfǎ jiēshòu bàopán.
除非你们减价百分之五，否则我们无法接受报盘。

Unless you reduce the price by 5%, we can't accept your offer.

Related Words

1	huánpán 还盘	counter offer	3	kǎnjià 砍价	to bargain; to beat down the price (colloquial)
2	fǎnhuánpán 反还盘	counter-counter offer	4	tǎojià-huánjià 讨价还价	to bargain

(Continued)

5	jiǎnjià 减价	to reduce price	8	lìrùn 利润	profit
6	jiàngjià 降价	to lower price	9	zuò shēngyi 做生意	to do business
7	tíjià 提价	to raise price	10	jìngzhēngxìng 竞争性	competitiveness

Cultural Navigation

When going shopping, many Chinese love to try "kǎnjià (beating down the price)." Actually, what "huánpán (counter offer)"and "fǎnhuánpán (counter-counter offer)" mean in business negotiation is the same, which is "tǎojià-huánjià (to bargain)." When doing business, one cannot avoid "tǎojià-huánjià (bargaining)." There is an old Chinese proverb handed down from the past, "Màntiān yàojià, jiùdì huánqián." (The seller can ask for a sky-high price, and the buyer can make a rock-bottom offer.) It not only indicates that "bargaining" has been considered as a matter of course by Chinese businessmen, but also reflects a sort of mindset based on speculation and fluke that originated from the business culture of old times.

37 Counter-Counter Offers

Key Sentence

Kǎolǜdào nín shì wǒmen de lǎo kèhù, wǒmen yuànyì bǎ
考虑到您是我们的老客户，我们愿意把
jiàgé zài xiàtiáo sān gè bǎifēndiǎn.
价格再下调三个百分点。

Taking into consideration that you are a long-term client of ours, we are willing to lower the price by another three percent.

Substitution

xīn kèhù
新客户
new client

chángqī hézuò huǒbàn
长期合作伙伴
long-term (business) partner

bǎi fēn zhī wǔ
百分之五
five percent

èrshí kuài
二十块
20 yuan

yī chéng
一成
ten percent

Extension

1. Guì gōngsī de huánpán chāochūle wǒ gōngsī nénggòu chéngshòu de jiàgé fànwéi.
贵公司的还盘超出了我公司能够承受的价格范围。
Your company's counter offer has exceeded the price range that our company can bear.

2. Wǒmen xīwàng nénggòu zhǎodào yí gè shuāngfāng dōu néng jiēshòu de jiàgé.
我们希望能够找到一个双方都能接受的价格。
We hope that we can find an acceptable price for both sides.

3. Zhèyàng de jiàgé wǒmen zhēnde méi fǎ jiēshòu.
这样的价格我们真的没法接受。
We really cannot accept a price like this.

4. Rúguǒ wǒmen yǐ 200 yuán yì tái de jiàgé ná 15000 tái, zhège jiàgé kěyǐ jiēshòu ma?
如果我们以200元一台的价格拿15000台，这个价格可以接受吗?
If we purchase 15,000 units at the price of 200 yuan per unit, is this price acceptable?

Dialogue

A: Guì gōngsī de huánpán chāochūle wǒmen nénggòu chéngshòu de jiàgé fànwéi.
贵公司的还盘超出了我们能够承受的价格范围。
Your company's counter offer has exceeded the price range that we can bear.

Wǒmen yě xīwàng nénggòu zhǎodào yí gè shuāngfāng dōu néng jiēshòu de jiàgé.
B: 我们也希望能够找到一个双方都能接受的价格。

We hope that we can find an acceptable price for both sides too.

Kěshì zhèyàng de jiàgé wǒmen zhēnde méi fǎ jiēshòu.
A: 可是这样的价格我们真的没法接受。

We really cannot accept a price like this.

Rúguǒ wǒmen yǐ 200 yuán yì tái de jiàgé ná 15000 tái, yě jiùshì duō gòumǎi 5000 tái, zhège jiàgé kěyǐ jiēshòu ma?
B: 如果我们以200元一台的价格拿15000台，也就是多购买5000台，这个价格可以接受吗？

If we purchase 15,000 units at the price of 200 yuan per unit, which means to purchase 5,000 units more, is this price acceptable?

Zhèyàng ba, kǎolǜdào nín shì wǒmen de lǎo kèhù, wǒmen yuànyì bǎ jiàgé zài xiàtiáo sān gè bǎifēndiǎn. Nín juéde zěnmeyàng?
A: 这样吧，考虑到您是我们的老客户，我们愿意把价格再下调三个百分点。您觉得怎么样？

Well, taking into consideration that you are a long-term client of ours, we are willing to lower the price by another three percent. What do you think?

Nín juéde hái yǒu qítā de rànglì kōngjiān ma?
B: 您觉得还有其他的让利空间吗？

Do you think there is any room for lowering the price?

Hěn bàoqiàn. Zhè shì wǒmen mùqián néng tígōng de zuì yōuhuì bàopán le.
A: 很抱歉。这是我们目前能提供的最优惠报盘了。

I'm sorry. This is the most favorable offer that we are currently able to make.

Related Words

1	bǎifēndiǎn 百分点	percentage	6	rànglì kōngjiān 让利空间	room for profit slash; room for giving a discount
2	xiàtiáo 下调	to lower; to adjust downward	7	jiàngjià kōngjiān 降价空间	room for price reduction
3	jiàgé fànwéi 价格范围	price range	8	xiāoshòuliàng 销售量	sales volume
4	jiàwèi 价位	price level	9	shìchǎng cèlǜ 市场策略	market strategy
5	dà pīliàngdìnggòu 大批量订购	to order in bulk			

Cultural Navigation

The idea of "bólì-duōxiāo (small profits but high volume)" is one of the market strategies that Chinese manufacturers and sellers often exercise. They are very adept at using this strategy. By lowering the price appropriately, manufacturers and sellers may effectively retain the competitiveness of their products and achieve the goal of attracting buyers and clients as well as raising sales volume and market shares. In fact, "bólì-duōxiāo" is beneficial to both the seller side and buyer side. It is a "win-win" choice.

38 Reaching an Impasse

Key Sentence

Nín de zhège huánpán, ràng wǒmen (huíqu) zài yánjiū yánjiū.
您的这个还盘，让我们（回去）再研究研究。

As for your counter offer, please allow us to (go back and) discuss it again.

Substitution

yāoqiú
要求
request

jiànyì
建议
suggestion

tiáojiàn
条件
condition

bàojià
报价
quote offer

kǎolǜ kǎolǜ
考虑考虑
consider

xiǎng yì xiǎng
想一想
think about

qǐngshì yíxià
请示一下
ask for instructions

huìbào yíxià
汇报一下
report (to the superior)

Extension

1. Zhège jiàgé wǒmen hěn nán jiēshòu.
这个价格我们很难接受。
This price is very difficult for us to accept.

2. Zhè jǐ nián de shìchǎng hángqíng, nín yīnggāi shì qīngchu de.
这几年的市场行情，您应该是清楚的。
You should know well about the market price in recent years.

3. Zhè zhǒng chǎnpǐn de jiàgé yìzhí zài kànzhǎng.
这种产品的价格一直在看涨。
The price of this product is always expected to rise.

4. Wǒmen shì xìn de guò guì gōngsī de chǎnpǐn de.
我们是信得过贵公司的产品的。
We do trust your company's products.

Dialogue

A: Shíhuà shuō, zhège jiàgé wǒmen háishi hěn nán jiēshòu.
实话说，这个价格我们还是很难接受。
To tell the truth, this price is still very difficult for us to accept.

B: Zhè jǐ nián de shìchǎng hángqíng, nín yīnggāi shì qīngchu de.
这几年的市场行情，您应该是清楚的。
You should know well about the market price in recent years.
Zhè zhǒng shāngpǐn de jiàgé yìzhí zài kànzhǎng.
这种商品的价格一直在看涨。
The price of this product is always expected to rise.

A: Zhè yì diǎn wǒmen dōu liǎojiě, búguò zuìjìn zhè zhǒng chǎnpǐn de shìchǎng yǐjīng jiējìn bǎohé le.
这一点我们都了解，不过最近这种产品的市场已经接近饱和了。
Both of us know that. However, the market of this product has been approaching its saturation point recently.

B: Huà suìrán zhème shuō, kěshì mùqián wǒmen de chǎnpǐn háishi gōngbúyìngqiú.
话虽然这么说，可是目前我们的产品还是供不应求。

Nevertheless, currently the supply of our products still can't meet the demand.

A: Dāngrán, dāngrán,wǒmen shì xìn de guògui gōngsī de chǎnpǐn de.
当然，当然，我们是信得过贵公司的产品的。

Of course, we do trust your company's products.

Zhèyàng ba, nín de zhège huánpán, ràng wǒmen huíqu zài yánjiū yánjiū.
这样吧，您的这个还盘，让我们回去再研究研究。

Well then, as for your counter offer, please allow us to go back and discuss it again.

Related Words

1	gōngbúyìngqiú 供不应求	demand exceeds supply	7	zhìxiāo 滞销	unsalable; unmarketable
2	gōngguòyúqiú 供过于求	supply exceeds demand	8	chàngxiāo 畅销	to sell well
3	shìchǎng hángqíng 市场行情	market condition; market quotation; market price	9	hōngtái jiàgé 哄抬价格	to drive up prices
4	xūqiú qiángjìng 需求强劲	strong demand	10	qīngxiāo 倾销	to dump (goods)
5	xūqiú píruò 需求疲弱	weak demand	11	pāoshòu 抛售	to undersell; underselling
6	quēhuò 缺货	to run out of stock	12	qūshì 趋势	trend

Cultural Navigation

During an international trade talk, there may be some misunderstanding due to different cultural backgrounds of two parties. When this happens, patience and understanding are indispensable. According to the traditional Chinese way of thinking, people often express their opinions in a tactful way instead of saying something that hurts one's self-esteem or makes him/her lose face. For instance, the other party would probably not reject you directly. Instead, they would say "Wǒmen zài yánjiū yánjiū" (We'll discuss it again), "Wǒ zài kǎolǜ kǎolǜ" (I'll think about it again), or "Ràng wǒ qǐngshì yíxià" (Let me ask for instructions). You have to figure out what he/she truly means.

39 Methods of Payment

Key Sentence

Wǒmen yāoqiú (nǐmen) yùfù bǎi fēn zhī sānshí de
我们要求（你们）预付百分之三十的
dìngjīn, shèngxia de cǎiyòng fùkuǎnjiāodān de fāngshì.
定金，剩下的采用“付款交单”的方式。

We request you to pay 30% as a deposit in advance, and the rest will be paid by D/P.

Substitution

yíbàn
一半
a half; 50%

xìnyòngzhèng
信用证
letter of credit; L/C

chéngduì jiāodān
承兑交单
D/A

yí cì fùqīng
一次付清
pay off in one lump sum

1. Qǐngwèn guì gōngsī yìbān cǎiyòng nǎ zhǒng fùkuǎn fāngshì?
请问贵公司一般采用哪种付款方式？
May I ask which payment method your company usually uses?

2. Nǐmen jiēshòu gēn dān tuōshōu huòzhě xìnyòngzhèng de jiésuàn fāngshì ma?
你们 接受 “跟 单 托收” 或者 “信 用 证”（的 结 算 方式）吗？
Do you accept “documentary collection” or “letter of credit” (as a method of settling up)?

3. Rúguǒ shì cǎiyòng gēn dān tuōshōu, wǒmen zhǐ jiēshòu fùkuǎn jiāo dān de fāngshì.
如果（是）采用 “跟 单 托收”，我们只接受 “付款 交 单” 的方式。
If using “documentary collection,” we only accept “document against payment.”

4. Wǒ fāng kěyǐ yùfù bùfen huòkuǎn.
我 方 可以预付部分 货 款。
Our side can pay partial payment in advance.

Dialogue

A: Qǐngwèn guì gōngsī yìbān cǎiyòng nǎ zhǒng fùkuǎn fāngshì?
请 问 贵公司一般采 用哪 种 付款方式？
May I ask which payment method your company usually uses?

B: Wǒmen qīngxiàngyú cǎiyòng yùfù huòkuǎn de fāngshì.
我们 倾 向 于 采用 “预付货款” 的方式。
We prefer to use the method of “cash before delivery.”

A: Nàme, nǐmen jiēshòu gēn dān tuōshōu huòzhě xìnyòngzhèng ma?
那么，你们接受 “跟 单 托收” 或者 信 用 证 吗？
Then, do you accept “documentary collection” or letter of credit?

B: Rúguǒ cǎiyòng gēn dān tuōshōu, wǒmen zhǐ jiēshòu fùkuǎn jiāodān de fāngshì.
如果采用 “跟 单 托收”，我们只接受 “付款 交 单” 的方式。
If using “documentary collection,” we only accept “document against payment.”

Dāngrán wǒmen yě huānyíng yòng jíqī xìnyòngzhèng jiésuàn.
当然，我们也欢迎用"即期信用证"结算。

Of course, we also welcome the use of "sight letter of credit" to settle up an account.

Wǒ jiànyì zhézhōng yíxià. Wǒ fāng kěyǐ yùfù bùfen huòkuǎn, shèngxia de cǎiyòng fùkuǎn jiāo dān huòzhě xìnyòngzhèng
A: 我建议折中一下。我方可以预付部分货款，剩下的采用"付款交单"或者信用证。

I suggest to compromise a little bit. Our side can pay partial payment in advance, and the rest will be paid by using "D/P" or letter of credit.

Rúguǒ shì nàyàng dehuà, wǒmen yāoqiú nǐmen yùfù bǎi fēn zhī sānshí de dìngjīn, shèngxia de cǎiyòng fùkuǎn jiāo dān de fāngshì.
B: 如果是那样的话，我们要求你们预付百分之三十的定金，剩下的采用"付款交单"的方式。

If it's the case, we request you to pay 30% as a deposit in advance, and the rest will be paid by using "document against payment."

Related Words

1	jiésuàn 结算	to settle up; to close an account	5	diànhuì 电汇	telegraphic transfer; T/T
2	yùfù 预付	to pay in advance	6	yùfù huòkuǎn 预付货款	cash before delivery
3	dìngjīn 定金/ dìngjīn 订金	deposit	7	huò dào fùkuǎn 货到付款	cash on delivery; C.O.D.
4	huìpiào 汇票	draft; bill of exchange	8	gēn dān tuōshōu 跟单托收	documentary collection

(Continued)

9	fùkuǎn jiāo dān 付款交单	document against payment; D/P	11	jíqī xìnyòng-zhèng 即期信用证	sight letter of credit; letter of credit at sight
10	chéngduì jiāo dān 承兑交单	document against acceptance; D/A	12	bù kě chèxiāo xìnyòngzhèng 不可撤销信用证	irrevocable letter of credit

Cultural Navigation

In today's international trade and business transactions, Chinese have generally adopted those payment methods which are used internationally. However, on the other hand, many small-and-medium-sized businesses still like to settle an account in the way of "domestic trade." They often demand the buyer to pay 50%–60% of the total amount as a deposit in advance, and then when goods are shipped, the buyer will pay the rest by using the "document against payment" method. There might be two reasons why they do this: one is the problem of capital turnover, and the other is that they haven't put their trust in the other side. If you ever come across this type of problem, please do not lose your patience. As long as you are willing to communicate with the other side and try to know what they really think while letting them know your position, many issues can eventually be solved.

40 Reaching a Deal

Key Sentence

Zhège jiàgé, wǒmen kěyǐ jiēshòu.
这个价格，我们可以接受。
We can accept this price.

Substitution

jiàwèi
价位
price level

bàopán
报盘
offer

tiáojiàn
条件
condition

tóngyì
同意
agree

qiānyuē
签约
sign (a contract)

xiàdān
下单
place an order

Extension

1. Rúguǒ guì gōngsī néng kǎolǜ jìnyíbù tiáozhěng bàojià, wǒmen kěyǐ duō dìnggòu liǎngwàn tào.
如果贵公司能考虑进一步调整报价，我们可以多订购两万套。

If your company may consider adjusting the quoted offer further, we can purchase 20,000 more units.

2. Wèile biǎoshì wǒmen de chéngyì, wǒmen yuànyì zài ràng liǎng gè diǎn.
为了表示（我们的）诚意，我们愿意再让两个点。
To show (our) sincerity, we are willing to offer another 2% discount.

3. Kànlái wǒmen kěyǐ xiàdān qiānyuē le.
看来我们可以下单签约了。
It seems that we can place an order and sign the contract now.

4. Zhùhè wǒmen shùnlì chéngjiāo!
祝贺我们顺利成交！
Congratulations to us on reaching the deal smoothly.

Dialogue

A: Rúguǒ guì gōngsī néng kǎolǜ jìnyíbù tiáozhěng bàojià, wǒmen kěyǐ duō dìnggòu yíwàn tào.
如果贵公司能考虑进一步调整报价，我们可以多订购一万套。
If your company may consider adjusting the quoted offer further, we can purchase 10,000 more units.
Bólì-duōxiāo ma, duì bú duì?
薄利多销嘛，对不对？
It's small profits but high sales volume, isn't it?

B: Xíng, jìrán nín zhèyàng shuō, wèile biǎoshì chéngyì, wǒmen yuànyì zài ràng liǎng gè diǎn. Nín juéde zěnmeyàng?
行，既然您这样说，为了表示诚意，我们愿意再让两个点。您觉得怎么样？
OK, if you say so, we are willing to offer another 2% discount to show our sincerity. What do you think?

A: Zhège jiàgé wǒmen kěyǐ jiēshòu.
这个价格我们可以接受。
We can accept this price.

Búguò wǒmen yǒu yí gè tiáojiàn, wǒmen yāoqiú suǒyǒu huòwù nénggòu zài
不过我们有一个条件，我们要求所有货物能够在
xià gè yuè 1 hào zhīqián zhuāngchuán.
下个月1号之前装船。

But we have one condition. We request that all the goods can be loaded on board by the 1st of next month.

Èng, zhège tiáojiàn wǒmen yě kěyǐ jiēshòu.
B: 嗯，这个条件我们也可以接受。

Oh, we can accept it too.

Nàhǎo, kànlái wǒmen kěyǐ xiàdān qiānyuē le.
A: 那好，看来我们可以下单签约了。

That's good. It seems that we can place an order and sign the contract now.

Lái zhùhè wǒmen shùnlì chéngjiāo!
B: 来，祝贺我们顺利成交！

Come on, congratulations to us on reaching the deal smoothly!

Related Words

1	chéngjiāo 成交	to make a deal	6	gàizhāng 盖章	to stamp; to seal
2	hétong 合同	contract	7	gōngzhāng 公章	official seal
3	dìng (huò) dān 订（货）单	purchase order	8	zhèngběn 正本	original (of a document)
4	qiānzì 签字	to sign (on a document)	9	fùběn 副本	duplicate (of a document)
5	qiānmíng 签名	to sign one's name	10	fùyìnjiàn 复印件	Xerox; photocopy

(Continued)

11	yí shì 一式 liǎng fèn 两份	in duplicate; with a duplicate copy	12	yǐtuì-以退 wéijìn 为进	to retreat in order to advance; to make concessions in order to gain advantages

Cultural Navigation

The idea of "yǐtuìwéijìn (to retreat in order to advance)" originates from ancient Chinese philosophy, and means that people should make proper concessions at a proper time in order to achieve the final goal. It teaches us to make compromises and concessions if necessary. It is the philosophy of life as well as a technique to survive a dilemma. Moreover, you may find many examples of using the idea of "retreating in order to advance" in matters of politics, economy, military and international relations too. It is also a useful strategy in a business negotiation.

41 Failed Transactions

Key Sentence

Rúguǒ nǐmen jiānchí zhège jiàgé, wǒmen zhǐhǎo fàngqì zhè bǐ jiāoyì le.
如果你们坚持这个价格，我们只好放弃这笔交易了。

If you insist on this price, we have to give up this deal.

Substitution

yuánlái de bàopán
原来的报盘
the original offer

zhèxiē tiáojiàn
这些条件
these conditions

zhè dān shēngyi
这单生意
the deal

zhè xiàng cǎigòu
这项采购
the purchase

xiàdān
下单
place an order

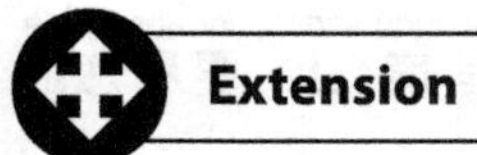

Extension

1. Jīnnián de bàojià bǐ qùnián de jiàgé gāo.
今年的报价比去年的价格高。
This year's quoted price is higher than last year's price.

2. Jīnnián yuáncáiliào de jiàgé bǐ qùnián zhǎngle bǎifēnzhīsānshí.
今年 原材料的价格比去年 涨了 百分之三十。
The price of raw and semi-finished materials this year has increased by 30% compared to that of last year.

3. Wǒmen bìxū tiáozhěng wǒmen de chǎnpǐn jiàgé.
我们必须 调 整 (我们的) 产 品 价格。
We must adjust the price of (our) products.

4. Wǒmen néng bù néng chéngjiāo, hěn dà chéngdù shang yào kàn nín de jiàgé.
我们 能 不 能 成 交，很大程 度 上 要 看 您的价格。
Whether we can make a deal or not depends on your price to a great extent.

Dialogue

A: Wáng xiānsheng, nǐmen jīnnián de bàojià bǐ qùnián de jiàgé gāo a!
王 先 生，你们今年的报价比去年的价格高啊！
Mr. Wang, your quoted price this year is higher than last year's price.

B: Jīnnián yuáncáiliào de jiàgé bǐ qùnián zhǎngle bǎi fēn zhī wǔshí. Wǒmen bùdébù tiáozhěng chǎnpǐn jiàgé.
今年 原材料的价格比去年涨了百分之五十。我们不得不 调 整 产 品 价格。
The price of raw and semi-finished materials this year has increased by 50% compared to that of last year. We have to adjust the price of products.

A: Búguò wǒmen néng bù néng chéngjiāo, hěn dà chéngdù shang yào kàn nín de jiàgé.
不过我们能不能成交，很大程度上要看您的价格。

But whether we can make a deal or not depends on your price to a great extent.

B: Bù hǎoyìsi. Zhè yǐjīng shì wǒmen néng gěi nín de zuì dī jiàgé le.
不好意思。这已经是我们能给您的最低价格了。

I'm really sorry. This is already the lowest price that we can offer.

A: Rúguǒ nín jiānchí zhège jiàgé, wǒmen zhǐhǎo fàngqì zhè bǐ jiāoyì le.
如果您坚持这个价格，我们只好放弃这笔交易了。

If you insist on this price, we have to give up this deal.

B: Tài yíhàn le. Wǒ xīwàng xià cì néng yǒu hézuò de jīhuì.
太遗憾了。我希望下次能有合作的机会。

What a pity. I hope there will be another opportunity for cooperation next time.

Related Words

1	qǔxiāo 取消	to cancel	6	bèipò 被迫	to be forced
2	fàngqì 放弃	to give up	7	bùdéyǐ 不得已	to have no alternative but to
3	jùjué 拒绝	to reject; to refuse	8	ràngjià 让价	to make a concession in price
4	chèdān 撤单	to withdraw an order	9	dǐjià 底价	minimum price; base price
5	chéngjiāo 成交	to strike a deal; to close a deal	10	qǔjuéyú 取决于	to be decided by; to depend on

Cultural Navigation

In ancient Chinese business culture, there is a rational and practical principle: "Shēngyi bù chéng qíngyì zài." (We are still tied by friendship even though the business deal failed.) There is gain and loss when people do business, and there is success and failure when people negotiate a business. Only when friendship exists, will there be the chance for cooperation next time. A smart businessman would never take an unsuccessful negotiation to heart or even turn shame into anger.

Around the Office

42 Work Hours

Key Sentence

Yīnwèi lùshang dǔchē, wǒ chídàole shí fēnzhōng.
因为路上堵车，我迟到了十分钟。

Because of the traffic jam, I was 10 minutes late.

Substitution

nàozhōng méi xiǎng
闹钟没响

The alarm clock didn't work.

chē huài le
车坏了

The car has broken down.

jiāli yǒushì
家里有事

family business

dàxuě
大雪

heavy snow

bàn gè xiǎoshí
半个小时

half an hour

yíhuìr
一会儿

a little while

jǐ fēnzhōng
几分钟

a few minutes

Extension

Yǐjīng guòle jiǔ diǎn le, nǐ zěnme cái lái a?

1. 已经过了九点了，你怎么才来啊?

It has already passed 9 o'clock. Why have you just arrived?

Xiànzài kāichē de rén duō, zǎogāofēng chángcháng dǔchē.

2. 现在开车的人多，早高峰常常堵车。

Since many people drive to work now, there are often traffic jams during the morning rush hours.

Yǐhòu wǒ bǎozhèng zhǔndiǎn shàngbān.

3. 以后我保证准点上班。

I promise that I'll come to work on time in the future.

Rúguǒ xià cì shàngbān zài chídào, shì yào kòu nǐ gōngzīde!

4. 如果下次上班再迟到，是要扣你工资的！

If you are late for work again next time, your salary will be reduced!

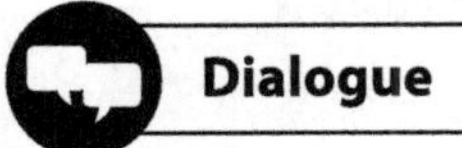

Dialogue

Yǐjīng guòle jiǔ diǎn le, nǐ zěnme cái lái a?

A: 已经过了九点了，你怎么才来啊?

It has already passed 9 o'clock. Why have you just arrived?

Bù hǎoyìsi, jīnglǐ! Yīnwèi lùshang dǔchē, wǒ chídàole shí fēnzhōng.

B: 不好意思，经理！因为路上堵车，我迟到了十分钟。

I'm sorry, Manager! Because of the traffic jam, I was 10 minutes late.

Xiànzài kāichē de rén duō, zǎogāofēng chángcháng dǔchē.

A: 现在开车的人多，早高峰常常堵车。

Since many people drive to work now, there are often traffic jams during morning rush hours.

Xià cì jìde zǎodiǎnr chūmén!
下次记得早点儿出门!
Remember to leave home earlier next time!

Zhīdào le. Yǐhòu wǒ bǎozhèng zhǔndiǎn shàngbān.
B: 知道了。以后我 保 证 准 点 上 班。
I know. I promise that I'll come to work on time in the future.

Rúguǒ xià cì shàngbān zài chídào, shì yào kòu nǐ jiǎngjīn de!
A: 如果下次 上 班 再迟到，是要 扣你奖金的!
If you are late for work again next time, your bonus will be reduced!

Related Words

1	kǎoqín 考勤	to check on work attendance	7	bānchē 班车	shuttle bus
2	chūqín 出勤	to be on duty; to turn out for work	8	wùchē 误车	to miss the bus
3	kǎoqín jìlù 考勤记录	attendance record	9	wǎndiǎn 晚点	late; behind the schedule
4	kǎoqínzhōng 考勤钟	time clock; telltale clock	10	zhǔnshí 准时	on time
5	kǎoqínkǎ 考勤卡/ chūqínkǎ 出勤卡/ jìshíkǎ 记时卡	time card; time sheet	11	jiāotōng shìgù 交通事故	traffic accident
6	gōngjiāochē 公交车	bus			

Cultural Navigation

China has implemented an eight-hour-day working system. Working hours of corporations and enterprises are usually "zhāojiǔ-wǎnwǔ (from 9 o'clock in the morning to 5 o'clock in the afternoon)." Working hours of government departments and public institutions are often a little earlier, normally starting at 8 o'clock or 8:30 in the morning and ending at 5 o'clock or 5:30 in the afternoon. There is a one-hour lunch break at noon. However, the rules of each province and city may not be exactly the same. Besides, state-run corporations and private enterprises may not have the completely same working hours. No matter where you work, there is one thing for certain: no one would like an employee who is often late for work.

43 Coffee Breaks

Key Sentence

Wǒ qù hē (yì) bēi kāfēi, nǐ (yě) qù ma?
我去喝（一）杯咖啡，你（也）去吗?

I'm going to have a cup of coffee. Are you going (too)?

Substitution

hē (yì) bēi shuǐ
喝（一）杯水

drink a glass of water

dào (yì) bēi chá
倒（一）杯茶

pour a cup of tea

mǎi (yì) diǎnr chī de
买（一）点儿吃的

buy something to eat

chōu (yì) zhī yān
抽（一）支烟

smoke a cigarette

Extension

1. Gōngzuòle kuài yì tiān le, wǒmen xiūxi bàn xiǎoshí ba.
工作了快一天了，我们休息半小时吧。
We have been working for almost the whole day. Let's take a break for half an hour.

2. Zài diànnǎo qián zuò de shíjiān cháng le, wǒ de bózi dōu jiāng le.
在电脑前坐的时间长了，我的脖子都僵了。
I have been sitting in front of the computer (screen) for a long time, and my neck is stiff.

3. Nǐ néng bāng wǒ dài yì bēi kāfēi ma?
你能帮我带一杯咖啡吗？
Could you bring me a cup of coffee?

4. Huódòng huódòng shēntǐ néng tígāo gōngzuò xiàolǜ.
活动活动身体能提高工作效率。
Stretching your body can increase work efficiency.

Dialogue

A: Gōngzuòle kuài yí gè shàngwǔ le, wǒmen xiūxi shí fēnzhōng ba.
工作了快一个上午了，我们休息十分钟吧。
We have been working for almost the whole morning. Let's take a break for ten minutes.

B: Shì a, zài diànnǎo qián zuò de shíjiān cháng le, wǒ de bózi dōu jiāng le.
是啊，在电脑前坐的时间长了，我的脖子都僵了。
You are right. I have been sitting in front of the computer (screen) for a long time, and my neck is stiff.

A: Wǒ qù hē bēi kāfēi, nǐ yě qù ma?
我去喝杯咖啡，你（也）去吗？
I'm going to have a cup of coffee. Are you going (too)?

B: Wǒ háishi zài gàn yíhuìr ba. Nǐ néng bāng wǒ dài yì bēi (kāfēi) ma?
我还是再干一会儿吧。你能帮我带一杯（咖啡）吗？

I'd better work for a while longer. Could you bring me a cup (of coffee)?

A: Háishi yìqǐ qù ba. Huódòng huódòng shēntǐ néng tígāo gōngzuò xiàolǜ.
还是一起去吧。活动活动身体能提高工作效率。

Come on, let's go together. Stretching your body can increase work efficiency.

Related Words

1	kāfēijī 咖啡机	coffee maker; coffee machine	7	pàochá 泡茶	to make tea
2	yǐnshuǐjī 饮水机	water dispenser	8	chōng kāfēi 冲咖啡	to make instant coffee
3	yǐnshuǐ pēntóu 饮水喷头	drinking fountain	9	zhǔ kāfēi 煮咖啡	to make coffee
4	zìdòng shòuhuòjī 自动售货机	vending machine	10	yǐnliào 饮料	beverage
5	xiūxishì 休息室	lounge	11	xiǎochī/língshí 小吃/零食	snack
6	xīyānqū 吸烟区	smoking area	12	gōngzuòcān 工作餐	working meal

Cultural Navigation

"Gōngjiāncāo" is a kind of group exercise during a break at work. In China, some factories, companies, government departments and public institutions have a break of 15 to 20 minutes during every workday for this exercise. Employees line up in the playground, the courtyard, or even the porch or the hallway, doing exercises together along with loud music. It makes for quite an energetic spectacle.

44 Working Overtime

Key Sentence

Zhèfèn jìhuà hái méi zuòwán, jīntiān wǒ zhǐhǎo jiābān le.
这份计划还没做完，今天我只好加班了。
This proposal has not been finished yet and I have to work overtime today.

Substitution

shǒutóu de gōngzuò
手头的工作
work at hand

yǒu fèn jíjiàn
有份急件
there is an urgent document

zhème duō shìqing
这么多事情
so many things

lǎobǎn fēnpài de rènwu
老板分派的任务
the work that the boss has assigned

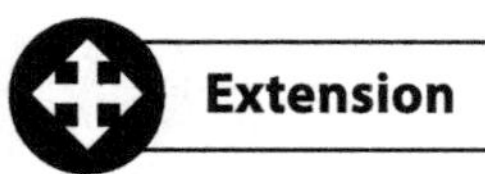

1. Yǐjīng dào xiàbān de shíjiān le, nǐ hái bù zǒu ma?
已经到下班的时间了，你还不走吗？
It is already the time to get off work. Aren't you leaving?

2. Nǐmen bùmén zuìjìn hǎoxiàng chángcháng jiābān, shì bú shì?
你们部门最近好像常常加班，是不是？
Your department seems to often work overtime recently, doesn't it?

3. Zhège xiàngmù bìxū zài zhège yuèdǐ wánchéng.
这个项目必须在这个月底完成。
The project has to be completed by the end of this month.

4. Nǐ jiābān zhìshǎo yǒujiǎngjīn, zhè yě búcuò a.
（你）加班至少有奖金，这也不错啊。
You'll have a bonus for working overtime at least. That's not bad.

Dialogue

A: Yǐjīng dào xiàbān de shíjiān le, nǐ hái bù zǒu ma?
已经到下班的时间了，你还不走吗？
It's already the time to get off work. Aren't you leaving?

B: Zhè fèn jìhuà méi zuòwán, jīntiān wǒ zhǐhǎo jiābān le.
这份计划没做完，今天（我）只好加班了。
This proposal has not been finished yet and I have to work overtime today.

A: Nǐmen bùmén zuìjìn hǎoxiàng chángcháng jiābān, shì bú shì?
你们部门最近好像常常加班，是不是？
Your department seems to often work overtime recently, doesn't it?

B: Méi bànfǎ. Zhège xiàngmù kèhù yào de jí, bìxū zài zhège yuèdǐ wánchéng.
没办法。这个项目客户要得急，必须在这个月底完成。
We have no choice. The client needs this project to be finished urgently. It has to be completed by the end of this month.

A: Búguò jiābān zhìshǎo yǒu jiǎngjīn, zhè yě búcuò a.
不过加班至少有奖金，这也不错啊。
But you'll have a bonus for working overtime at least. That's not bad.

B: Nǐ kāi wánxiào ba? Wǒ nìngyuàn dàodiǎn xiàbān huíjiā, búyào jiǎngjīn.
你开玩笑吧？我宁愿到点下班回家，不要奖金。
You are kidding me, aren't you? I would rather go home on time than have an overtime bonus.

Related Words

1	dàodiǎn 到点	it is time; time is up	7	jiābānfèi 加班费	overtime pay
2	chāoshí 超时	to exceed the time limit	8	jiābān gōngzī 加班工资	overtime wage
3	gǎngōng 赶工	to hurry at work; to hurry to finish a task in time	9	jiābān jiǎngjīn 加班奖金	overtime bonus
4	kāi yèchē 开夜车	to work late until midnight; to burn midnight oil	10	wúcháng jiābān 无偿加班	unpaid overtime
5	dàigōng 怠工	to slow down work; to goof off	11	tiáoxiū 调休	to switch a day off; to exchange a day off (with a fellow worker)
6	jiābān jiādiǎn 加班加点	to work extra shifts and extra hours			

Cultural Navigation

Labor Contract Law is a short form of *Labor Contract Law of the People's Republic of China*. It is the most important law among the labor-related laws and regulations in China currently. *Labor Contract Law* applies to all enterprises, including foreign or foreign-funded enterprises, individual economic organizations and private non-enterprise entities within Chinese territory. It has specific rules regarding working overtime, including the upper limit on overtime work per day or per month, and the standard for overtime pay.

45 Asking for Leave

Key Sentence

Xià gè xīngqī wǒ xiǎng qǐng sān tiān jià.
下个星期我 想 请 三 天 假。
I want to ask for three-day leave next week.

Substitution

zhège yuè xiàxún
这个月 下旬
the last ten days of this month

Qīyuèfèn
七月份
July

shàngbànnián
上 半 年
the first half of the year

xiàbànnián
下半年
the second half of the year

qǐng liǎngtiān shìjià
请 两 天事假
ask for two-day leave of absence

tiáoxiū yì tiān
调休一 天
have a day off switched

xiū niánjià
休年假
take one's annual leave

Extension

1. Nǐ yǒu shénme tèshū yuányīn xūyào qǐngjià ma?
你有 什么特殊原因（需要）请假 吗?
Do you have any particular reasons to ask for leave of absence?

2. Wǒ péngyou cóng Měiguó lái kànwǒ, wǒxiǎng qǐng jǐ tiān jià péipei tā.
我 朋 友 从 美国来看我，我 想 请几天假陪陪他。
My friend has come to see me from the USA, so I want to take a few days off to accompany him.

3. Bié wàngle bǎ nǐ de qǐngjiàtiáo gěiwǒ.
别 忘了把你的请假条给我。
Don't forget to give me your written request for leave.

4. Nǐ huíjiā hǎohǎo xiūxi xiūxi ba.
（你）回家好好休息休息吧。
(You should) go home and take a good rest.

Dialogue

A: Jīnglǐ, xià gè xīngqī wǒ xiǎng qǐng sān tiān jià
经理，下个星期我 想 请 三 天 假。
Manager, I want to ask for three-day leave next week.

B: Nǐ yǒu shénme tèshū yuányīn xūyào qǐngjià ma?
你有 什 么特殊原 因需要请假吗?
Do you have any particular reasons to ask for leave of absence?

A: Wǒ fùmǔ cóng Měiguó lái kàn wǒ. Wǒ xiǎng qǐng jǐ tiān jià péipei tāmen.
我父母 从 美 国来看 我。我 想 请几天假陪陪他们。
My parents have come to see me from the USA. I want to take a few days off to accompany them.

B: Hǎoba. Bié wàngle bǎ nǐ de qǐngjiàtiáo gěi wǒ.
好吧。别忘了把你的请假条给我。

OK. Don't forget to give me your written request for leave.

C: Jīnglǐ, wǒ juéde bú tài shūfu. Wǒ xiǎng zǎodiǎnr xiàbān, qǐng yí gè xiǎoshí bìngjià.
经理，我觉得不太舒服。我想早点儿下班，请一个小时病假。

Manager, I don't feel very well. I want to get off work earlier and ask for one-hour sick leave.

B: Nà jiù huíjiā hǎohǎo xiūxi xiūxi ba. Zǒu de shíhou jìzhe dǎkǎ!
那就回家好好休息休息吧。走的时候记着打卡！

If so, you should go home and take a good rest. Please remember to punch the time clock when you leave!

Related Words

1	qǐngjià 请假	to ask for leave	6	gōngxiū rì 工休(日)	day off (from one's work)
2	xiūjià 休假	vacation leave; to have a holiday/vacation leave	7	niánjià 年假	annual leave
3	shìjià 事假	leave of absence (for personal reasons)	8	dàixīn xiūjià 带薪休假	vacation with pay
4	bìngjià 病假	sick leave	9	chǎnjià 产假	maternity leave
5	gōngxiū rì 公休(日)	general/official holiday			

(Continued)

10	tànqīn-jià 探亲假	home visit leave (The vacation enjoyed by employees working in enterprises or non-profiting institutions allows them to visit their spouses or relatives living in other places.)
11	kuànggōng 旷工	to skip work; absence from one's work without permission

Cultural Navigation

According to Chinese law, employees of enterprises and governmental staff work eight hours per day and five days per week. In addition, there are eleven days of national official holiday in China each year, which are New Year's Day (Yuándàn), a three-day holiday for the Spring Festival (Chūnjié), the Tomb Sweeping Day (Qīngmíngjié), the International Labor Day on May 1st (Láodòngjié), the Dragon Boat Festival (Duānwǔjié), the Mid-autumn Festival (Zhōngqiūjié) and a three-day holiday for the National Day on Oct 1st (Guóqìngjié). Moreover, female employees can enjoy 14-week maternity leave.

46 Newbie on the Road

Key Sentence

Wǒ shì xīnshǒu, jīnhòu yídìng qǐng nín duōduō zhǐjiào.
我是新手，今后一定请您多多指教。
I'm a new recruit, and definitely need much advice from you in the future.

Substitution

shíxíshēng
实习生
intern

dì-yī cì lái Zhōngguó
第一次来中国
the first time someone comes to China

xué diànnǎo zhuānyè de
学电脑专业的
computer science major

cóng shìchǎngbù diào guolai de
从市场部调过来的
transferred from the Marketing Department

Extension

Zhè wèi shì nǐ xīn lái de tóngshì.
1. 这位是（你）新来的同事。

This is your new colleague.

Huānyíng jiārù wǒmen de tuánduì!
2. 欢迎加入我们的团队！

Welcome to join our team!

Tā shì wǒmen zhèr de zhuānjiā.
3. 他是我们这儿的专家。

He is our expert here.

Jīnhòu dàjiā hùxiāng xuéxí.
4. 今后大家互相学习。

We'll learn from each other from now on.

Dialogue

Wáng gōng, zhèwèi shì xīn lái de tóngshì, Màikè.
A: 王工，这位是新来的同事，麦克。

Engineer Wang, this is a new colleague, Michael.

Ò, huānyíng huānyíng! Huānyíng jiārù wǒmen de tuánduì!
B: 哦，欢迎欢迎！欢迎加入我们的团队！

Oh, welcome! Welcome to join our team!

Wáng gōng shì wǒmen zhèr de zhuānjiā, nǐ yǒu shénme wèntí dōu kěyǐ wèn tā.
A: 王工是我们这儿的专家，你有什么问题都可以问他。

Engineer Wang is our expert here. You can ask him if you have any questions.

C: Nà tài hǎo le! Wǒ shì xīnshǒu, jīnhòu yídìng qǐng nín duōduō zhǐjiào.
那太好了！我是新手，今后一定请您多多指教。
That'll be great! I'm a new recruit, and I definitely need much advice from you in the future.

B: Bú kèqi. Jīnhòu dàjiā dōu shì tóngshì, wǒmen hùxiāng xuéxí.
不客气。今后大家都是同事，我们互相学习。
Not at all. We are colleagues from now on, and we'll learn from each other.

Zhèyàng ba, wǒ xiān lǐng nǐ shúxī shúxī huánjìng.
这样吧，我先领你熟悉熟悉环境。
Then let me show you around first.

Related Words

1	xīnshǒu 新手	new hand; novice; new recruit	7	bùmén 部门	department
2	lǎoshǒu 老手	old hand; veteran; experienced/skillful person in a field	8	gǎngwèi 岗位	post; station
3	línshí gōngzuò 临时工作	temporary job	9	chējiān 车间	workshop
4	duǎnqī gōngzuò 短期工作	short-term job	10	xiàngmù 项目	project
5	zhèngshì yuángōng 正式员工	regular employee	11	jīngyàn fēngfù 经验丰富	very experienced; skillful
6	hétonggōng 合同工	contract worker	12	quēfá jīngyàn 缺乏经验	lack of experience; inexperience

Cultural Navigation

There are two interesting terms in Chinese: "xīnshǒu (new hand or novice)" and "lǎoshǒu (old hand or veteran)." The original meaning of "xīnshǒu shànglù" refers to a fresh driver who has just learned how to drive. If a person who has just been hired or transferred from other places without any needed experience, this person can be called a "new hand" too. It is very normal that a "new hand" is not familiar with his job. Confucius once said: "Zhī zhī wéi zhī zhī, bù zhī wéi bù zhī, shì zhì yě." (Being aware of what you know and what you don't know is wisdom.) If you are new to your job, please don't feel embarrassed to seek advice from those "old hands." You'll find that most Chinese are happy to give a hand to a newcomer or "a new hand."

47 Office Equipment

Key Sentence

Nǐ zhīdào zěnme yòng zhè tái fùyìnjī ma?
你知道怎么用这台复印机吗?
Do you know how to use this copy machine?

Substitution

zhège ruǎnjiàn
这个软件
this software

zhè tái dǎyìnjī
这台打印机
this printer

zhè tái tóuyǐngjī
这台投影机
this projector

nà tái sǎomiáojī
那台扫描机
that scanner

Extension

1. Zhè tái xīn jīqì yǒudiǎn fùzá.
这台新机器有点复杂。
This new machine is a little bit complicated.

2. Wǒ zuótiān gāng xuéhuì zěnme yòng.
我昨天刚学会怎么用。
I just learned how to use it yesterday.

3. Nǐ gǎnkuài jiāo wǒ yíxià zěnme yòng ba.
（你）赶快教我一下（怎么用）吧。
Please teach me (how to use it) now.

4. Nǐ děi xiān shūrù nǐ de mìmǎ, zài ànzhào tíshì yí bù yí bù zuò.
你得先输入你的密码，再按照提示一步一步做。
You must enter your password first, and then follow the instructions step by step.

Dialogue

A: Nǐ zhīdào zěnme yòng zhè tái fùyìnjī ma?
你知道怎么用这台复印机吗?
Do you know how to use this copy machine?

B: Èng, zhè tái xīn jīqì yǒudiǎn fùzá. Wǒ zuótiān gāng xuéhuìle zěnme yòng tā.
嗯，这台新机器有点复杂。我昨天刚学会了怎么用它。
Yes, this new machine is a little bit complicated. I just learned how to use it yesterday.

A: Shìma? Nà nǐ gǎnkuài jiāowǒ yíxià zěnme yòng ba.
是吗? 那你赶快教我一下怎么用吧。
Really? Then teach me how to use it now.

B: Nǐ děi xiān shūrù nǐ de mìmǎ, zài ànzhào tíshì yí bù yí bù zuò.
你得先输入你的密码，再按照提示一步一步做。
You must enter your password first, and then follow the instructions step by step.

A: Wǒ shì àn nǐ gāngcái shuō de zuò de a! Bú shì jīqì yǒu wèntí ba?
我是按你（刚才）说的做的啊！不是机器有问题吧?
I did exactly what you (just) said! Is it possible that the machine has some problems?

Related Words

1	dānmiàn 单面	one-sided; single-sided	7	dìngshūjī 订书机	stapler
2	shuāngmiàn 双面	two-sided	8	dìngshūdīng 订书钉	staple
3	jiā zhǐ 加纸	to load paper	9	huíxíngzhēn 回形针	paper clip
4	dǔ zhǐ 堵纸/ kǎ zhǐ 卡纸	paper jam	10	tòumíng jiāodài 透明胶带	scotch tape
5	wénjiànjiā 文件夹	folder	11	túgǎiyè 涂改液/ xiūzhèngyè 修正液	correction fluid
6	huóyè (wénjiàn) jiā 活页(文件)夹	binder	12	mò (fěn) hé/tàn (fěn) hé 墨(粉)盒/碳(粉)盒	toner cartridge

Cultural Navigation

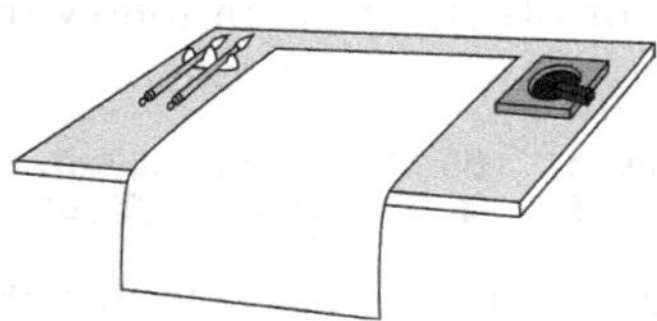

Have you ever heard about "wénfáng sì bǎo (four treasures of the study)?" They are four kinds of traditional Chinese stationery, including "máobǐ (the writing brush)," "mò (ink stick)," "yàntái (ink slab)"

and "zhǐ (paper)." Chinese have been using these "four treasures of the study" for about two thousand years. Generally speaking, in history, "Húbǐ," writing brushes made in Huzhou of Zhejiang Province, "Huīmò," ink sticks made in Huizhou (now known as Jixi, Tunxi, Shexian County, etc. of Anhui Province), "Duānyàn," ink slabs made in Duanzhou (now known as Zhaoqing of Guangdong Province) and "Xuānzhǐ," high quality paper made in Xuancheng (now known as Jingxian County of Anhui Province) were considered the best in quality. Among them, "Xuānzhǐ" is listed as Intangible Cultural Heritage by UNESCO (United Nations Educational, Scientific and Cultural Organization).

48 Assigning Tasks

Key Sentence

Qǐng nǐ bǎ zhè fèn xiàngmù shíshī jìndùbiǎo yòng yóujiàn fāgěi gège bùmén.
请你把这份项目实施进度表用邮件发给各个部门。

Please send this project implementation schedule to each department by e-mail.

Substitution

gōngzuò jìndù bàobiǎo
工作进度报表
work progress chart

shēngchǎn tǒngjì bàogào
生产统计报告
production statistical report

xiāoshòu tǒngjìbiǎo
销售统计表
statistical table of sales

jìdù zīchǎn fùzhàibiǎo
季度资产负债表
quarterly balance sheet

1. Xià gè yuè yuē tóuzīfāng jiànmiàn de shìqing nǐ ānpái le ma?
下个月约投资方见面的事情（你）安排了吗？
Have you arranged next month's meeting with the investors?

2. Shíjiān hé dìdiǎn dōu ānpái hǎo le.
时间和地点都安排好了。
Time and location have both been settled.

3. Wǒmen xūyào jǐnkuài zhǔnbèihǎo suǒyǒu de zīliào.
我们需要尽快准备好所有的资料。
We need to have all the information ready as soon as possible.

4. Zhège rènwu jiù jiāogěi nǐ le.
这个任务就交给你了。
Now this job is yours.

A: Zhāng zǒng, nín zhǎo wǒ ma?
张总，您找我吗？
General Manager Zhang, are you looking for me?

B: Shìde. Qǐng nǐ bǎ zhèfèn xiàngmù shíshī jìndùbiǎo yòng yóujiàn fāgěi gège bùmén.
是的。请你把这份项目实施进度表用邮件发给各个部门。
Yes. Please send this project implementation schedule to each department by e-mail.

A: Hǎo, wǒ mǎshàng qù zuòzhè jiàn shì.
好，我马上去做这件事。
OK, I'll do this right away.

B: Xià xīngqī yuē tóuzīfāng jiànmiàn de shìqing nǐ ānpái le ma?
下星期约投资方见面的事情你安排了吗?
Have you arranged next week's meeting with the investors?

A: Méi wèntí, shíjiān hé dìdiǎn dōu ānpái hǎo le.
没问题，时间和地点都安排好了。
No problem. Time and location have both been settled.

B: Nàme wǒmen xūyào jǐnkuài zhǔnbèihǎo suǒyǒu de zīliào.
那么，我们需要尽快准备好所有的资料。
Well then, we need to have all the information ready as soon as possible.

Zhège rènwu jiù jiāogěi nǐ le.
这个任务就交给你了。
Now this job is yours.

Related Words

1	jìhuà 计划	plan; to plan	7	cáiwù bàobiǎo 财务报表	financial statement
2	tiáozhěng 调整	to adjust	8	jìndùbiǎo 进度表	progress chart
3	wánchéng 完成	to accomplish; to complete	9	tǒngjìbiǎo 统计表	statistical table
4	gōngzuòliàng 工作量	workload	10	shíjiānbiǎo 时间表	time table
5	zhǐpài 指派	to appoint; to name; to designate	11	línshí ānpái 临时安排	temporary arrangement
6	rénshǒu búgòu/zú 人手不够/足	to be short of hands	12	gǎngwèi zérènzhì 岗位责任制	system of post responsibility

Cultural Navigation

"Chī dàguōfàn" is a term unique to China. Literally, it means "everyone shares the food prepared in a large canteen cauldron." Chinese use this term as a metaphor when employees receive exactly the same salary and compensation regardless of the quality of their work or level of their contribution. Since the economic reform of 1979, China has abandoned this approach of egalitarianism. Now every employee is paid according to his/her work and contribution. The ideas of getting rich through hard work, getting rich through knowledge and getting rich through fair competition have been widely accepted by every industry and individual. Obviously, this change is one of the driving forces for the booming economy of China.

49 Disputes at Work

Key Sentence

Zhè cì shìgù bù yīnggāi guài wǒ.
这次事故不应该怪我。
I'm not to blame for this accident.

Substitution

gēn wǒ méi guānxi
跟我没关系
have nothing to do with me

bú shì wǒ de zérèn
不是我的责任
not my responsibility

bú shì wǒ zàochéng de
不是我造成的
not caused by me

Extension

1. Gāngcái jīnglǐ lái diànhuà, tā shuō shàng xīngqī de nà pī huò (wǒmen) fācuò le!
刚才经理来电话，他说上星期的那批货（我们）发错了！
The manager just called and he said that we shipped out the wrong goods last week!

Zhè xià hǎo le, zhège yuè de jiǎngjīn méi le!
2. 这下好了，这个月的奖金没了！

That's too bad! This month's bonus is gone!

Wèi shénme yào kòu dàjiā de jiǎngjīn?
3. 为什么要扣大家的奖金？

Why is everyone's bonus being deducted?

Gǎnkuài kànkan cǎiqǔ shénme bǔjiù cuòshī ba!
4. 赶快看看采取什么补救措施吧！

Let's see what could be done to fix it right now!

Dialogue

A: Gāngcái jīnglǐ lái diànhuà, tā shuō shàngxīngqī de nà pī huò wǒmen fācuò le!
刚才经理来电话，他说上星期的那批货（我们）发错了！

The manager just called and he said that we shipped out the wrong goods last week!

B: Zhèxià hǎo le, zhège yuè de jiǎngjīn méi le!
这下好了，这个月的奖金没了！

That's too bad! This month's bonus is gone!

C: Wèi shénme yào kòu dàjiā de jiǎngjīn? Nà zhāng dān shì shéi jīngshǒu de?
为什么要扣大家的奖金？那张单是谁经手的？

Why is everyone's bonus being deducted? Who handled that order?

D: Shì wǒ. Kěshì wǒ shì wánquán àn jīnglǐ de fēnfu bàn de. Zhè cì shìgù bù yīnggāi guài wǒ.
是我。可是我是完全按经理的吩咐办的。这次事故不应该怪我。

It was me. But I did exactly what the manager told me. I'm not to blame for this accident.

A: Hǎo le, bié zhēng le! Gǎnkuài kànkan cǎiqǔ shénme bǔjiù cuòshī ba!
好了，别争了！赶快看看采取什么补救措施吧！
OK, stop arguing! Let's see what could be done to fix it right now!

Related Words

1	zérèn 责任	responsibility	7	gōngzuòkuáng 工作狂	workaholic; workaholism
2	fùzé 负责	responsible for; in charge of	8	rènzhēn 认真	serious(ly); earnest(ly)
3	chéngdān zérèn 承担责任	to take responsibility	9	qínfèn 勤奋	diligent(ly)
4	tuīxiè zérèn 推卸责任	to shirk responsibility; to pass the buck	10	mǎhu 马虎	careless(ly)
5	tōulǎn 偷懒	lazy	11	zhànxiǎopiányi 占小便宜	to gain petty advantages (at others' expense)
6	móyánggōng 磨洋工	loaf on the job	12	zhùrén-wéilè 助人为乐	to find pleasure in helping others

Cultural Navigation

Unexpected problems pop up all the time at work. It is unrealistic to expect that disagreements and disputes between colleagues can be avoided every time. When a problem happens, your attitude towards solving the problem is very important. This attitude of "yán yǐ lǜjǐ, kuān yǐ dàirén (being strict with oneself and lenient towards others)" has always been considered as a virtue in traditional Chinese culture. If one can practice this virtue at work, he/she will certainly win respect and friendship of his/her coworkers.

50 Submitting an Expense Account for Reimbursement

Key Sentence

Wǒ lái bàoxiāo wǒ shàng gè yuè de chāilǚfèi.
我来报销（我）上个月的差旅费。
I'm here to get reimbursement for (my) last month's travel expenses.

Substitution

jīpiào
机票
airplane ticket

kèhù jiēdàifèi
客户接待费
expense for receiving clients

cānzhǎn fèiyong
参展费用
expense for participating in the exhibition

bàngōng yòngpǐn cǎigòufèi
办公用品采购费
expense for purchasing office supplies

xīnchǎnpǐn fābùhuì de huāfèi
新产品发布会的花费
expense for the new product release conference

Extension

1. Nǐ bǎ fāpiào dōu dàilai le ma?
你把发票都带来了吗?
Do you bring all receipts with you?

2. Zhè xiàng kāizhī àn guīdìng bù néng bào.
这项开支按规定不能报。
According to the regulations, this expenditure cannot be reimbursed.

3. Zhèshì Wáng zhǔrèn pīzhǔnde.
这是王主任批准的。
This was approved by Director Wang.

4. Nǐ xūyào zhǎo jīnglǐ qiān gè zì.
你需要找经理签个字。
You need to get a signature from the manager.

Dialogue

A: Wáng kuàijì, Wǒ lái bàoxiāo shàng gè yuè de chāilǚfèi.
王会计，我来报销上个月的差旅费。
Accountant Wang, I'm here to get reimbursement for last month's travel expenses.

B: Ò, nǐ bǎ fāpiào dōu dàilai le ma?
哦，你把发票都带来了吗?
Oh, do you bring all receipts with you?

A: Dōu dài le. Zhè shì fèiyong qīngdān. Nín kàn yí kàn shì bú shì dōu quán le.
都带了。这是费用清单。您看一看是不是都全了。
Yes. This is the detailed list of expenses. Could you take a look and see if everything needed is here?

B: Hǎode, ràngwǒ héduì yíxià.
好的，让我核对一下。
Good. Let me check.

Zhè xiàng kāizhī àn guīdìng bù néng bào.
这 项 开支按规定不 能 报。
According to the regulations, this expenditure cannot be reimbursed.

A: kěshì, zhè shì Chén zǒng pīzhǔn de a.
可是，这是 陈 总 批准的啊。
But this was approved by General Manager Chen.

B: Nàyàng dehuà, nǐ xūyào zhǎo lǎobǎn qiān gè zì.
那 样 的话，你需要 找 老板 签 个字。
If so, you need to get a signature from the boss.

Related Words

1	zhīchū 支出	to expend; expenditure	7	jīntiē 津贴	subsidy; allowance
2	shōurù 收入	income	8	qiānmíng 签 名	signature; to sign (one's name)
3	qīngdān 清 单	detailed list	9	gàizhāng 盖 章	to stamp; to affix one's seal
4	bàobiǎo 报 表	form to report statistics	10	pīzhǔn 批准	to approve; to ratify
5	cáiwù 财务 guīdìng 规 定	financial regulation	11	báitiáo 白条	unofficial receipt (with little binding force)
6	chāozhī 超 支	to overspend	12	záxiàng fèiyong 杂 项 费 用	miscellaneous expenses

Cultural Navigation

There are three different types of common receipts related to receiving money, making payments or purchasing, which are "fāpiào," "shōujù" and "xiǎopiào." To be brief, both "fāpiào" and "shōujù" are original receipts for sales and purchase or transaction of funds. The difference is that "fāpiào" is an original proof that documents cost, expense or income, and can be used to get a reimbursement as well as be a proof for taxation. "Shōujù" is only used to document a transaction of funds. Usually, it cannot be used as a proof of cost, expense or income, and therefore cannot be used for the purpose of reimbursement or taxation. "Xiǎopiào" is a sales check or invoice which is broadly used at stores, shopping centers and supermarkets.

51 Office Gossip

Key Sentence

Zhēnde, zhè shì kěkào de nèibù xiāoxi.
真的，这是可靠的内部消息。
It's true. This is reliable inside information.

Substitution

qiānzhēn-wànquè
千真万确
absolutely true

juéduì zhǔnquè
绝对准确
absolutely accurate

xiāngxìn wǒ
相信我
trust me

zuì xīn xiāoxi
最新消息
latest news

dì-yī shǒu qíngbào
第一手情报
first-hand intelligence

xìnxī láiyuán
信息来源
information channel/source

Extension

1. Nǐ tīngshuō le ma? Shìchǎngbù de Xiǎo Lǐ yǒu xīn nánpéngyou le!
(你) 听说了吗? 市场部的小李有新男朋友了!
Have you heard about it? Xiao Li at the Marketing Department has a new boyfriend!

2. Tīngshuō shì jìshùbù de Wáng gōng.
听说是技术部的王工。
I've heard that it's Engineer Wang from the Technology Department.

3. Wǒ kàn shì xiǎodào xiāoxi ba.
我看是小道消息吧。
I think that's hearsay.

4. Zhè shì diǎnxíng de bāguà!
(这是) 典型的八卦!
(This is) typical gossip!

Dialogue

A: Tīngshuō le ma? Shìchǎngbù de Xiǎo Lǐ yǒu xīn nánpéngyou le!
听说了吗? 市场部的小李有新男朋友了!
Have you heard about it? Xiao Li at the Marketing Department has a new boyfriend!

B: Nǐ zǒngshì yǒu xīnwén. Shì shéi?
你总是有新闻。是谁?
You always have some news. Who is he?

A: Tīngshuō shì jìshùbù de Wáng gōng.
听说是技术部的王工。
I've heard that it's Engineer Wang from the Technology Department.

B: Wǒ juéde bù kěnéng.
我觉得不可能。
I don't think that's possible.

A: Zhēnde, zhèshì kěkào de nèibù xiāoxi.
真的，这是可靠的内部消息。
It's true. This is reliable inside information.

B: Wǒkànshìxiǎodào xiāoxi ba. Diǎnxíng de bāguà!
我看是小道消息吧。典型的八卦！
I think that's hearsay. Typical gossip!

Related Words

1	guǎn xiánshì 管闲事	to meddle; to poke one's nose into other people's business	7	qiánguīzé 潜规则	hidden rule
2	dǎtàn 打探	to make inquiries discreetly	8	shuōcháng-dàoduǎn 说长道短	to criticize others (often irresponsibly); to gossip
3	yǐnsī 隐私	privacy	9	tiānyóu-jiācù 添油加醋	to add spice; to embroider the facts
4	zàoyáo 造谣	to start a rumor	10	liúyán-fēiyǔ 流言蜚语	rumors and slanders
5	kǎnyé 侃爷	a talkative man (colloquial)	11	wúzhōng-shēngyǒu 无中生有	purely fictitious; fabricated
6	chángshé-fù 长舌妇	a nosey/inquisitive woman (colloquial)	12	bānnòng shìfēi 搬弄是非	to sow discord; to tell tales

Cultural Navigation

Have you ever chatted with your Chinese colleagues or coworkers in Chinese? If the answer is "no," then you really should give a try. Local weather, restaurants and food, a new movie or a recent popular song, all of these things can be used to start a friendly conversation. You will realize surprisingly that the language barrier is not as a big problem as you thought. You will also find out that today Chinese are very open. You may chat about any topics you want. Chatting with Chinese can help you make friends and know Chinese people and society better. These may also benefit your work in China. However, there is one thing that should not be forgotten: wandering around and chatting at work is not allowed by any companies. There is no exception in China either.

Having a Meeting

52 Being Notified of a Meeting

Key Sentence

Míngtiān xiàwǔ sì diǎn zài sān lóu huìyìshì kāihuì
明天下午四点在三楼会议室开会。
There will be a meeting in the conference room on the 3rd floor at 4:00 pm tomorrow.

Substitution

Xīngqīyī
星期一
Monday

Wǔyuè shí hào
五月十号
May 10th

jīntiān wǎnshang
今天晚上
tonight

jīnglǐ bàngōngshì
经理办公室
manager's office

gōngsī zǒngbù
公司总部
company headquarters

shīgōng xiànchǎng
施工现场
construction site

Extension

1. Nǐ shōudàole zhòngyào huìyì de tōngzhī méiyǒu?
你收到了 重 要 会议的通知 没有?
Have you received the message about the important meeting?

2. Jùshuō shì guānyú chǎnpǐn zhìliàng wèntí de huì.
据说是关于 产品 质量问题的会。
It is said that the meeting is about product quality.

3. Kāihuì tōngzhī shì jīntiān shàngwǔ yòng yóujiàn fāchū de.
开会 通知 是今天 上 午 用 邮件发出的。
The meeting notice was sent by e-mail this morning.

4. Wǒ děi gǎnjǐn chá yíxià wǒ de yóujiàn.
我 得赶紧 查一下我的 邮 件。
I have to check my e-mail right away.

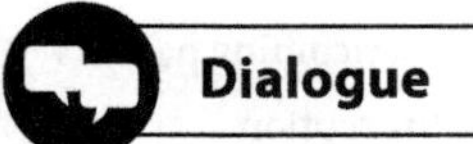

Dialogue

A: Nǐ shōudào míngtiān huìyì de tōngzhī méiyǒu?
你 收 到 明 天 会议的通 知 没有?
Have you received the message about tomorrow's meeting?

B: Méiyǒu a. Míngtiān shénme shíhou kāihuì?
没 有啊。明天 什 么 时候开会?
I haven't. When will the meeting be held tomorrow?

A: Míngtiān xiàwǔ sì diǎn zài sānlóu huìyìshì kāihuì
明 天 下午四 点 在三楼会议室（开会）。
The meeting will be held in the conference room on the 3rd floor at 4:00 pm tomorrow.

B: Nǐ zhīdào kāi shénme huì ma?
你知道 开 什 么 会 吗?
Do you know what this meeting is about?

Jùshuō shì guānyú chǎnpǐn zhìliàng wèntí de huì.
A: 据说是关于产品质量问题的会。
It is said that the meeting is about product quality.

Kāihuì tōngzhī shì jīntiān shàngwǔ yòng yóujiàn fāchū de.
开会通知是今天上午用邮件发出的。
The meeting notice was sent by e-mail this morning.

Hǎoba, wǒ děi gǎnjǐn chá yíxià wǒ de yóujiàn.
B: 好吧，我得赶紧查一下我的邮件。
Well, I have to check my e-mail right away.

Related Words

1	jǔxíng zhàokāi huìyì 举行/召开会议	to hold a meeting	7	zhāodàihuì 招待会	reception
2	zhàojí huìyì 召集会议	to call a meeting	8	huānyínghuì 欢迎会	welcoming party/ reception
3	diànhuà huìyì 电话会议	teleconference	9	qìngzhùhuì 庆祝会	celebration meeting
4	shìpín huìyì 视频会议	video conference	10	yántǎohuì 研讨会	seminar; symposium
5	xīnwén fābùhuì 新闻发布会	news conference	11	yuángōng dàhuì/zhígōng dàhuì 员工大会/职工大会	all employees' general meeting; all staff meeting; workers' assembly
6	jìzhě zhāodàihuì 记者招待会	press conference	12	niánzhōng zǒngjiéhuì 年终总结会	year-end summary meeting

Cultural Navigation

In Chinese, an invitation letter is called "yāoqǐngxìn" or "yāoqǐnghán." The words of "xìn" and "hán" have the same meaning in modern Chinese language, but it will sound more formal if the word "hán" is used. In fact, some people even prefer to use more traditional terms, such as "qǐngjiǎn" or "qǐngtiě," to show politeness and respect. Based on the specific needs and recipients of your letter, you may choose to use an e-invitation letter or traditional letter of invitation. The former is more convenient and faster while the latter is more formal and serious.

53 Participants of the Meeting

Key Sentence

Míngtiān de huì gè bùmén fùzérén (dōu) bìxū cānjiā.
明天的会各部门负责人（都）必须参加。
The person in charge from each department has to attend tomorrow's meeting.

Substitution

quántǐ yuángōng
全体员工
all the employees

bùmén jīnglǐ
部门经理
department manager

zhōngcéng jīnglǐ
中层经理
middle manager

zhōngcéng gànbù
中层干部
middle-level cadre

dǒngshìhuì chéngyuán
董事会成员
member of the board of directors

1. Míngtiān de huì měi gè rén dōu bìxū cānjiā ma?
   明天的会每个人都必须参加吗?
   Does everyone have to attend tomorrow's meeting?
2. Zhǐ yǒu wǒmen lǐngdǎo qù cānjiā.
   只有我们领导去参加。
   Only our leader is going to attend.
3. Nǐ bù yě shì lǐngdǎo ma?
   你不也是领导吗?
   Aren't you a leader too?
4. Wǒ nǎr shì shénme lǐngdǎo!
   我哪儿是什么领导!
   How come I am a leader?

A: Míngtiān de huì měi gè rén dōu bìxū cānjiā ma?
明天的会每个人都必须参加吗?
Does everyone have to attend tomorrow's meeting?

B: Míngtiān de huì gè bùmén fùzérén dōu bìxū cānjiā.
明天的会各部门负责人都必须参加。
The person in charge from each department has to attend tomorrow's meeting.

A: Ò, nàyàng dehuà, wǒmen lǐngdǎo qù jiù xíng le.
哦，那样的话，我们领导去就行了。
Oh, in that case, it will be fine that only our leader attends.

B: Nǐ bù yě shì lǐngdǎo ma?
你不也是领导吗?
Aren't you a leader too?

Kāi shénme wánxiào, wǒ nǎr shì shénme lǐngdǎo!
A: 开什么玩笑，我哪儿是什么领导！
Are you joking? How come I am a leader?

Zàishuō, kuài xiàbān cái kāihuì, shéi zhīdào yào kāidào shénme shíhou ne!
再说，快下班才开会，谁知道要开到什么时候呢！
Besides, the meeting will start almost at the end of the day. Who knows how long it will take!

Related Words

1	cānjiā 参加	to attend; to participate; to join	6	sànhuì 散会	to end a meeting
2	chūxí 出席	to attend	7	huìyì 会议 dìdiǎn 地点	location of a meeting
3	yīngù 因故	for some reason; due to unforeseen circumstance	8	huìyì 会议 yìtí 议题	theme of a meeting
4	quēxí 缺席	absent	9	nèiróng 内容	content
5	lièxí 列席	to attend as an observer	10	yùhuìzhě 与会者	conferee; participant

Cultural Navigation

In Chinese, "chūxí huìyì" and "cānjiā huìyì" sound the same. However, there are some slight differences between "chūxí" and "cānjiā." Literally, "chūxí" means "to appear in one's seat." It is normally used for attending meetings or gatherings only, especially in attending a formal meeting. Therefore, the tone of "chūxí" tends to be more formal. When it is used with "lièxí (to attend as an observer)" together, "chūxí" especially applies to those representatives who have the right to speak and vote. And "cānjiā" puts the emphasis on "to participate" and "to interact." Therefore, it can not only be used for attending meetings, but also in participating in all kinds of activities and organizations (i.e. to become a member). Since the tone of "cānjiā" is not as formal as "chūxí," "cānjiā" is used more frequently when regular meetings are involved.

54 In Preparation for a Meeting

Key Sentence

Xiàzhōu de chǎnpǐn fābùhuì zhǔnbèi de zěnmeyàng le?
下周的产品发布会准备得怎么样了?
How is the preparation work going for next week's product release conference?

Substitution

chǎnpǐn tuījièhuì
产品推介会
product release and promotion conference

zhāobiāohuì
招标会
competitive bidding; public bidding

gāoxīn jìshù yántǎohuì
高新技术研讨会
new and high-tech symposium

niándù dìnghuòhuì
年度订货会
annual pre-order show

Extension

1. Yāoqǐngxìn yǐjīng dōu fā chuqu le.
邀请信已经都发出去了。
All the invitation letters are already sent out.

2. Chūgǎo yǐjīng chūlai le, búguò hái xūyào zuò yìxiē xiūgǎi.
初稿已经出来了，不过还需要做一些修改。
The first draft has already come out, but it still needs some revisions.

3. Zhè fèn zīliào xūyào dǎyìn duōshao fèn?
这份资料需要打印多少份?
How many copies of this material need to be printed?

4. Hái yǒu yí jiàn shì, (qǐng) tōngzhī Chén jīnglǐ dào shíhou ānpái rén bùzhì huìchǎng.
还有一件事，（请）通知陈经理到时候安排人布置会场。
One more thing. (Please) notify Manager Chen that he should assign someone the job of setting up the meeting place when the time comes.

Dialogue

A: Xiàzhōu de chǎnpǐn fābùhuì zhǔnbèi de zěnmeyàng le?
下周的产品发布会准备得怎么样了?
How is the preparation work going for next week's product release conference?

B: Yāoqǐngxìn yǐjīng dōu fā chuqu le.
邀请信已经都发出去了。
All the invitation letters are already sent out.

Yǎnshì yòng de huàndēng bàogào zuòhǎo le ma?
A: 演示 用 的 幻 灯 报告 做好了吗?
Is the PPT for the demonstration ready?

Chūgǎo yǐjīng chūlai le, búguò hái xūyào zuò yìxiē xiūgǎi.
B: 初稿已经出来了，不过还需要做一些修改。
The first draft has already come out, but it still needs some revisions.

Nàhǎo, dìnggǎo yǐhòu fāgěi wǒ kàn yí kàn.
A: 那好，定稿以后发给我 看一看。
That's good! Once it has been done, please send the final version to me to look at.

Wǒ xiǎng wèn yíxià zhèfèn zīliào xūyào dǎyìn duōshao fèn?
B: 我 想 问一下这份资料需要打印多 少 份?
Could I ask how many copies of this material need to be printed?

Sānbǎi fèn yīnggāi gòu le. Háiyǒu yí jiànshì, qǐng tōngzhī Chén jīnglǐ dào shíhou ānpái rén bùzhì huìchǎng.
A: 三百份应该够了。还有一件事，请通知 陈 经理到时候安排人布置会场。
300 copies should be enough. One more thing. Please notify Manager Chen that he should assign someone the job of setting up the meeting place when the time comes.

Related Words

1	dǎyìn 打印	to print	3	cǎiyìn 彩印	color printing
2	fùyìn 复印	to copy; to duplicate	4	huàndēngjī 幻灯机	slide projector; overhead projector

(Continued)

5	jiǎngtái 讲台	platform; rostrum; dais	9	yuánzhuō 圆桌 tǎolùnhuì 讨论会	round table discussion
6	zhǔxítái 主席台	platform; rostrum for the chairman and board	10	tōngzhī 通知 shū (书)	notice; notification (letter)
7	huìyì- 会议 zhuō 桌	board room/ conference room table	11	bàomíng 报名	to enter one's name; to sign up
8	yuánzhuō 圆桌	round table	12	bàodào 报到/ qiāndào 签到	to register; to check in

Cultural Navigation

If you ever have a chance to participate in a seminar or a formal meeting in China, there are three things to keep in mind. First of all, make sure to bring a box of business cards with you. After greetings and shaking hands, Chinese businessmen are used to exchanging business cards with each other. There is no doubt that attending a conference is a good opportunity to establish social connections. Second, wear proper attire. Just as the old saying goes, "Rén kào yīfu mǎ kào ān." (Clothes make the man.) Today in China, businessmen often wear Western-style business suits and businesswomen often wear suits and matching skirts. Moreover, keep Chinese seating rules in your mind. Unless you are told where to sit in advance, most conferees would not tend to sit in the center seats at a meeting table or the front row at a conference hall. The humble and low-key attitude will always be approved and praised in Chinese traditional culture.

55 Meeting Agenda

Key Sentence

Wǒ rènwéi yīnggāi bǎ běntǔhuà wèntí liè wéi huìyì yìchéng de dì-yī yìtí.
我认为应该把"本土化"问题列为（会议议程的）第一议题。

I think that the issue of "localization" should be listed as the first item (on the agenda).

Substitution

jiànyì
建议
suggest

zhǔzhāng
主张
advocate

jiānchí
坚持
insist

juéde
觉得
feel; think

yuángōng péixùn
员工培训
employee training

zhìliàng guǎnlǐ
质量管理
quality control

bìnggòu
并购
merger and acquisition

gōngsī shàngshì
公司上市
company goes public

xīn gǔ shǒufā
新股首发
IPO

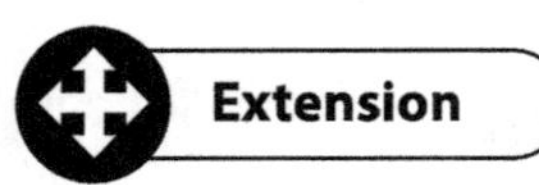

Extension

1. Zhèshì huìyì de zàndìng yìchéng.
这是会议的暂定议程。
This is a tentative agenda for the meeting.

2. Yìchéngshang yígòng yǒu wǔxiàng yìtí, shì bú shì pái de tài mǎn le?
（议程上）一共有五项议题，是不是排得太满了？
There are five items (on the agenda) in total. Is it too full?

3. Wǒmen shìfǒu kěyǐ bǎ sì, wǔ liǎng xiàng bìng wéi yí xiàng?
（我们）是否可以把四、五两项并为一项？
Can we combine Items 4 and 5 into one?

4. Xiūgǎi yǐhòu nǐ zài bǎ yìchéng sònggěi Zhāng zǒng guòmù.
修改以后你再把议程送给张总过目。
After the modifications have been done, please deliver the agenda to General Manager Zhang for approval.

Dialogue

A: Jīnglǐ, zhèshì huìyì de zàndìng yìchéng, nín kànkan shìfǒu héshì.
经理，这是会议的暂定议程，您看看是否合适。
Manager, this is a tentative agenda for the meeting. Could you take a look and see if it's appropriate?

B: Yígòng yǒu wǔxiàng yìtí, shì bú shì pái de tài mǎn le?
一共有五项议题，是不是排得太满了？
There are five items in total . Is it too full?

A: Nàme, wǒmen shìfǒu kěyǐ bǎ sì, wǔ liǎng xiàng bìng wéi yí xiàng?
那么，我们是否可以把四、五两项并为一项？
Well then, can we combine Items 4 and 5 into one?

B: Wǒ juéde kěxíng. Lìngwài, wǒ rènwéi yīnggāi bǎ "běntǔhuà" wèntí liè wéi dì-yī yìtí.
我觉得可行。另外，我认为应该把"本土化"问题列为第一议题。

I think that will work. In addition, I think that the issue of "localization" should be listed as the first item.

A: Hǎode. Wǒ mǎshàng jiù zuò tiáozhěng.
好的。我马上就做调整。

Good. I'll make adjustments immediately.

B: Xiūgǎi yǐhòu nǐ zài bǎ yìchéng sònggěi Zhāng zǒng guòmù.
修改以后你再把议程送给张总过目。

After the modifications have been done, please deliver the agenda to General Manager Zhang for approval.

Related Words

1	lièrù 列入	to be listed/ included in	7	zhǔchí huìyì 主持会议	to preside over a meeting
2	yìshì rìchéng 议事日程	agenda	8	zhǔchírén 主持人	host; hostess
3	yìchéng xiàngmù 议程项目	agenda item	9	tèyāo dàibiǎo 特邀代表	specially invited representative
4	zàndìng yìchéng 暂定议程	tentative agenda	10	guìbīn/ jiābīn 贵宾/嘉宾	distinguished guest
5	huìyìshì 会议室	meeting/ conference room	11	zhǔtí fāyánrén 主题发言人	keynote speaker
6	huìyìtīng 会议厅	conference/ assembly hall	12	yǎnjiǎng jiābīn 演讲嘉宾	guest speaker

Cultural Navigation

When you attend a conference in China, there will often be two extra activities you can expect: a conference banquet and after-conference sightseeing. Chinese people believe that the host has the responsibility to treat guests well. Conference organizers take this opportunity to show their hospitality, while hoping to establish better relationships at the same time. Just as some people say, "Eat well, have fun and do well in business." Maybe it does make sense.

56 Work Briefing

Key Sentence

Wǒ yào xiān xiàng zàizuò gèwèi huìbào yíxià wǒmen de xiāoshòu yèjì.
我要先向在座各位汇报一下我们的销售业绩。

Firstly, I'll report our sales performance to everyone present.

Substitution

dàjiā
大家
everyone

gèwèi tóngshì
各位同事
every colleague

gèwèi lǐngdǎo
各位领导
every leader

gèwèi dàibiǎo
各位代表
every representative

gèwèi tóngháng
各位同行
everyone of the same profession

shēngchǎn jìhuà
生产计划
production plan

tánpàn jiéguǒ
谈判结果
negotiation result

wàibāo xiàngmù
外包项目
outsourcing project

gōngchéng jìnzhǎn
工程进展
progress of the construction

Extension

Xiàmiàn qǐng Lǐ jīnglǐ jiǎndān jièshào yíxià gōngsī mùqián de jīngyíng yèjì.
1. 下面请李经理简单介绍一下公司目前的经营业绩。
Next, we'll ask Manager Li to brief us on the company's current operating performance.

Zīliào hái yǒu ma? Zhè biān hái quē yí fèn.
2. 资料还有吗？这边还缺一份。
Is there an extra copy? There's one copy short here.

Qǐng nín gēn pángbiān de rén hé kàn yí fèn ba.
3. 请您跟旁边的人合看一份吧。
Could you please share one with the person next to you?

Xiànzài píngmù shang xiǎnshì de shì wǒmen gōngsī jīnnián de yèjì mùbiāo.
4. 现在屏幕上显示的是我们公司今年的业绩目标。
Now what we see from the screen is our company's performance objectives of this year.

Dialogue

Xiàmiàn qǐng Lǐ jīnglǐ jiǎndān jièshào yíxià gōngsī mùqián de jīngyíng yèjì.
A: 下面请李经理简单介绍一下公司目前的经营业绩。
Next, we'll ask Manager Li to brief us on the company's current operating performance.

Dàjiā hǎo, wǒ yào xiān xiàng zàizuò gèwèi huìbào yíxià wǒmen de xiāoshòu yèjì.
B: 大家好，我要先向在座各位汇报一下我们的销售业绩。
Hello, everyone! Firstly, I'll report our sales performance to everyone present.

Máfan nín chuándì yíxià zhèfèn zīliào.
麻烦您传递一下这份资料。

Would you please pass on this material?

Zīliào hái yǒu ma? Zhè biān hái quē yí fèn.
C: 资料还有吗？这边还缺一份。

Is there an extra copy? There's one copy short here.

Bù hǎoyìsi. Qǐng nín gēn pángbiān de rén hé kàn yí fèn ba.
B: 不好意思。请您跟旁边的人合看一份吧。

I'm sorry. Could you please share one with the person next to you?

Hǎo! Xiànzài píngmù shang xiǎnshì de shì wǒmen gōngsī jīnnián de yèjì mùbiāo.
好！现在屏幕上显示的是我们公司今年的业绩目标。

OK! Now what we see from the screen is our company's performance objectives of this year.

Related Words

1	zàizuò 在座	present	5	jìxiào 绩效	performance and achievement
2	dàochǎng 到场	to show up; present	6	jìxiào mùbiāo 绩效目标	performance and achievement goal
3	yèjì 业绩	outstanding achievement	7	běn qī jīngyíng yèjì 本期经营业绩	operating performance of this period
4	xiàoyì 效益	beneficial result	8	gōngsī yèjì 公司业绩	company performance

(Continued)

9	yèjì 业绩 mùbiāo 目标	performance objective	11	yèjì 业绩 pínggū 评估	performance evaluation
10	yèjì 业绩 kǎohé 考核	performance assessment	12	jìxiào 绩效 biāozhǔn 标准	standard of performance and achievement

Cultural Navigation

Generally, the words "huìbào (to summarize and report)" and "qǐngshì (to ask for instructions)" are used when you report something to a higher-level authority or ask for instructions from your boss. They are used not only to show respect but also to express a serious and conscientious attitude. In terms of giving a speech at a meeting, it is common to use neutral words like "bàogào (to report)" or "tōngbào (to notice publicly)." You can also use "huìbào" to show your modesty and respect to the audience. However, words like "qǐngshì" or "huìbào" are often not used among colleagues of the same rank. If your officemate suddenly uses the words like "qǐngshì" or "huìbào" to talk to you, either it is a harmless joke or he/she has a bone to pick with you.

57 Discussion during a Meeting

Key Sentence

Zhège tí'àn fēicháng hǎo, wǒ zànchéng.
这个提案非常好，我赞成。
This proposal is very good, and I endorse it.

Substitution

jiànyì
建议
suggestion

xiǎngfǎ
想法
idea

yìjiàn
意见
opinion

jìhuà
计划
plan

zhǔzhāng
主张
proposition

wánquán kěxíng
完全可行
totally workable

hěn yǒuchuàngyì
很有创意
very creative

zhídé kǎolǜ
值得考虑
worth considering

bú qiè shíjì
不切实际
unrealistic

háowú xīnyì
毫无新意
nothing new; without the least innovation

tóngyì
同意
agree

zhīchí
支持
support

fǎnduì 反对 oppose	yǒu yíwèn 有疑问 have a doubt

1. Wǒ zhīchí zhège tí'àn.
我支持这个提案。
I support this proposal.

2. Wǒ de kànfǎ gēn nǐmen de bú tài yíyàng.
我的看法跟你们（的）不太一样。
My view is not exactly the same as yours.

3. Wǒ juéde tí'àn de dì-èr bùfen bú tài shíjì.
我觉得提案的第二部分不太实际。
I think that the second part of the proposal is not realistic.

4. Zhège bùfen de lùnzhèng búgòu, zīliào shōují yě bù chōngfèn.
这个部分的论证不够，资料收集也不充分。
The argument and evidence in this part are not enough, and the data collection is not sufficient either.

A: Zhège tí'àn fēicháng hǎo, wǒ zànchéng.
这个提案非常好，我赞成。
This proposal is very good, and I endorse it.

B: Wǒ tóngyì. Wǒ yě zhīchí zhège tí'àn.
我同意。我也支持这个提案。
I agree. I support this proposal too.

C: Wǒ de kànfǎ gēn nǐmen de bú tài yíyàng.
我的看法跟你们的不太一样。

My view is not exactly the same as yours.

Wǒ juéde tí'àn de dì-èr bùfen bú tài shíjì.
我觉得提案的第二部分不太实际。

I think that the second part of the proposal is not realistic.

A: Nǐ néng shuōshuo nǐ de jùtǐ yìjiàn ma?
你能说说你的具体意见吗?

Can you talk about your opinions specifically?

C: Zhège bùfen de lùnzhèng búgòu, zīliào shōují yě bù chōngfèn.
这个部分的论证不够，资料收集也不充分。

The argument and evidence in this part are not enough, and the data collection is not sufficient either.

B: Wǒ néng tí gè jiànyì ma?
我能提个建议吗?

Can I make a suggestion?

Related Words

1	tǎolùn xiǎozǔ 讨论小组	discussion panel	5	jiànyì 建议	to suggest; suggestion
2	tíjiāo 提交	to submit	6	zhǔzhāng 主张	to advocate; to stand for; view; position
3	fāng'àn 方案	scheme; plan; project	7	guāndiǎn 观点	point of view; standpoint
4	tíyì 提议	to propose; to suggest; motion; proposal; suggestion	8	quánmiàn 全面	overall; comprehensive

(Continued)

9	piànmiàn 片面	unilateral; one-sided	11	bǎoshǒu 保守	conservative
10	dàdǎn 大胆	audacious; brave			

Cultural Navigation

Have you ever heard the Chinese phrase "wénshān-huìhǎi"? It means "endless paperwork and meetings." A more literal translation is "a mountain of paperwork and a sea of meetings." For quite a long time, the Chinese meeting style has been criticized by many people. These meetings are often long and tedious. They lack interaction among participants and are often inefficient. However, this kind of situation is now gradually improving. Many routine meetings at companies and government departments have become more efficient. Interaction among participants is becoming a necessary part of meetings. People are more willing to offer different opinions. Even "brainstorm" has been brought to many meetings.

58 Making a Decision

Key Sentence

Rúguǒ méiyǒu biéde wèntí, zhèjiànshì jiù zhèyàng
如果没有别的问题，这件事就这样
juédìng le.
决定了。

If there are no more questions, this is the decision about this matter.

Substitution

qítā yìjiàn
其他意见
other ideas

bù tóng kànfǎ
不同看法
different opinions

biéde jiànyì
别的建议
other suggestions

zhèxiàng tí'àn
这项提案
this proposal

zhètiáoguīdìng
这条规定
this regulation

yìyì
异议
objection

zhèxiàng jìhuà
这项计划
this plan

zhègexiàngmù
这个项目
this project

Extension

1. Zhè jiànshì bù néng zài tuō le.
   这 件事不 能 再拖了。
   This issue cannot be delayed any more.

2. Dàjiā tóupiào biǎojué ba.
   大家投票 表决 吧。
   Let's decide by taking a vote.

3. Biǎojué de jiéguǒ shì sān piào fǎnduì, wǔ piào tóngyì.
   表决的结果是三 票 反对，五 票 同意。
   The result of the vote is three nays and five yeas.

4. Jìrán duōshù rén zànchéng, wǒ zhíxíng zhàobàn jiùshì le.
   既然多数 人 赞 成，我 执行 照 办 就是了。
   Since the majority has approved it, I will carry it out accordingly.

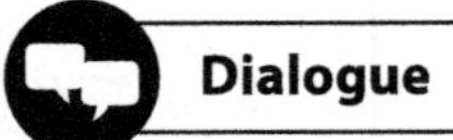

Dialogue

A: Zhè jiànshì bù néng zài tuō le, wǒmen bìxū lìkè zuòchū juédìng.
这 件事不 能 再拖了，我们必须立刻做出 决定。
This issue cannot be delayed any more. We have to make a decision right now.

B: Dàjiā tóupiào biǎojué ba.
大家投票 表决 吧。
Let's decide by taking a vote.

A: Biǎojué de jiéguǒ shì sān piào fǎnduì, wǔ piào tóngyì. Tí'àn tōngguò.
表决的结果是三 票 反对，五 票 同意。提案 通 过。
The result of the vote is three nays and five yeas. The proposal has been approved.

B: Wáng gōng, nín hái yǒu shénme yào bǔchōng de ma?
王 工，您还有 什 么 要 补 充 的吗?
Engineer Wang, is there anything that you would like to add?

C: Jìrán duōshù rén zànchéng, wǒ zhíxíng zhàobàn jiùshì le.
既然多数人赞成，我执行照办就是了。
Since the majority has approved it, I will carry it out accordingly.

A: Hǎo! Rúguǒ méiyǒu biéde wèntí, zhè jiàn shì jiù zhèyàng (jué) dìng le!
好！如果没有别的问题，这件事就这样（决）定了！
Good! If there are no more questions, this is the decision about this matter!

Related Words

1	jǔshǒu 举手 biǎojué 表决	to vote by raising hands	7	fǎnduìpiào 反对票	dissenting vote
2	bú jìmíng 不记名 tóupiào 投票	secret ballot	8	qìquán 弃权	to waive one's rights; to abstain from voting
3	tōngguò 通过	to pass; to carry (a motion/ legislation)	9	chí bǎoliú 持保留 yìjiàn 意见	with reservations; to have qualified opinions
4	fǒujué 否决	to veto; to overrule	10	duōshù 多数	majority
5	qǔxiāo 取消	to cancel; to abolish	11	shǎoshù 少数	minority
6	zànchéngpiào 赞成票	affirmative vote	12	huìyì 会议 jìlù 记录	records of a meeting; minutes

Cultural Navigation

If there are no calculating devices or machines, do you know how Chinese count the number of votes? It's quite simple. They write the character "正(zhèng)" on the blackboard. The Chinese character "正(zhèng)" contains five strokes. Therefore, each character "正(zhèng)" represents five votes or ballots. You just count how many "正(zhèng)" that you wrote, and you will easily know how many votes you got. Besides, the character "正(zhèng)" also means "zhèngzhí (honest and upright)," "zhèngzhí (proper and legitimate)," "zhèngdàng (positive)," "zhèngmiàn (decent)" and so on. Isn't that interesting?

59 Comments after a Meeting

Key Sentence

Wǒ hěn huáiyí zhèyàng de fāng'àn shìfǒu xíng de tōng.
我很怀疑这样的方案是否行得通。
I really doubt whether this kind of scheme will work.

Substitution

xiǎng zhīdào
想 知道
wonder

xiǎngkànkan
想看看
want to see

bú quèdìng
不确定
not sure

hàoqí
好奇
curious

jìhuà
计划
plan

yāoqiú
要求
request

rènwu
任务
assignment

guīdìng
规定
regulation

xiànshí
现实
realistic

hélǐ
合理
reasonable

néng shíxiàn
能 实现
can be achieved

néng wánchéng
能 完成
can be accomplished

néng shíshī
能 实施
can be put into practice

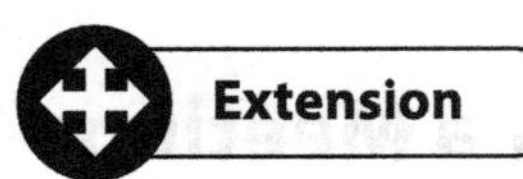

1. Jīntiān de huì nǐ juéde zěnmeyàng?
今天的会你觉得怎么样?
What do you think about today's meeting?

2. Wǒ juéde háishi Wáng gōng de tí'àn bǐjiào hélǐ.
我觉得还是 王 工 的提案比较合理。
I think that Engineer Wang's proposal is still relatively reasonable.

3. Jīnglǐ de yìsi nǐ hái kàn bù chūlái ma?
经理的意思你还看不出来吗?
Can't you see what the manager wants?

4. Shéi yuànyì qù zìtǎo-méiqù!
谁 愿意去自讨没趣!
Who would want to court a rebuff?

A: Shuō zhēnde, jīntiān de huì nǐ juéde zěnmeyàng?
说 真 的，今天的会你觉得怎么样?
Tell me the truth, what do you think about today's meeting?

B: Hái bú shì lǎo yí tào. Shuō de hǎotīng, shíjì shang shénme doū zuò bú dào.
还不是老一套。说得好听，实际 上 什 么 都 做不 到。
It's still the same old stuff. It sounds good, but actually nothing is going to work.

C: Shì a, wǒ yě hěn huáiyí zhèyàng de fāng'àn shìfǒu xíng de tōng.
是啊，我也很怀疑这 样 的 方 案是否 行 得通。
I agree. I also really doubt whether this kind of scheme will work.

A: Wǒ juéde háishi Wáng gōng de tí'àn bǐjiào hélǐ.
我觉得还是王工的提案比较合理。

I think that Engineer Wang's proposal is still relatively reasonable.

D: Jìrán nǐmen yǒu zhème duō yìjiàn, wèi shénme zài huì shang bù tí chulai ne?
既然你们有这么多意见，为什么在会上不提出来呢？

Since you have so many objections, why didn't you propose them at the meeting?

B: Hèng, lǎobǎn de yìsi nǐ hái kàn bù chūlái ma? Shéi yuànyì qù zìtǎo-méiqù!
哼，老板的意思你还看不出来吗？谁愿意去自讨没趣！

Humph, can't you see what the boss wants? Who would want to court a rebuff?

Related Words

1	yǒuyī-shuōyī 有一说一	to tell the whole truth	5	yǒu yìjiàn 有意见	to have an objection or a different opinion; to have something to say
2	shíshì-qiúshì 实事求是	to seek the truth from facts; practical and realistic	6	yáoyán 谣言	rumor; gossip
3	yìlùn-fēnfēn 议论纷纷	all sorts of comments; widespread comments	7	fēngyán-fēngyǔ 风言风语	groundless talk; slanderous gossip
4	bùmǎn 不满	dissatisfied; resentful	8	shuōcháng-dàoduǎn 说长道短	to criticize others in an annoying way

(Continued)

9	fā láosāo 发牢骚	to complain; to grouse	11	zhǐsāng-màhuái 指桑骂槐	to make oblique accusations; to scold sb. indirectly
10	fēngliáng-huà 风凉话	irresponsible and sarcastic remarks			

Cultural Navigation

There are quite a few Chinese idioms that are related to the way of expressing opinions or objections. What's interesting is that some of these idioms involve "numbers." For example, "shuōyī-bú'èr" has the numbers "yī (one)" and "èr (too)." It has a meaning of "what one says." It also means "to act arbitrarily," namely "never to consider the others' opinions and always do things by one's own way." The second idiom is "shuōsān-dàosì." It contains the numbers "sān (three)" and "sì (four)." The meaning of this idiom is "to make irresponsible remarks" or "to gossip." The third idiom "qīzuǐ-bāshé" has the numbers "qī (seven)" and "bā (eight)." The idiom literally means "seven mouths and eight tongues." Can you guess its real meaning? It means "everyone talks at same time." It may also suggest that "when there are many people, opinions differ."

60 Weekly Meetings

Key Sentence

Jīntiān de chénhuì wǒ yào xiān shuō yí gè hǎo xiāoxi.
今天的晨会我要先说一个好消息。
At today's morning meeting, I would like to announce a piece of good news first.

Substitution

xuānbù yí gè juédìng
宣布一个决定
announce a decision

jiějué yí gè jùtǐ wèntí
解决一个（具体）问题
solve a (specific) problem

zǒngjié yíxià shàngzhōu de gōngzuò
总结一下上周的工作
summarize last week's work

tōngbào yíxià tánpàn jìnzhǎn
通报一下谈判进展
inform (sb.) of the progress of negotiation

Extension

1. Shàng gè xīngqī wǒmen bùmén de yèjì shì quán gōngsī dì-yī míng!
上个星期我们部门的业绩是全公司第一名！
Last week our department's performance was Number One in the entire company!

2. Dì-yī míng yǒu jiǎngjīn ma?
第一名有奖金吗？
Is there a bonus for (being) Number One?

3. Nà yào kàn wǒmen quán nián de zuìhòu chéngjì zěnmeyàng le.
那要看我们全年的最后成绩怎么样了。
That depends on our final achievement of the whole year.

4. Wǒ juéde xiǎng yào bǎochí dì-yī, wǒmen zhìshǎo yào náxia yībǎi wàn yuán de (chǎnpǐn) dìngdān.
我觉得想要保持第一，我们至少要拿下一百万元的（产品）订单。
I think that we need to get at least one million yuan in (product) orders if we want to stay at Number One.

Dialogue

A: Dàjiā zǎo! Jīntiān de chénhuì wǒ yào xiān gàosu dàjiā yí gè hǎo xiāoxi.
大家早！今天的晨会我要先告诉大家一个好消息。
Good morning, everyone! At today's morning meeting, I would like to announce a piece of good news first.

Shàng gè xīngqī wǒmen bùmén de yèjì shì quán gōngsī dì-yī míng!
上个星期我们部门的业绩是全公司第一名！
Last week our department's performance was Number One in the entire company!

B: Tài hǎo le! Jīnglǐ, dì-yī míng yǒu jiǎngjīn ma?
太好了！经理，第一名有奖金吗？
Great! Manager, is there a bonus for being Number One?

A: Nà yào kàn wǒmen quán yuè de zuìhòu chéngjì zěnmeyàng le.
那要看我们全月的最后成绩怎么样了。
That depends on our final achievement of the whole month.

C: Wǒ juéde yào xiǎng bǎochí dì-yī, wǒmen zhìshǎo yào náxia yībǎi wàn yuán de dìngdān.
我觉得要想保持第一，我们至少要拿下一百万元的订单。
I think that we need to get at least one million yuan in (product) orders if we want to stay at Number One.

B: Méi wèntí! Wǒmen dàjiā yìqǐ jiāyóu!
没问题！我们大家一起加油！
No problem! We'll work harder together!

Related Words

1	lìhuì 例会	regular meeting	6	nèibù tōngxùn 内部通讯	internal newsletter
2	chénhuì 晨会	morning meeting	7	chuándá 传达	to pass on; to convey (instruction, information, etc.)
3	zhōuhuì 周会	weekly meeting	8	dòngyuán 动员	to mobilize; to arouse
4	zhōubào 周报	weekly report	9	tǎolùn 讨论	to discuss; discussion
5	gōngsījiǎnbào 公司简报	company bulletin	10	zhēngqiú yìjiàn 征求意见	to seek opinions; to solicit others' views

(Continued)

11	gèshūjǐjiàn 各抒己见	each airs his own views; everyone speaks his mind	12	ānpái gōngzuò 安排工作	to arrange work

Cultural Navigation

"Zhōuhuì (weekly meeting)" in Chinese is also called "lìhuì (regular meeting)." Since it is often held on Monday morning, some people call it "chénhuì (morning meeting)." Besides, there is a very unique kind of "morning meeting" in China. Many retail and service industries have such a system: Every morning before work, the store manager or department manager gathers all the employees and they spend about 5–10 minutes doing certain activities together, such as reciting the operation principle of the company, singing a company song or doing exercises for warm-up. Many managers believe that this kind of "morning meeting" can raise the morale of employees, elevate the energy and strengthen the team spirit.

61 Video Conferences

Key Sentence

Nǐ nà biān huìchǎng de shēngyīn qīngchu ma?
你那边 会 场的声 音 清楚吗?
Is the voice clear in your conference room?

Substitution

shìpín wěndìng
视频稳 定
video image is stable

wǎngsù liúchàng
网 速 流 畅
network speed is fast

túxiàng móhu
图 像模糊
image is blurred

liánjiē yǒu wèntí
连接有问题
connection has a problem

Běijīng hé Guǎngzhōu de tóngshìmen, nǐmen hǎo!
1. 北京和 广　州 的同事们，你们好!
Hello, colleagues in Beijing and Guangzhou!

2. Shēngyīn hěn qīngchu.
声音很清楚。
The voice is clear.

3. Shēngyīn zhìhòu kěnéng shì wǎngluò de wèntí.
声音滞后可能是网络的问题。
The lagging of sound is probably due to a problem with the Internet connection.

4. Nǐ kěyǐ shìshi chóngxīn liánjiē yí cì.
你可以试试重新连接一次。
You may try to reconnect it one more time.

Dialogue

A: Shànghǎi hé Shēnzhèn de tóngshìmen, nǐmen hǎo!
上海和深圳的同事们，你们好！
Hello, colleagues in Shanghai and Shenzhen!

B: Nǐ hǎo! Nǐ nà biān huìchǎng de shēngyīn qīngchu ma?
你好！你那边会场的声音清楚吗？
Hello! Is the voice clear in your conference room?

A: Shēngyīn hěn qīngchu, búguò yǒu yìdiǎn zhìhòu.
声音很清楚，不过有一点滞后。
The voice is clear, but it is slightly lagging.

B: Shēngyīn zhìhòu kěnéng shì wǎngluò de wèntí.
声音滞后可能是网络的问题。
The lagging of sound is probably due to a problem with the Internet connection.

Nǐ kěyǐ shìshi chóngxīn liánjiē yí cì.
你可以试试重新连接一次。
You may try to reconnect it one more time.

C: Qǐng děng yíxià. Wǒmen zhè biān zhǐ néng tīngjiàn shēngyīn, kěshì méiyǒu túxiàng.
请等一下。我们这边只能听见声音，可是没有图像。

Please wait for a moment. We can only hear (your) voice, but have no image.

Ò, xiànzài hǎo le!
哦，现在好了！

OK, now everything is fine!

A: Hǎo. Nàme, wǒmen xiànzài kāishǐ jīntiān de Shànghǎi, Shēnzhèn, Luòshānjī sān fāng shìpín huìyì.
好。那么，我们现在开始今天的上海、深圳、洛杉矶三方视频会议。

Well then, now let's begin today's three parties' video conference of Shanghai, Shenzhen and Los Angeles.

Related Words

1	tōnghuà 通话	to communicate by telephone	6	huàmiàn 画面 tài àn 太暗	the picture is too dim
2	tōnghuà 通话 qǔxiāo 取消	call canceled	7	bèijǐng tài liàng 背景太亮	the background is too bright
3	huàtǒng 话筒	microphone	8	wǎngluò liánjiē 网络连接	network connection
4	wǎngluò 网络 shèxiàngtóu 摄像头	webcam; web camera	9	wǎngsù 网速	network speed
5	yīnliàng 音量	volume	10	wǎngluòliúliàng (网络)流量	(network) data flow

Cultural Navigation

Chinese are familiar with Skype. Skype was officially launched in China in 2004. Chinese users can download a Chinese version of Skype software for free to a computer, cell phone or tablet, and then use it to call someone anywhere in the world or to chat online. Skype also provides VoIP services for Chinese business enterprises, such as video conferences, etc. Now in China more and more companies and enterprises are using Skype as a means of business communication.

Human Resources

62 Recruitment Information

Key Sentence

Wǒ zhīdào yǒu jiā chuánméi gōngsī xūyào zhāo yì
我知道有家传媒公司需要招一
míng xiāoshòu jīnglǐ.
名销售经理。

I know there is a media company that needs to recruit a sales manager.

Substitution

Yíjiā
宜家
IKEA

Xīménzǐ
西门子
SEIMENS

Fēngtián
丰田
TOYOTA

Wò'ěrmǎ Zhōngguó
沃尔玛(中国)
Wal-Mart China

Huāqí Yínháng Shànghǎi Fēnháng
花旗银行上海分行
Shanghai Branch of Citibank

kuàijìshī
会计师
accountant

gōngchéngshī
工程师
engineer
zǒngcái zhùlǐ
总裁助理
assistant of CEO
diànnǎo chéngxùyuán
电脑程序员
computer programmer
Yīngyǔ hǎo de gōngguān rényuán
英语好的公关人员
PR personnel with good English ability

1. Nǐ zuìjìn zài zhǎo xīngōngzuò ma?
   你最近在找新工作吗?
   Have you been looking for a new job recently?

2. Nǐ yǒu shénme zhāopìn xìnxī ma?
   你有什么招聘信息吗?
   Do you have any recruitment information?

3. Nǐ shì zài nǎr dédào zhège xiāoxi de?
   你是在哪儿得到这个消息的?
   Where did you get this information?

4. Tāmen de zhāopìn guǎnggào jiù zài wǎngshang.
   他们的招聘广告就在网上。
   Their employment advertisement is right here on the Internet.

Tīngshuō nǐ zuìjìn zài zhǎo xīn gōngzuò, shì ma?
A: 听说你最近在找新工作，是吗？
I've heard that you are looking for a new job recently, right?

Shì a. Nǐ yǒu shénme zhāopìn xìnxī ma?
B: 是啊。你有什么招聘信息吗？
Yes. Do you have any recruitment information?

Wǒ zhīdào yǒu jiā chuánméi gōngsī xūyào zhāo yì míng xiāoshòu jīnglǐ.
A: 我知道有家传媒公司需要招一名销售经理。
I know there is a media company that needs to recruit a sales manager.

Zhēn de? Nǐ shì zài nǎr dédào zhège xiāoxi de?
B: 真的？你是在哪儿得到这个消息的？
Really? Where did you get this information?

Tāmen de zhāopìn guǎnggào jiù zài wǎngshang.
A: 他们的招聘广告就在网上。
Their employment advertisement is right here on the Internet.

Guòlai! Nǐ kěyǐ zìjǐ kànkan duì zhège zhíwèi yǒu méi yǒu xìngqù.
过来！你可以自己看看对这个职位有没有兴趣。
Come here! You can have a look by yourself and see whether you are interested in this position.

Related Words

1	shēnqǐng 申请	to apply; application	7	zhāopìn jīgòu 招聘机构	recruitment agency
2	zhāorén 招人	to recruit people	8	zhōngjiè rén 中介(人)	agent; middleman
3	zhíwèi kòngquē 职位空缺	job opening	9	zhōngjiè gōngsī 中介公司	agency
4	zhāopìn guǎnggào 招聘广告	employment advertisement	10	zhōngjièfèi 中介费	agency commission
5	zhāopìnkǎoshì 招聘考试	recruitment examination	11	yòngrén dānwèi 用人单位	employer
6	zhāopìnhuì 招聘会	job fair	12	réncái shìchǎng 人才市场	employment market; job market

Cultural Navigation

Today many foreign companies are recruiting people in China while they do business here. At the same time, more and more Chinese companies are starting to recruit professionals from all over the world. If foreign companies plan to recruit new employees or if foreigners want to find a job in China, they can check related information on the Internet. There are a lot of websites offering such information in China, such as 51job.com and ChinaHR.com. These two websites both have Chinese and English versions, providing professional information in job hunting and recruitment nationwide. ChinaHR is also a member of the premier global online employment solution provider Monster.com. If you are in China now, you may also check some local publications. For example, you can get a free copy of *City Weekend* in many upscale hotels in Beijing, Shanghai, Guangzhou and other big cities. It is published in English biweekly. It has a lot of interesting and useful local information, including job openings.

63 On-Site Recruiting

Key Sentence

Wǒ xiǎng shēnqǐng guìgōngsī shìchǎng kāifā fāngmiàn de gōngzuò.
我想申请（贵公司）市场开发方面的工作。

I want to apply for the job in market development (at your company).

Substitution

shìchǎng cèhuà
市场策划
market planning

shìchǎng diàoyán
市场调研
market research

guǎnggào cèhuà
广告策划
advertisement planning

gōnggòng guānxì
公共关系
public relations

gǎngwèi
岗位
post; job

zhíwèi
职位
position

zhíwù
职务
post; duties

Extension

1. Zhè hǎibào shang shuō nǐmen zhèngzài zhāopìn hǎiwài shìchǎng yíngxiāo rén-
这海报上 说你们正在招聘海外市场营销人
yuán, shì ma?
员，是吗？
The poster says that you are recruiting salespersons for the overseas market, right?

2. Bù zhīdào nǐ duì nǎge zhíwèi gǎn xìngqù?
不知道你对哪个职位感兴趣？
I wonder which position you are interested in.

3. Wǒ jīnnián gāng bìyè, xué de shì shìchǎng yíngxiāo.
我今年刚毕业，学的是市场营销。
I just graduated this year, and my major is marketing.

4. Wǒ dāngguo liǎng nián shìchǎng yíngxiāo de shíxíshēng.
我当过两年市场营销的实习生。
I have worked as a marketing intern for two years.

Dialogue

A: Nín hǎo! Wǒ jiào Dàiwéi. Hǎibào shang shuō nǐmen zhèngzài zhāopìn
您好！我叫戴维。海报上 说你们正在招聘
hǎiwài shìchǎng yíngxiāo rényuán, shì ma?
海外市场营销人员，是吗？
Hello! My name is David. The poster says that you are recruiting salespersons for the overseas market, right?

B: Duì! Bù zhīdào nǐ duì nǎge jùtǐ zhíwèi gǎnxìngqù?
对！不知道你对哪个具体职位感兴趣？
Right! I wonder which particular position you are interested in.

A: Wǒ xiǎng shēnqǐng shìchǎng kāifā fāngmiàn de gōngzuò.
我想申请市场开发方面的工作。

I want to apply for the job in market development.

B: Nǐ guòqù yǒu zhè fāngmiàn de gōngzuò jīngyàn ma?
你过去有这方面的工作经验吗?

Do you have any work experiences in this field?

A: Wǒ jīnnián gāng bìyè, xué de shì shìchǎng yíngxiāo. Wǒ dāngguo liǎng nián shìchǎng yíngxiāo de shíxíshēng.
我今年刚毕业，学的是市场营销。我当过两年市场营销的实习生。

I just graduated this year, and my major is marketing. I have worked as a marketing intern for two years.

B: Hǎo. Nǐ xiān tián yíxià shēnqǐngbiǎoba.
好。你先填一下申请表吧。

Good. Please fill out the application form first.

Related Words

1	rénshì bùmén 人事部门	personnel department	6	yuángōng 员工	staff; personnel
2	rénshì zhǔguǎn 人事主管	personnel director	7	wěituō 委托	to entrust; to commission
3	réncái jiāoliú 人才交流	talent exchange; professional resources exchange	8	liètóu gōngsī 猎头公司	head-hunting company; recruiting firm
4	qiúzhí 求职	to apply for a job	9	zhāopìnhuì 招聘会	job fair
5	gùyòng 雇用	to employ; to hire	10	zhǔbàn 主办	to sponsor; to host

Cultural Navigation

“Zhāopìnhuì (a job fair)” is also called “réncái shìchǎng (a talent market).” In China, job fairs have become the popular places for people to find a job and for companies to recruit new employees. Driven by the growing economy, there are numerous job fairs of different types and scales held in China each year. Many of these job fairs are sponsored or supported by government departments of different levels. A number of foreign companies have also joined the Chinese HR market in recent years. You may give it a try if you need an employment solution in China.

64 Interview Notification

Key Sentence

Wǒmen xiǎng ānpái nín xià Xīngqīsān xiàwǔ liǎngdiǎn lái miànshì.
我们想安排您下星期三下午两点来面试。

We want to arrange an interview with you at 2:00 pm next Wednesday.

Substitution

tōngzhī
通知
notify

qǐng
请
ask (in polite way); invite

yuē
约
make an appointment with

zhège Xīngqīwǔ
这个星期五
this Friday

Liùyuè qī hào
六月七号
on June 7th

hòutiān zǎoshang jiǔ diǎn
后天早上九点
at 9:00 am the day after tomorrow

1. Wéi, wǒ shì Dōngnán Tōngxìn Gōngsī rénlì zīyuánbù.
喂，我是东南通信公司人力资源部。
Hello, this is the Human Resources Department of Southeast Communication Company.

2. Nín de shēnqǐng cáiliào shōudào le.
您的申请材料收到了。
Your application materials have been received.

3. Nín hái xūyào shénme qítā bǔchōng zīliào ma?
您还需要什么其他补充资料吗?
Do you need any supplemen-tary materials?

4. Mùqián bù xūyào shénme le.
目前不需要什么了。
There is no need for that at present.

A: dǎ diànhuà Mǎ xiānsheng ma? Wǒ shì Dōngnán Tōngxìn Gōngsī rénlì zīyuán bù.
(打电话): 马先生吗? 我是东南通信公司人力资源部。
(On the phone) Is that Mr. Ma? This is the Human Resources Department of Southeast Communication Company.

B: Nín hǎo. Wǒ shì Mǎ Zhìwěi. Qǐngwèn yǒu shénme shì?
您好。我是马志伟。请问有什么事?
Hello. This is Ma Zhiwei. What can I do for you?

A: Nín de shēnqǐng cáiliào shōudào le. Wǒmen duì nín de shēnqǐng hěn gǎn xìngqù.
您的申请材料收到了。我们对您的申请很感兴趣。

Your application materials have been received. We are very interested in your application.

B: Xièxie! Nín hái xūyào shénme qítā bǔchōng zīliào ma?
谢谢！您还需要什么其他补充资料吗？
Thank you! Do you need any supplementary materials?

A: Ò, mùqián bù xūyào shénme le.
哦，目前不需要什么了。
Oh, there is no need for that at present.

Wǒmen xiǎng ānpái nín xià Xīngqīsān xiàwǔ liǎng diǎn lái miànshì.
我们想安排您下星期三（下午）两点来面试。
We want to arrange an interview with you at 2:00 pm next Wednesday.

B: Tài hǎo le! wǒ yídìng zhǔnshí dào.
太好了！我一定准时到。
Great! I'll be there on time.

Related Words

1	qiúzhíxìn 求职信	application letter	6	lǚlì 履历	curriculum vitae; CV
2	shēnqǐngbiǎo 申请表	application form	7	jiǎnlì 简历	résumé; brief curriculum vitae
3	tuījiànxìn 推荐信	recommendation letter	8	tián biǎo 填表	to fill in a form
4	shēnqǐngrén 申请人	applicant	9	zhùyì shìxiàng 注意事项	matters needing attention
5	shēnqǐngfèi 申请费	application fee	10	jiézhǐ rìqī 截止日期	deadline

Cultural Navigation

Filling out an application form is a necessary part of the job application procedure. The format of a typical Chinese application form is quite similar to an English one, but with some differences in content. In addition to your name, age, gender and contact information, information like your birthplace or native place, marital status, hobbies, religious beliefs and political status, and even your height and weight, may need to be provided. In China, it is a very common practice to be asked for this type of personal information when one applies for a job.

65 The Job Interview

Key Sentence

Wǒ juéde wǒ duì diànzǐ shāngwù bǐjiào shúxī.
我觉得我对电子 商 务 比较熟悉。
I think that I'm more familiar with e-commerce.

Substitution

hǎiwài shìchǎng
海外 市 场
overseas market

Měiguó xiāofèizhě
美国 消费者
American consumers

wùliú guǎnlǐ
物流管理
logistics management

guójì màoyì
国际贸易
international trade

Extension

1. Nǐ néng yòng Zhōngwén gēn wǒmen shuō yíxià nǐ de gèrén qíngkuàng ma?
   你能用中文跟我们说一下你的个人情况吗？
   Can you use Chinese to tell us about yourself briefly?

2. Wǒ de zhuānyè shì qǐyè guǎnlǐ.
   我的专业是企业管理。
   My major is business management.

3. Zuò zhè fèn gōngzuò, nǐ juéde nǐ de qiángxiàng shì shénme?
   做这份工作，你觉得你的强项是什么？
   What strengths do you think you have suited for doing this job?

4. Wǒ yě liǎojiě niánqīng xiāofèizhě xǐhuan shénme.
   我（也）了解年轻消费者喜欢什么。
   I (also) understand what young consumers like.

Dialogue

A: Nǐ néng yòng Zhōngwén gēn wǒmen shuō yíxià nǐ de gèrén qíngkuàng ma?
你能用中文跟我们说一下你的个人情况吗？
Can you use Chinese to tell us about yourself briefly?

B: Hǎode. Wǒ jiào Lín Jié. Wǒ de zhuānyè shì qǐyè guǎnlǐ.
好的。我叫林杰。我的专业是企业管理。
OK. I'm Lin Jie. My major is business management.

A: Nǐ yǒu nǎxiē gōngzuò jīnglì?
你有哪些工作经历？
What kind of work experiences do you have?

B: Wǒ zài Yàmǎxùn gōngzuòguo sān nián.
我在亚马逊工作过三年。

I worked at Amazon for three years.

A: Zuò zhè fèn gōngzuò, nǐ juéde nǐ de qiángxiàng shì shénme?
做这份工作，你觉得你的强项是什么？

What strengths do you think you have suited for doing this job?

B: Wǒ juéde wǒ duì diànzǐ shāngwù bǐjiào shúxī, yě liǎojiě niánqīng xiāofèizhě xǐhuan shénme.
我觉得我对电子商务比较熟悉，也了解年轻消费者喜欢什么。

I think that I'm more familiar with e-commerce, and also understand what young consumers like.

A: Shùnbiàn wèn yí jù, nǐ wèi shénme xiǎng zài Zhōngguó gōngzuò?
顺便问一句，你为什么想在中国工作？

By the way, why do you want to work in China?

Related Words

1	zhǎo gōngzuò 找工作	to look for a job	6	zhuānyè 专业	academic major; profession
2	miànshì 面试	interview; to interview	7	zhuānyè jìnéng 专业技能	professional skill
3	xuéshì/běnkē xuélì 学士/本科学历	Bachelor degree	8	zhuānyè péixùn 专业培训	professional/specialized training
4	shuòshì 硕士	Master degree	9	zhuānyè zhèngshū 专业证书	professional certificate
5	bóshì 博士	PhD. degree	10	gèxìng 个性	individuality; personality

Cultural Navigation

In Chinese, "gōngzuò jīnglì" and "gōngzuò jīngyàn" are not exactly the same. The first one refers to one's "career history" or "employment history." It mainly includes the job or jobs this person once had and currently has, and for how long. The second phrase means the knowledge and skills that one has gained from his work. However, you don't need to feel embarrassed if you got confused by these two phrases. Actually, there are quite a few Chinese who are often unsure about how to use these phrases properly.

66 Salary and Benefits

Key Sentence

Zhège zhíwèi de qǐxīn shì duōshao?
这个职位的起薪是多少？
What is the entry-level salary of this position?

Substitution

xīnshui
薪水
salary

niánxīn
年薪
annual salary

zuì dī gōngzī
最低工资
minimum wage

píngjūn gōngzī
平均工资
average salary

gōngzī biāozhǔn
工资标准
wage standard

1. Qǐxīn shì měiyuè shuì qián 5000 yuán.
起薪是（每月）税前5000元。
The entry-level salary (per month) is 5,000 yuan before tax.

2. Yuángōng fúlì bāokuò yīliáo bǎoxiǎn hé tuìxiū yǎnglǎojīn.
员工福利包括医疗保险和（退休）养老金。
Employee benefits include medical insurance and retirement pension.

3. Gōngzuò mǎn shí'èr gè yuè yǐhòu, yì nián yǒu wǔ tiān dàixīn niánjià.
工作满十二个月以后，一年有五天带薪年假。
Once you have worked for 12 months, you will have 5 days of paid vacation each year.

4. Nǐ de gōnglíng yuè cháng, xiūjià yuè duō.
（你的）工龄越长，休假越多。
The more working years you have, the more vacation days you will have.

Dialogue

A: Wǒ néng wèn yíxià zhège zhíwèi de qǐxīn shì duōshao ma?
我能问一下这个职位的起薪是多少吗?
May I ask about the entry-level salary of this position?

B: Qǐxīn shì měi yuè shuì qián 5000 yuán.
起薪是每月税前5000元。
The entry-level salary per month is 5,000 yuan before tax.

A: Gōngsī yǒu nǎxiē fúlì ne?
公司有哪些福利呢?
What benefits does the company have?

B: Yuángōng fúlì bāokuò yīliáo bǎoxiǎn hé tuìxiū yǎnglǎojīn.
员工福利包括医疗保险和退休养老金。
Employee benefits include medical insurance and retirement pension.

A: Yuángōng de niánjià yǒu shénme guīdìng?
员工的年假有什么规定?
What are the rules for employees' annual vacation?

B: Gōngzuò mǎn shí'èr gè yuè yǐhòu, yì nián yǒu wǔ tiān dàixīn niánjià.
工作满十二个月以后，一年有五天带薪年假。
Gōnglíng yuè cháng, xiūjià yuè duō.
工龄越长，休假越多。

Once you have worked for 12 months or more, you will have 5 days of paid vacation each year. The more working years you have, the more vacation days you will have.

Related Words

1	xīnshui gōngzī 薪水/工资	salary; wage	7	zhèngcè 政策	policy
2	hétong 合同/ héyuē 合约	contract	8	yībǎo 医保/ yīliáo bǎoxiǎn 医疗保险	medical insurance
3	shìyòngqī 试用期 jiān (间)	probation period	9	shuì qián 税前	before tax
4	zhuǎnzhèng 转正	(a temporary or probationary worker) to become a regular worker	10	shuì hòu 税后	after tax
5	xùyuē 续约	to renew a contract/ treaty	11	kòushuì 扣税	to deduct tax
6	guīdìng 规定	regulation; rule	12	tuìxiū 退休	to retire

Cultural Navigation

Chinese law and government regulations require that all employers must provide insurance and retirement welfare for their employees. The welfare includes endowment insurance, medical insurance, unemployment insurance, worker's compensation injury insurance, and maternity insurance, as well as a housing accumulation fund. These benefits together are called "five insurance and one fund." According to the law, the employer and the employee share the premiums for endowment insurance, medical insurance and unemployment insurance, while the employer is required to pay for worker's compensation injury insurance and maternity insurance. In addition, both the employer and the employee need to make a monthly contribution to the housing accumulation fund at the same percentage.

67 Decision of Hiring

Key Sentence

Wǒ rènwéi tā de zhuānyè zhīshi hěn shìhé zhège gōngzuò.
我认为他的专业知识很适合这个工作。
I think that his professional knowledge is very suitable to this job.

Substitution

gèxìng
个性
personality

zhuānyè xùnliàn
专业训练
professional training

gōngzuò jīngyàn
工作经验
work experience

gè fāngmiàn nénglì
各方面能力
overall capability

Zhōngwén shuǐpíng
中文水平
Chinese language proficiency

Extension

1. Cóng jiǎnlì hé miànshì kàn, zhè liǎngwèi shēnqǐngrén dōu hěn búcuò.
从简历和面试看，这两位申请人都很不错。
Based on the resumes and interviews, these two applicants are both good.

2. Zhè cì wǒmen zhǐnéng zhāopìn yí gè rén.
这次我们只能招聘一个人。
This time we can only recruit one person.

3. Tā de biǎodá gōutōng nénglì hěnqiáng.
他的表达沟通能力很强。
He is very good at expression and communication.

4. Rúguǒ méiyǒu fǎnduì yìjiàn, wǒmen jiù zhèngshì juédìng lùyòng tā le.
如果没有反对意见，我们就正式决定录用他了。
If there is no objection, we'll officially decide to hire him.

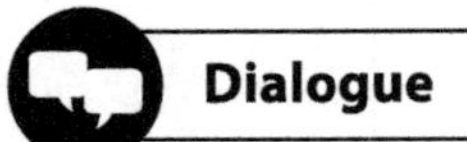

Dialogue

A: Cóng jiǎnlì hé miànshì kàn, zhè liǎng wèi shēnqǐngrén dōu hěn búcuò.
从简历和面试看，这两位申请人都很不错。
Based on the resumes and interviews, these two applicants are both good.

B: Shì a. Kěxī zhè cì wǒmen zhǐnéng zhāopìn yí gè rén.
是啊。可惜这次我们只能招聘一个人。
Yes. Unfortunately, this time we can only recruit one person.

A: Nàme, nín gèng qīngxiàngyú tiāoxuǎn shéi?
那么，您更倾向于挑选谁?
In that case, which one do you prefer to choose?

B: LínJié. Wǒ rènwéi tā de zhuānyè zhīshi hěn shìhé zhège gōngzuò.
林杰。我认为他的专业知识很适合这个工作。
Lin Jie. I think that his professional knowledge is very suitable to this job.

A: Wǒ tóngyì. Tā de biǎodá gōutōng nénglì hěn qiáng, zhè yì diǎn gěi wǒ de yìnxiàng fēicháng shēn.
我同意。他的表达沟通能力很强，(这一点) 给我的印象非常深。

I agree. He's very good at expression and communication, and I was very impressed (by this).

B: Hǎo. Rúguǒ méiyǒu fǎnduì yìjiàn, wǒmen jiù zhèngshì juédìng lùyòng tā le!
好。如果没有反对意见，我们就正式决定录用他了！

Good. If there is no objection, we'll officially decide to hire him!

Related Words

1	yōudiǎn 优点/ chángchu 长处	merit; strong point	7	kànhǎo 看好	to have a good prospect of
2	quēdiǎn 缺点/ duǎnchu 短处	defect; shortcoming	8	huáiyí 怀疑	to doubt; to suspect; doubt; suspicion
3	ruòdiǎn 弱点	weakness	9	shāixuǎn 筛选	to select; to screen
4	hégé 合格	to qualify; qualified	10	hòuxuǎnrén 候选人	candidate
5	mǎnyì 满意	satisfied	11	lùyòng 录用	to employ; to hire
6	kànzhòng 看中	to settle on; to choose	12	pìnyòng 聘用	to employ; to hire; to appoint to a position

Cultural Navigation

How to find the most suitable person through recruitment? Since the ancient times, Chinese have adopted a set of principles about recruitment as well as how to utilize people's talents. First of all, Chinese people believe that it is very important to "liàngcái-lùyòng (give someone a job according to his/her abilities)." Second, when employers assign work to employees, it is wise to make them to "yángcháng-bìduǎn (play up their strengths and avoid their weaknesses)," so they can do what they are good at. Finally, it is crucial for the boss to trust his/her employees. Just as the old saying goes, "Yòngrén bù yí, yírén bú yòng." (Don't suspect your employees. If one is suspicious, don't employ him/her.)

68 Training and Advanced Studies

Key Sentence

Wǒ dǎsuàn qù (jìn) xiū yì mén diànzǐ shāngwù kè.
我打算去（进）修一门电子商务课。

I plan to take an e-business class.

Substitution

guójì màoyì
国际贸易
international trade

qǐyè guǎnlǐ
企业管理
enterprise management

qǐyè wénhuà
企业文化
corporate culture

wùliú guǎnlǐ
物流管理
logistics management

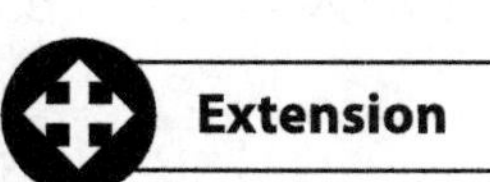

1. Gōngsī zuìjìn duì yuángōng péixùn yǒule xīn guīdìng.
公司最近对员工培训有了新规定。
The company has a new regulation about employee training.

2. Měi gè jìdù měi rén bìxū cānjiā wǔtiān de zhuānyè péixùn.
每个季度每人必须参加五天的专业培训。
Everyone has to attend five days of professional training each season.

3. Péixùn hé jìnxiū de jiéguǒ hái yào lièrù niánzhōng kǎohé.
培训和进修的结果还要列入年终考核。
The result of the training and advanced studies will be included in the year-end assessment too.

4. Xiànzài hěn duō lǐngyù de zhīshi gēngxīn hěn kuài.
现在很多领域的知识更新很快。
Now knowledge of many fields is updated rapidly.

Dialogue

A: Gōngsī zuìjìn duì yuángōng péixùn yǒule xīnguīdìng.
公司最近对员工培训有了新规定。
The company has a new regulation about employee training.

B: Wǒ yě tīngshuō le. Měi nián měi rén bìxū cānjiā sān zhōu de zhuānyè péixùn.
我也听说了。每年每人必须参加三周的专业培训。
I've heard it too. Everyone has to attend three weeks of professional training each year.

A: Bùjǐn rúcǐ, péixùn hé jìnxiū de jiéguǒ hái yào lièrù niánzhōng kǎohé ne!
不仅如此，培训和进修的结果还要列入年终考核呢！
Not only that. The result of the training and advanced studies will be included in the year-end assessment too!

B: Dì-yī qī péixùn nǐ dǎsuàn bàomíng ma?
第一期培训你打算报名吗?
Are you going to sign up for the first training session?

Shì a, wǒ dǎsuàn qù xiū yì mén diànzǐ shāngwù kè.
A: 是啊，我打算去修一门电子商务课。

Yes, I plan to take an e-business class.

Wǒ yě dǎsuàn qù. Xiànzài hěn duō lǐngyù de zhīshi gēngxīn hěn kuài. Bù gěi zìjǐ chōngdiàn jiùyào luòhòu le.
B: 我也打算去。现在很多领域的知识更新很快。不给自己充电就要落后了。

I plan to take it too. Now knowledge in many fields is updated rapidly. You will fall behind if you don't "recharge" your knowledge.

Related Words

1	xiūkè 修课/ shàngkè 上课	to take a class; to attend a class	7	jìshù géxīn 技术革新	technological innovation
2	tígāo 提高	to raise; to increase; to improve	8	jìshù gémìng 技术革命	technological revolution
3	zēngqiáng 增强	to strengthen; to enhance	9	zhīshi bàozhà 知识爆炸	knowledge explosion
4	gēngxīn 更新	to update; to replace	10	zhīshi gēngxīn 知识更新	update of one's knowledge
5	yèwù shuǐpíng 业务水平	professional skill; vocational level	11	jiéyè zhèngshū 结业证书	course-completion certificate
6	gōngzuò nénglì 工作能力	capacity of work			

Cultural Navigation

In recent decades, demand for adult continuing education has been very strong in China. Online colleges, education channels, evening schools, weekend schools and all kinds of professional training programs are all over China. Due to the factors like rapidly advancing technology, fast economic growth and intense competition in the job market as well as at workplaces, more and more people are taking advantage of every opportunity to take new courses and learn new knowledge, in order to continuously reinforce themselves. Many companies have made professional training and advanced studies as a kind of benefit as well as a requirement for their employees.

69 Job Transfer and Promotion

Key Sentence

Chén gōng xià gè yuè yào diàodào zǒngbù qù le.
陈 工 下个月 要 调 到 总部去了。
Engineer Chen will transfer to the headquarters next month.

Substitution

tā
他
he

wǒ
我
I

Lǐ xiānsheng
李 先 生
Mr. Li

wǒmen zhǔguǎn
我们 主 管
our director

chǎnpǐn yánfābù
产 品 研发部
department of product development

kèfúbù
客服部
department of customer service

péixùnbù
培训部
department of job training

biéde bùmén
别的部门
another department

Extension

1. Xiǎo Wáng shì bú shì yǒu shénme tèshū guānxì a?
小王是不是有什么特殊关系啊?
Does Xiao Wang have some kind of special connections?

2. Tā yíxiàng gōngzuò chéngjì tūchū, dédào shēngqiān shì yīnggāi de.
他一向工作成绩突出，得到升迁是应该的。
He always has outstanding performance in the job and deserves a promotion.

3. Wáng jīnglǐ yào qù lìng yì jiā gōngsī zuò le.
王经理要去另一家公司做了。
Manager Wang is going to work for another company soon.

4. Zuìjìn tiàocáo de rén bù shǎo a!
最近跳槽的人不少啊!
There are quite a few people job-hopping recently!

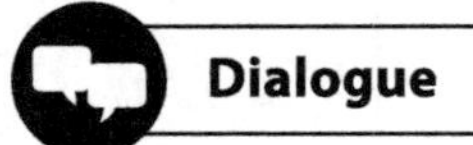

Dialogue

A: Tīngshuō Chén gōng xià gè yuè yào diàodào zǒngbù qù le!
听说陈工下个月要调到总部去了!
I've heard that Engineer Chen will transfer to the headquarters next month!

B: Zhēn de ma? Tā shì bú shì yǒu shénme tèshū guānxì a?
真的吗? 他是不是有什么特殊关系啊?
Really? Does he have some kind of special connections?

A: Tā yíxiàng gōngzuò chéngjì tūchū, dédào shēngqiān shì yīnggāide.
他一向工作成绩突出，得到升迁是应该的。
He always has outstanding performance in the job and deserves a promotion.

B: Wǒ tīngshuō háiyǒu biéde rén yàozǒu le.
我听说还有别的人要走了。
I've heard that someone else is going to leave.

A: Shéi?
谁？
Who?

B: Wáng jīnglǐ yào qù lìng yì jiā gōngsī zuò le.
王经理要去另一家公司做了。
Manager Wang is going to work for another company soon.

A: Wa, zuìjìn tiàocáo de rén bù shǎo a!
哇，最近跳槽的人不少啊！
Wow, there are quite a few people job-hopping recently!

Related Words

1	tíshēng 提升/ tíbá 提拔	to promote; promotion	7	jiǎnglì 奖励	to reward; reward
2	jiàngjí 降级	to demote; demotion	8	jīhuì 机会	opportunity; chance
3	tíxīn 提薪	to raise salary	9	huàn gōngzuò 换工作	to change jobs
4	jiàngxīn 降薪	to reduce salary	10	wā (zǒu) réncái 挖（走）人才	to skim off the best minds/people
5	dàiyù yōuhòu 待遇优厚	excellent pay and conditions	11	tiàocáo 跳槽	job-hopping; to change to a better job
6	dàiyù guò dī 待遇过低	underpaid	12	yòngrén dānwèi 用人单位	employing unit; employer

Cultural Navigation

"Tiàocáo" and "xiàhǎi" are two unique words. Both of them are related to changing jobs or changing careers. Originally, "tiàocáo" means that a horse is lured by better fodder and jumps over to another manger. Now this word means that a person is attracted by a better position and has decided to change his job. The original meaning of "xiàhǎi" is very straight forward. It means to go out to sea (for fishing or sailing). Now it means that one gives up his original career and engages in business or starts his own business. It certainly needs courage to make a career change. Just like sailing on the ocean, there are both opportunities and risks. The development of China's economy has many profound impacts on Chinese culture and people's life. Even the daily language and words are no exception. "Tiàocáo" and "xiàhǎi" are very good examples.

70 Decision of Resignation

Key Sentence

Yīnwèi mǒuxiē yuányīn, wǒ xiǎng cóng xià gè yuè qǐ jiù
因为某些原因，我想从下个月起就
bù lái shàngbān le.
不来上班了。

For certain reasons, I won't come to work from next month.

Substitution

gèrén
个人
personal

jiātíng
家庭
family

jiànkāng
健康
health

Liùyuè yī hào
六月一号
June 1st

Yuándàn yǐhòu
元旦以后
after New Year

yuèdǐ
月底
at the end of the month

míngtiān
明天
tomorrow

Extension

1. Nǐ yào cízhí ma?
   你要辞职吗?

   Do you want to resign?

2. Nǐ shì wǒmen de yèwù jiānzi a!
   你是 我们 的业务尖子啊!

   You are our top-notch professional person!

3. Wǒ xiǎng xiūxi yí duàn shíjiān, zài chóngxīn kāishǐ.
   我 想 休息一 段 时间，再 重 新 开始。

   I want to take a break for a while, and then start over.

4. Xièxie nín yìzhí yǐlái duì wǒ de guānzhào!
   谢谢您一直以来对我的关 照!

   Thank you for always looking after me!

Dialogue

A: Jīnglǐ, yīnwèi mǒuxiē yuányīn, wǒ xiǎng cóng xià gè yuè qǐ jiù bù lái shàngbān le.
经理，因为某些原因，我 想 从 下个月起就不来上 班 了。

Manager, for certain reasons, I won't come to work from next month.

B: Zěnme? Nǐ yào cízhí ma?
怎么? 你要辞职吗?

How come? Do you want to resign?

A: Bù hǎoyìsi. Zhè shì wǒ de cízhíxìn.
不好意思。这是我的辞职信。

I'm sorry. This is my resignation letter.

B: Nǐ shì wǒmen de yèwù jiānzi a! Shì lìngyǒu gāojiù ma?
你是我们的业务尖子啊！是另有高就吗？
You are our top-notch professional person! Did you get a better offer elsewhere?

A: Búshì. Wǒxiǎng xiūxi yí duànshíjiān, zài chóngxīn kāishǐ.
不是。我想休息一段时间，再重新开始。
No. I want to take a break for a while, and then start over.

Xièxiè nín yìzhí yǐlái duìwǒ de guānzhào!
谢谢您一直以来对我的关照！
Thank you for always looking after me!

Related Words

1	qǐngcí 请辞	to request permission to resign	7	jiěgù 解雇	to discharge; to dismiss
2	cízhí 辞职	to resign; to quit	8	kāichú 开除	to expel; to fire
3	cízhíxìn 辞职信/ bàogào 报告	letter of resignation	9	chǎo 炒 yóuyú 鱿鱼	to dismiss; to fire (literally: to fry a squid)
4	tíngxīn 停薪 liúzhí 留职	to retain the job but suspend the salary; to leave without pay	10	shīyè 失业	to lose one's job; out of work; unemployed
5	tíngzhí 停职	to suspend from duty	11	tuìxiū 退休	to retire
6	xiàgǎng 下岗	to be laid off due to restructuring	12	fǎnpìn 返聘	to rehire after retirement

Cultural Navigation

There is an ancient Chinese story called "sàiwēng-shīmǎ (the old frontiersman loses his horse)." There was an old man living at the northern frontier. One day he lost his horse. His neighbors came to comfort him. The old man said, "How do you know that this won't be good luck?" After a few months, the horse returned with some other good horses. His neighbors came to congratulate him. The old man said, "How do you know this won't be bad luck?" One day, his son fell from the horse and broke his leg. Those people came to console him again. The old man said, "How do you know this won't be good luck (again)?" Soon after, enemies invaded the region, and many young men died in battles. Since his son was a cripple and couldn't go into battle, both father and son escaped unharmed. This story represents a thought from ancient Chinese philosophy, namely "fúhuò-xiāngyī (fortune and misfortune are interrelated)." If you just quit your job or lose your job and feel upset, why don't you tell yourself this old Chinese story? You may realize that it might be a new beginning in your life!

71 Year-End Assessment

Key Sentence

Jīnnián de niánzhōng kǎohé yǒu nǎxiē fāngmiàn a?
今年的年终考核有哪些方面（啊）?
What aspects will this year's year-end assessment need to cover?

Substitution

gōngzuò zǒngjié
工作总结
job performance summary

niándù zǒngjié
年度总结
annual summary

zìwǒ pínggū
自我评估
self-evaluation

jìxiào kǎohé
绩效考核
performance/achievement assessment

xiàngmù
项目
item

nèiróng
内容
content

yāoqiú
要求
requirement

guīdìng
规定
rule; regulation

Extension

1. Nǐ shuō huā zhème duō shíjiān xiě zhèxiē yǒu shénme yòng?
你说花这么多时间写这些有什么用？
Can you tell me if there is any use in spending so much time writing these?

2. Nǐ míngnián de shēngjí tíxīn quánkào tā le!
你明年的升级、提薪全靠它了！
Your promotion and salary raise next year all depend on it!

3. Wǒ juéde jīběnshang gēn qùnián yíyàng.
（我觉得）基本上跟去年一样。
(I think that) it is almost the same as last year's.

4. Nǐ de nònghǎole jiègěi wǒ chāochao dé le!
你的弄好了借给我抄抄得了！
(I think that) it is almost the same as last year's.

Dialogue

A: Ài, yòu gāi jiāo niánzhōng kǎohé bàogào le. Nǐ shuō huā zhème duō shíjiān xiě zhèxiē yǒu shénme yòng?
唉，又该交年终考核报告了。你说花这么多时间写这些有什么用？
Alas, it's time to turn in the year-end assessment report again. Can you tell me if there is any use in spending so much time writing these?

B: Dāngrán yǒuyòng! Nǐ míngnián de shēngjí tíxīn quán kào tā le!
当然有用！你明年的升级、提薪全靠它了！
Of course it is useful! Your promotion and salary raise next year all depend on it!

A: Jīnnián de niánzhōng kǎohé yǒu nǎxiē fāngmiàn a?
今年的年终考核有哪些方面啊?

What aspects will this year's year-end assessment need to cover?

B: Xiāoshòu yèjì chūqínlǜ zhuānyè péixùn, jīběnshang gēn qùnián de yíyàng.
销售业绩、出勤率、专业培训，基本上跟去年的一样。

Sales performance, attendance rate, professional development. It is about the same as last year's.

A: Zhēn máfan! Nǐ de nònghǎole jiègěi wǒ chāochao dé le!
真麻烦! 你的弄好了借给我抄抄得了!

It's so troublesome! Could I borrow and copy yours when you are done?

B: Nàyàng zuò zěnme xíng! Nǐ shì kāiwánxiào ba?
那样做怎么行! 你是开玩笑吧?

That's not right! You are joking, right?

Related Words

1	gèrén 个人 biǎoxiàn 表现	personal performance	5	yìbān 一般 piān shàng 偏上	above average
2	yōuyì 优异	excellent	6	yìbān 一般 piānxià 偏下	below average
3	tūchū 突出	outstanding	7	chà 差	poor; bad
4	yìbān 一般	average; just so-so	8	luòhòu 落后	to fall behind

(Continued)

9	rènzhēn fùzé 认真负责	serious and responsible	11	yǒngyú chuàngxīn 勇于创新	eager to innovate; to have the courage to bring forth new ideas
10	lèyú hézuò 乐于合作	willing to collaborate with	12	niánzhōngjiǎng jīn 年终奖(金)	year-end bonus

Cultural Navigation

Starting from the end of last century, the performance assessment system has been adopted and implemented widely in China. Many enterprises and public institutions have established their own assessment systems and standards, and require their employees to have performance assessments at fixed periods, as well as to make personal year-end assessments. An employee's promotion and bonus all depend on his/her work performance. Today, egalitarianism has mainly been replaced by "jiǎngyōu-fáliè (rewarding the good and punishing the bad)."

72 Harassment and Discrimination

Key Sentence

Nǐ yīnggāi dāngmiàn gàosu tā zhè shì sāorǎo xíngwéi!
你应该当面告诉他这是骚扰行为!
You should tell him face to face that it is harassment!

Substitution

yánsù de
严肃地
seriously

qīngchu de
清楚地
clearly

zhíjié-liǎodàng de
直截了当地
directly

bú kèqi de
不客气地
ruthlessly; unreservedly

xìngsāorǎo
性骚扰
sexual harassment

xìngbié qíshì
性别歧视
sexual discrimination

niánlíng qíshì
年龄歧视
age discrimination
zhǒngzú qíshì
种族歧视
racial discrimination

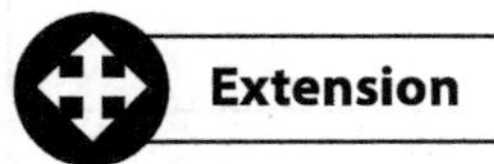

1. Wǒ zhēn shòubuliǎo le!
我真受不了了!
I really can't stand it anymore!

2. Gōngzuò shíjiān tā zǒngshì jiǎng yìxiē huángsè xiàohua.
工作时间他总是讲一些黄色笑话。
He always tells dirty jokes during work hours.

3. Tā chángcháng kànbuqǐ nǚtóngshì.
他常常看不起女同事。
He often looks down on female co-workers.

4. Wǒmen bù néng róngrěn zài gōngzuò chǎngsuǒ de zhè zhǒng sāorǎo xíngwéi!
我们不能容忍在工作场所的这种骚扰行为!
We cannot tolerate this kind of harassment in the workplace!

Dialogue

Wǒ zhēn shòubuliǎo le! Gōngzuò shíjiān tā zǒngshì jiǎng yìxiē huángsè xiàohua.

A: 我真受不了了！工作时间他总是讲一些黄色笑话。

I really can't stand it anymore! He always tells dirty jokes during work hours.

Wǒ yě tǎoyàn zhège rén! Tā chángcháng kànbuqǐ nǚtóngshì, shuō tāmen méinénglì.

B: 我也讨厌这个人！他常常看不起女同事，说她们没能力。

I dislike this person too! He often looks down on female co-workers and says they are incapable.

Wǒ rènwéi nǐ yīnggāi dāngmiàn gàosu tā zhèshì sāorǎo xíngwéi!

我认为你应该当面告诉他这是骚扰行为！

I think you should tell him face to face that it's harassment!

Wǒ shuō le, kěshì tā gēnběn bú dàng yì huí shì.

A: 我说了，可是他根本不当一回事。

I did, but he didn't take it seriously at all.

Nà nǐ jiù zhíjiē xiàng yǒuguān bùmén tóusù!

B: 那（你）就直接向有关部门投诉！

Then you should file a complaint directly to the department concerned!

Wǒ dào juéde tā yīnggāi qù kàn xīnlǐ yīshēng!

A: 我倒觉得他应该去看心理医生！

Instead, I think that he should go to see a psychologist!

Bùguǎn zěnmeyàng, wǒmen bù néng róngrěn zài gōngzuò chǎngsuǒ de zhè zhǒng sāorǎo xíngwéi!

B: 不管怎么样，我们不能容忍在工作场所的这种骚扰行为！

Anyway, we cannot tolerate this kind of harassment in the workplace!

Related Words

1	jùjué 拒绝	to refuse; to say no	7	xiàliú 下流	obscene; dirty
2	zhìzhǐ 制止	to prevent; to stop	8	sèqíng 色情	erotic; pornographic; sexy
3	pīpíng 批评	to criticize	9	tiáoqíng 调情	to flirt
4	zhǐzé 指责	to censure; to accuse; to criticize	10	tiáoxì 调戏	to harass a woman with obscenities
5	huángsè 黄色	pornography	11	liǎnpí hòu 脸皮厚	thick-skinned; shameless
6	huángduànzi 黄段子	dirty jokes; ribaldry	12	wúchǐ 无耻	shameless

Cultural Navigation

It is very easy to cause misunderstandings due to cultural differences. For instance, in China if you see two young people of the same sex are walking arm in arm or hand in hand on a street, it doesn't necessarily mean that they are a homosexual couple. Similarly, it is not easy for a foreigner with a different cultural background to distinguish between sexual harassment and off-color jokes, as well as the difference between discrimination and an unfriendly attitude. If you have doubts or feel uncomfortable with someone's words and actions, the best way is to tell him your feelings directly, or you can report the evidence to your supervisor.

Marketing

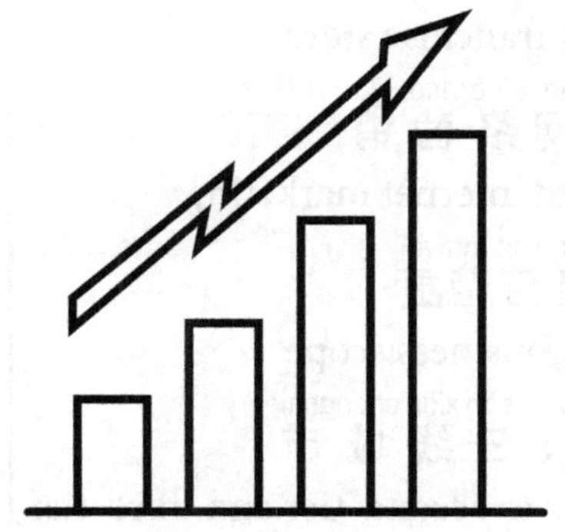

73 Marketing Strategies

Key Sentence

Tuīchū shēngjí chǎnpǐn shì yí gè yǒuxiào de cèlüè.
推出升级产品是一个有效的策略。
Bringing out an upgraded product is an effective strategy.

Substitution

jiàngdī jiàgé
降低价格
lower the price

fāzhǎn jiāméngdiàn
发展加盟店
expand franchise stores

tuīdòng wǎngluò yíngxiāo
推动网络营销
promote Internet marketing

kuòdà jīngyíng fànwéi
扩大经营范围
expand business scope

jìnjūn èr, sān xiàn chéngshì
进军二、三线城市
advance to second-tier and third-tier cities

kāituò hǎiwài shìchǎng
开拓海外市场
open up overseas market

tuìchū dīduān chǎnpǐn shìchǎng
退出低端产品市场
withdraw from low-end product market

búcuò
不错
not bad

míngzhì
明智
wise

zhèngquè
正确
correct

zhòngyào
重要
important

cuòwù
错误
wrong

kě gōng xuǎnzé
可供选择
alternative

zhídé kǎolǜ
值得考虑
worth considering

1. Yóuyú yíngxiāo cèlüè shīwù, gōngsī de lìrùn xiàhuále 30%.
由于营销策略失误，公司的利润下滑了30%。
Due to a mistake in marketing strategy, the company's profit has dropped by 30%.

2. Jīngjì zēngzhǎng huǎnmàn shì lìng yí gè yuányīn.
经济增长缓慢是另一个原因。
A sluggish economy is another reason.

3. Wǒmen bìxū gēnjù shìchǎng xūqiú, tiáozhěng gōngsī de yíngxiāo cèlüè.
我们必须根据市场需求，调整公司的营销策略。
We must adjust the company's marketing strategy according to the market demand.

Wǒmen yìqǐ lái yánjiū yánjiū xià yí bù de yíngxiāo cèlüè.
4. 我们一起来研究研究下一步的营销策略。

Let's come together and discuss our marketing strategy for the next step.

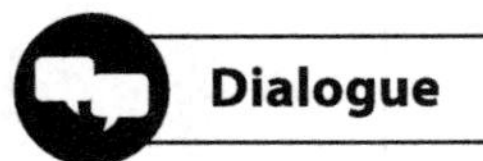

Yóuyú yíngxiāo cèlüè shīwù, shàng gè jìdù gōngsī de lìrùn xiàhuále 30%.
A: 由于营销策略失误，上个季度公司的利润下滑了30%。

Due to a mistake in marketing strategy, the company's profit has dropped by 30% last season.

Díquè rúcǐ, wǒmen duì jìngzhēng duìshǒu liǎojiě búgòu.
B: 的确如此，我们对竞争对手了解不够。

Indeed, we didn't know enough about our competitor.

Wǒ juéde jīngjì zēngzhǎng huǎnmàn yě shì yí gè yuányīn.
A: 我觉得经济增长缓慢也是一个原因。

I think that a sluggish economy is another reason too.

Wǒmen bìxū gēnjù shìchǎng xūqiú, tiáozhěng gōngsī de yíngxiāo cèlüè.
B: 我们必须根据市场需求，调整公司的营销策略。

We must adjust the company's marketing strategy according to the market demand.

Tuīchū shēngjí chǎnpǐn yěxǔ shì yí gè yǒuxiào de cèlüè.
A: 推出升级产品也许是一个有效的策略。

Bringing out upgraded products may be an effective strategy.

Wèile qǚdé gèng duō de shìchǎng fèn'é, wǒmen yě yīnggāi shǐ chǎnpǐn jiàgé gèng yǒu jìngzhēnglì.
B: 为了取得更多的市场份额，我们也应该使产品价格更有竞争力。

In order to take more market shares, we should also make the product's price more competitive.

A: Hǎo, wǒmen yìqǐ lái yánjiū yánjiū xià yí bù de yíngxiāo cèlüè.
好，我们一起来研究研究下一步的营销策略。
Good, let's come together and discuss our marketing strategy for the next step.

Related Words

1	xiāoshòu qúdào 销售渠道	distribution channel	7	jiàgé cèlüè 价格策略	pricing strategy
2	xiāoshòu wǎngluò 销售网络	sales network; distribution network	8	língshòu jiàgé 零售价格	retail price
3	liánsuǒdiàn 连锁店	chain store	9	pīfā jiàgé 批发价格	wholesale price
4	shítǐdiàn 实体店	physical shop/store; actual shop/store	10	gāoduān chǎnpǐn 高端产品	high-end product
5	wǎng luò diàn pù 网(络)店(铺)	online shop/store; Internet shop/store; virtual shop/store	11	shìchǎng bǎohé 市场饱和	market saturation
6	Táobǎowǎng 淘宝网	Taobao.com (the biggest e-commerce and e-auction website in China)			

Cultural Navigation

A booming economy, changes in lifestyle and Western influences everywhere have all been transforming China from a society with a tradition of thrift into a consumer society. Consumption concepts among the Chinese have also become diversified. Following the crowd and showing personality exist side by side, and the old custom of always laying stress on excellent goods at modest prices has no problems coexisting with the new fondness for fashion and name brands. In fact, no matter what kind of marketing strategies you adopt, it is always important to understand the conditions in China, and to know Chinese consumers and your competitors in the Chinese market. It is just like what Sun Tzu said in his book *The Art of War* more than two thousand years ago: only if you know yourself and know your opponent, will you never lose a battle.

74 Advertisement Planning

Key Sentence

Zhè cì wǒmen de guǎnggào yīnggāi tūchū pǐnpái xíngxiàng.
这次我们的广告应该突出品牌形象。
This time our advertisement should give prominence to brand image.

Substitution

chǎnpǐn tèsè
产品特色
special feature of the product

shíshàng cháoliú
时尚潮流
fashion trend

xiūxián fēnggé
休闲风格
casual style

lǜsè huánbǎo zhǔtí
绿色环保主题
environment-friendly motif/theme

Extension

1. Wǒmen jìhuà zài jìnqī tuīchū xīn yì lún guǎnggào xuānchuán huódòng.
我们计划在近期推出新一轮广告宣传活动。
We plan to push out a new round of advertisement promotions in the near future.

2. Wǒ jiànyì yāoqǐng yí wèi zhùmíng yǐngxīng dānrèn wǒmen de chǎnpǐn xíngxiàng dàiyánrén.
我建议邀请一位著名影星担任我们的产品形象代言人。

I suggest inviting a famous movie star to be the image spokesperson for our product.

3. Lìyòng míngrén xiàoyìng shì yí gè búcuò de fāngfǎ.
利用名人效应是一个不错的方法。

Using the celebrity effect is probably not a bad idea.

4. Ràng wǒmen zhǎo yì jiā yǒu jīngyàn de guǎnggào gōngsī zīxún yíxià.
让我们找一家有经验的广告公司咨询一下。

Let's find an experienced advertisement company for a consultation.

Dialogue

A: Gōngsī jìhuà zài xià gè jìdù tuīchū xīn yì lún guǎnggào xuānchuán huódòng.
公司计划在下个季度推出新一轮广告宣传活动。

The company plans to push out a new round of advertisement promotion next season.

B: Zhè cì de guǎnggào cèhuà yǒu shénme jùtǐ yāoqiú ma?
这次的广告策划有什么具体要求吗?

Is there any specific requirement for this advertisement scheme?

A: Zhè cì de guǎnggào yīnggāi tūchū pǐnpái xíngxiàng.
这次的广告应该突出品牌形象。

This time the advertisement should give prominence to brand image.

B: Wǒ jiànyì yāoqǐng yí wèi zhùmíng yǐngxīng dānrèn wǒmen de chǎnpǐn xíngxiàng dàiyánrén.
我建议邀请一位著名影星担任我们的产品形象代言人。

I suggest inviting a famous movie star to be the image spokesperson for our product.

A: Lìyòng míngrén xiàoyìng dàgài shì yí gè búcuò de fāngfǎ, yóuqí shì wǒmen chǎnpǐn de gùkè zhǔyào shì niánqīngrén.
利用名人效应大概是一个不错的方法，尤其是我们产品的顾客主要是年轻人。

Using the celebrity effect is probably not a bad idea, especially since our product's customers are mainly young people.

B: Ràng wǒmen xiān zhǎo yì jiā yǒu jīngyàn de guǎnggào gōngsī zīxún yíxià.
让我们先找一家有经验的广告公司咨询一下。

Let's first find an experienced advertisement company for a consultation.

Related Words

1	pǐnpái yìshi 品牌意识	brand awareness	5	píngmiàn guǎnggào 平面广告	graphic advertisement
2	pǐnpái tuīguǎng 品牌推广	brand promotion	6	diànshì guǎnggào 电视广告	television advertisement; TV commercial
3	shìchǎng tuīguǎng 市场推广	market promotion	7	gōngyì guǎnggào 公益广告	advertisement for public interests; charity ads
4	pǐnpái zhīmíngdù 品牌知名度	brand popularity	8	guǎnggào shèjì 广告设计	advertising design

(Continued)

9	guǎnggào 广告 chuàngyì 创意	advertising creativity	11	guǎnggào 广告 duìxiàng 对象	object of advertisement
10	guǎnggào 广告 yùsuàn 预算	budget for advertising	12	mùbiāo 目标 shìchǎng 市场	target market

Cultural Navigation

Although advertisements and commercials are ubiquitous in our life, it is still not easy to let your advertisement win Chinese consumers' hearts. Chinese often give a snort of contempt to an exaggerated and untrue advertisement. If a Chinese expresses his/her opinion about something by saying "that is advertising," that means he/she totally doesn't believe it. In addition, if you are doing an advertisement scheme for Chinese market, you must understand Chinese cultural traditions and value system. The Great Wall, Yellow River, Chinese dragon, Confucius, Tian'anmen and so on are considered symbols of China and Chinese culture. Chinese usually cannot accept a foreign product advertisement that uses these images to make funny jokes, play zany tricks or do weird things.

75 Sales Promotion

Key Sentence

Wèile dǎkāi shìchǎng, wǒmen jìhuà gǎo yí cì dàxíng (de) cùxiāo huódòng.
为了打开市场，我们计划搞一次大型（的）促销活动。

In order to open up the market, we plan to have a large-scale sales promotion.

Substitution

kāifā xīn shìchǎng
开发新市场
develop a new market

tígāo xiāoshòu'é
提高销售额
boost sales volume

tígāo zhīmíngdù
提高知名度
increase one's popularity

xīnpǐn shàngshì
新品上市
place new products into the market

kuòdà yǐngxiǎng
扩大影响
extend influence

tuīdòng wǎnggòu
推动网购
push online shopping

xīyǐn gùkè
吸引顾客
attract customers

quánguó fànwéi
全国范围
nationwide

mǎiyī-sòngyī
买一送一
buy one and get one free

jiérì
节日
holiday

wǎngshang
网 上
online

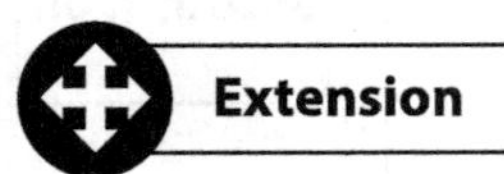

Extension

1. Wǒmen de xīn chǎnpǐn jiù kuài yàoshàngshì le.
我们的新产品就快要上市了。
Our new product will be on the market soon.

2. Zhè cì de cùxiāo huódòng fànwéi yǒuduō dà?
这次的促销活动范围有多大?
What is the scope of this sales promotion?

3. Zhè cì de cùxiāo huódòng jiāng zài quánguó gè dà chéngshì de méndiàn tóngbù jìnxíng.
这次的促销活动将在全国各大城市的门店同步进行。
This sales promotion will be carried out in step with stores in all big cities nationwide.

4. Wǎngshang de cùxiāo yīnggāi zuò de gèng yōuhuì yìxiē.
网上的促销应该做得更优惠一些。
The online sales promotion should offer more discounts.

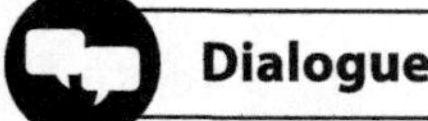

Dialogue

Xià gè yuè wǒmen de xīnchǎnpǐn jiùyào shàngshì le.
A: 下个月我们的新产品就要上市了。
Our new product will be on the market next month.

Gōngsī yǒu shénme xuānchuánzàoshì de jìhuà ma?
B: 公司有什么宣传造势的计划吗?
Does the company have any plans to build up publicity and promote sales?

Wèile dǎkāi shìchǎng, wǒmen jìhuà gǎo yí cì dàxíng cùxiāo huódòng.
A: 为了打开市场，我们计划搞一次大型促销活动。
In order to open up the market, we plan to have a large-scale sales promotion.

Zhè cì de cùxiāo huódòng fànwéi yǒu duō dà?
B: 这次的促销活动范围有多大?
What is the scope of this sales promotion?

Zhè cì de cùxiāo huódòng jiāng zài quánguó gè dà chéngshì de méndiàn tóngbù jìnxíng.
A: 这次的促销活动将在全国各大城市的门店同步进行。
This sales promotion will be carried out in step with stores in all big cities nationwide.

Lìngwài, gōngsī de guānwǎng yě huì tóngshí tuīchū cùxiāo huódòng.
另外，公司的官网也会同时推出促销活动。
In addition, the company's official website will also bring out the sales promotion at the same time.

Wǒ jiànyì wǎngshang de cùxiāo yīnggāi zuò de gēng yōuhuì yìxiē, bǐrú mǎiyī-sòngyī.
B: 我建议网上的促销应该做得更优惠一些，比如买一送一。
I suggest that the online sales promotion should offer more discounts. For example, buy one and get one free.

Related Words

1	wǎngluò cùxiāo 网络促销	sales promotion on the Internet	7	qīngcāng chǔlǐ/qīngcāng dàjiǎnjià 清仓处理/清仓大减价	clearance sale; inventory sale
2	shìchǎng dìngwèi 市场定位	market positioning	8	zhíxiāo 直销	direct distribution (i.e., selling products to customers without distributors)
3	xiāofèi qún tǐ 消费群(体)	consumer group; consumer base			
4	dǎzhé 打折	to make a discount	9	jīngpǐn 精品	top quality goods
5	jiǎnjià 减价	to reduce the price; to mark down	10	wùměi-jiàlián 物美价廉	excellent quality and reasonable price
6	rànglì 让利	to give up a share of the profits and offer a discount	11	dǎogòu fúwù 导购服务	shopping guide service

Cultural Navigation

A shopping guide or shopping consultant and a salesperson are two different kinds of sales job. In China, many big department stores, shopping centers, and specialty stores hire shopping guides. Since many of these shopping guides are young women, they are also called "dǎogòu xiǎojiě (Miss Shopping Guide)." Their job is to provide product information and purchase suggestions, and they can even accompany customers as they shop. A salesperson works for the manufacturer or the enterprise, and promotes sales of their products to relevant clients and possible consumers. There are many different kinds of ways in which a salesperson may promote the products. For instance, telephone sales, text message sales, mail sales or e-mail sales, and even door-to-door sales are all quite common in today's China.

76 The Market Survey

Key Sentence

Wèile liǎojiě xiāofèizhě yìjiàn, wǒmen jìhuà gǎo yí gè
为了了解消费者意见，我们计划搞一个
shìchǎng diàochá.
市场调查。

In order to find out consumer opinions, we plan to have a market survey.

Substitution

shìchǎng xūqiú
市场需求
market demand

shìchǎng dòngxiàng
市场动向
market trend

xiāofèi qīngxiàng
消费倾向
propensity to consume

xiāofèi xíguàn
消费习惯
habit of consumption

xiāofèizhě xǐhào
消费者喜好
consumer preference

jìngzhēng duìshǒu
竞争对手
competitor

Extension

1. Xiànzài jìngzhēng hěn jīliè, zhǎngwò shìchǎng xìnxī fēicháng zhòngyào.
现在竞争很激烈，掌握市场信息非常重要。
The competition right now is very intense, so it is very important to have the market information.

2. Wènjuàn de shèjì yuè jiǎnjié yuè hǎo.
问卷的设计越简洁越好。
The format and design of the questionnaire would be better if it is more succinct.

3. Shàng cì qǐng diàoyán gōngsī zuò de wènjuàn tài fùzá le.
上次请调研公司做的问卷太复杂了。
The previous questionnaire that we had a market research firm make was too complicated.

4. Wènjuàn chúle suí chǎnpǐn fēnfā yǐwài, yě yào fàng zài wǎngshang.
问卷除了随产品分发以外，也要放在网上。
In addition to being distributed with the product, the questionnaire will be placed online too.

Dialogue

A: Wèile liǎojiě xiāofèizhě yìjiàn, wǒmen jìhuà gǎo yí gè shìchǎng diàochá.
为了了解消费者意见，我们计划搞一个市场调查。
In order to find out consumer opinions, we plan to have a market survey.

B: Shì a, xiànzài jìngzhēng hěn jīliè, zhǎngwò shìchǎng xìnxī fēicháng zhòngyào.
是啊，现在竞争很激烈，掌握市场信息非常重要。
Yes, the competition now is very intense, so it is very important to have the market information.

A: Nǐ juéde zhèfèn diàochá wènjuàn yào bāokuò nǎxiē fāngmiàn de wèntí?
你觉得这份调查问卷要包括哪些方面的问题?
What kinds of questions do you think should be included in this questionnaire?

B: Wǒ jiànyì wènjuàn zhǔyào bāokuò sān gè fāngmiàn: pǐnpái xìngjiàbǐ hé shòuhòu fúwù.
我建议问卷主要包括三个方面：品牌、性价比和售后服务。
I suggest that the questionnaire mainly include three aspects: brand, performance-price ratio and after-sale service.

A: Wǒ tóngyì. Wènjuàn de shèjì yuè jiǎnjié yuè hǎo.
我同意。问卷的设计越简洁越好。
I agree. The format and design of the questionnaire would be better if it is more succinct.

B: Díquè rúcǐ. Shàng cì qǐng diàoyán gōngsī zuò de wènjuàn tài fùzá le.
的确如此。上次请调研公司做的问卷太复杂了。
Yes, indeed. The previous questionnaire that we had a market research firm make was too complicated.

A: Zhè cì wènjuàn chúle suí chǎnpǐn fēnfā yǐwài, yě yào fàng zài wǎngshang.
这次问卷除了随产品分发以外，也要放在网上。
This time, in addition to being distributed with the product, the questionnaire will be placed online too.

Related Words

1	tíwèn 提问	to question	3	shāngyè zīxún 商业咨询	business consulting
2	dá'àn 答案	answer	4	shìfēití 是非题	yes-no question

(Continued)

No.	Chinese	Pinyin	English
5	选择题	xuǎnzétí	multiple-choice question
6	随机抽样	suíjī chōuyàng	random sampling
7	消费模式	xiāofèi móshì	consumption pattern
8	特定消费群体	tèdìngxiāofèi qúntǐ	specific group of consumers
9	市场动向标志	shìchǎng dòngxiàng biāozhì	market indicator
10	市场趋势	shìchǎng qūshì	market tendency
11	人气	rénqì	popularity
12	人气产品	rénqì chǎnpǐn	popular product

Cultural Navigation

Although the market survey has become a common way to get market information and find out about consumer demands, Chinese consumers don't seem to be very interested in this kind of survey activities. Especially when market surveys take place on the spot, people often refuse to answer questions. If you come across a situation like this, you should not lose your patience. You might as well greet that person by saying "nín hǎo (hello)" with a smile, even handing over a small gift or sample that you have prepared to distribute, and then ask in a polite manner: "Wǒ néng máfan nín bāng gè máng ma?" (May I trouble you for a bit of help?) or "Néng wèn nín jǐ gè xiǎowèntí ma?" (May I ask you a couple of small questions?) or "Néng zhànyòng nín jǐ fēnzhōng shíjiān ma?" (Can I have a few minutes with you?) Normally in this kind of situation, a Chinese will be willing to answer your questions.

77 Sale Agency

Key Sentence

Wǒmen yìzhí shì Lántiān Shǒujī de dújiā dàilǐ.
我们一直是蓝天手机的独家代理。
We have always been Blue Sky Mobile Phone's sole agent.

Substitution

Fēngtián Qìchē
丰田汽车
Toyota Motor Corp.

zhège pǐnpái
这个品牌
this brand

zhèzhǒng chǎnpǐn
这种产品
this product

zhè jiā gōngsī
这家公司
this company

zǒngdàilǐ
总代理
general agency/agent

qūyù dàilǐ
区域代理
regional agency/agent

fēnxiāoshāng
分销商
distributor

jīngxiāoshāng
经销商
dealer

1. Wǒmen xīwàng néng chéngwéi guìgòngsī chǎnpǐn de zhǐdìng dàilǐshāng.
我们希望能成为贵公司产品的指定代理商。
We hope to become a designated agent of your company's products.

2. Wǒmen de yòngjīn biāozhǔn shì gēnjù shíjì xiāoshòu'é fēnwéi liǎng dàng de.
我们的佣金标准是根据实际销售额分为两档的。
Our commission standard is divided into 2 scales based on the actual volume of sales.

3. Wǒmen huì yòng shíjì de xiāoshòu chéngjì zhèngmíng wǒmen de jiàzhí.
我们会用实际的销售成绩证明我们的价值。
We'll prove our value by actual sales results.

4. Wǒmen lái tántan jùtǐ de tiáojiàn hé yāoqiú.
我们来谈谈具体的条件和要求。
Let's talk about conditions and requirements in detail.

A: Wǒmen Nánfāng Tōngxìn xīwàng néng chéngwéi guì gōngsī chǎnpǐn de zhǐdìng dàilǐshāng.
我们南方通信希望能成为贵公司产品的指定代理商。
South Communication hopes to become a designated agent of your company's products.

B: Nǐmen zài xiāoshòu dàilǐ fāngmiàn yǒu nǎxiē jīngyàn ne?
你们在销售代理方面有哪些经验呢?
What kind of experience do you have in the field of sales agency?

A: Guòqù jǐ nián, wǒmen yìzhí shì Lántiān Shǒujī de dújiā dàilǐ.
过去几年，我们一直是蓝天手机的独家代理。
During the past several years, we have always been Blue Sky Mobile Phone's sole agent.

Nín duì yòngjīn yǒu shénme yāoqiúma?
B: 您对佣金有什么要求吗?

Do you have any expectations for the commission?

Wǒmen de yòngjīn biāozhǔn shì gēnjù shíjì xiāoshòu'é wéi liǎng dàng de.
我们的佣金标准是根据实际销售额为两档的。

Our commission standard is divided into 2 scales based on the actual volume of sales.

Méiwèntí. Wǒmenhuìyòng shíjì dexiāoshòu chéngjì zhèngmíng wǒmen de jiàzhí.
A: 没问题。我们会用实际的销售成绩证明我们的价值。

This is not a problem. We'll prove our value by actual sales results.

Hǎo. Rúguǒ shì zhèyàng dehuà, wǒmen xiànzài lái tántan jùtǐ de tiáojiàn hé yāoqiú.
B: 好。如果是这样的话，我们现在来谈谈具体的条件和要求。

Good. If you say so, now let's talk about conditions and requirements in detail.

Related Words

1	quánquán dàilǐ 全权代理	universal agent/ agency	4	dàilǐ xiéyì 代理协议	agency agreement
2	fēndàilǐ 分代理	sub-agent; sub-agency	5	tèyuē jīngxiāo tèxǔ 特约经销/特许 jīngxiāoshāng 经销商	franchiser; franchised dealer
3	dàilǐquán 代理权	agency authority/right	6	liánsuǒjīngxiāo 连锁经销	chain of distribution

(Continued)

7	bǎifēnbǐ 百分比	percentage	10	yòngjīn bǐlǜ 佣金比率	commission ratio/rate
8	shòuquán 授权	to authorize	11	fēnhóng 分红	to get a bonus; to share profits
9	tíchéng 提成	commission; to deduct a percentage from a sum of money; to draw a percentage	12	lìrùn 利润	profit

Cultural Navigation

With regard to "sales," there are quite a few terms in Chinese that are easily confused. For instance, the term "yìbān dàilǐ (ordinary/commission agent)" is used to distinguish from "dújiā dàilǐ (sole agent)" while "zhǐdìng dàilǐ (designated agent)" means that the manufacturer has chosen and designated this agent to sell their products. The term "fēndàilǐ (sub-agent)" means sub-agents that are under "zǒngdàilǐ (general agent)," and it may also be further divided into "yī jí dàilǐ (Class A sub-agent)," "èr jí dàilǐ (Class B sub-agent)" and even "sān jí dàilǐ (Class C sub-agent)." The standard used to divide those sub-agents depends on either the size of the region or the volume of sales. Without doubt, it will help you to know who you are actually dealing with if you know what those terms mean.

78 Public Welfare and Charity Support

Key Sentence

Wǒmen gōngsī juédìng juānzèng gěi běndì xiǎoxué yīqiān
我们公司决定捐赠给本地小学一千
tái diànnǎo.
台电脑。

Our company has decided to donate 1,000 computers to local elementary schools.

Substitution

pínkùn dìqū
贫困地区
impoverished region

shòuzāi dìqū
受灾地区
disaster area

císhàn jīgòu
慈善机构
charity organization

xīwàng jiàoyù jījīn
希望教育基金
the Hope Education Foundation

yīliáo qìcái
医疗器材
medical equipment

yībǎiwàn yuán rénmínbì
一百万元人民币
one million yuan RMB

yídìng shùmù de qǐdòng jījīn
一定数目的启动基金
certain amount of startup fund
ruògān gè quán'é jiǎngxuéjīn
若干个全额奖学金
several full scholarships

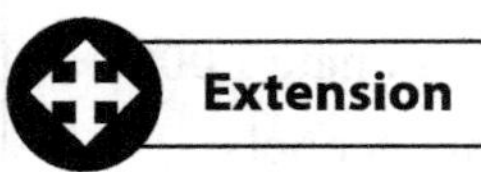

1. Wǒmen kěyǐ jièzhù zhège jīhuì ràng gōngzhòng duì wǒmen qǐyè hé chǎnpǐn yǒu gèng duō de liǎojiě.
我们可以借助这个机会让公众对我们企业和产品有更多的了解。
We can use this opportunity to make the general public know more about our corporation and products.

2. Huíkuì shèhuì shì wǒmen yīnggāi zuò de shì.
回馈社会是我们应该做的事。
It is our duty to repay society.

3. Gōngyì zànzhù duì qǐyè hé shèhuì shì yí jiàn shuāngyíng de hǎoshì.
公益赞助对企业和社会是一件双赢的好事。
Supporting public welfare is a win-win matter for both the enterprise and society.

4. Zuòhǎo zhè jiàn shì yídìng yào yǒu yí gè qièshí kěxíng de cāozuò fāng'àn.
做好这件事一定要有一个切实可行的操作方案。
In order to do this well, we definitely need a practical operating plan.

A: Jīnnián wǒmen gōngsī juédìng juānzènggěi běndì xiǎoxué yīqiān tái diànnǎo.
今年我们公司决定捐赠给本地小学一千台电脑。
This year our company has decided to donate 1,000 computers to local elementary schools.

B: Hěn hǎo.Wǒmen kěyǐ jièzhù zhège jīhuì ràng gōngzhòng duì wǒmen qǐyè hé chǎnpǐn yǒu gèng duō de liǎojiě.
很好。我们可以借助这个机会让公众对我们企业和产品有更多的了解。
That's very good. We can use this opportunity to make the general public know more about our corporation and products.

A: Huíkuì shèhuì shì wǒmen yīnggāi zuò de shì.
回馈社会是我们应该做的事。
It is our duty to repay society.

B: Wǒ tóngyì. Gōngyì zànzhù duì qǐyè hé shèhuì shì yí jiàn shuāngyíng de hǎoshì.
我同意。公益赞助对企业和社会是一件双赢的好事。
I agree. Supporting public welfare is a win-win matter for both the enterprise and society.

A: Búguò, zuòhǎo zhè jiàn shì yídìng yào yǒu yí gè qièshí kěxíng de cāozuò fāng'àn.
不过，做好这件事一定要有一个切实可行的操作方案。
However, in order to do this well, we definitely need a practical operating plan.

B: Wǒ jiànyì wǒmen de gōngguānbù yīnggāi jièrù zhè cì huódòng de xuānchuán hé zhíxíng guòchéng.
我建议我们的公关部应该介入这次活动的宣传和执行过程。

I suggest that our Public Relations Department should get involved in the process of publicizing and operating this campaign.

Related Words

1	juānkuǎn 捐款	to contribute money; contribution; donation	4	wùzī 物资	material; goods
2	juānzèng 捐赠	to contribute (as a gift); to donate	5	zījīn 资金	fund
3	zīzhù 资助	to aid financially; to subsidize	6	shànkuǎn 善款	money for charity
7	gōngguān cèlüè 公关策略	public relations strategy	9	gōngyì guǎnggào 公益广告	advertisement for public interests; charity ads
8	chǎngshāng zànzhù 厂商赞助	supported or sponsored by manufacturers or business corporations	10	gōngyìxìntuō jījīn 公益信托基金	public trust fund; charitable trust fund

Cultural Navigation

More and more Chinese businesses have learned to make charity or public welfare support projects as a campaign for their public relations. This kind of activity not only benefits the general public but also helps the business to win trust from the general public as well as to build up a good image. However, how a business takes part in a charity activity still needs careful consideration. There is an old saying in China: "Wù yǐ shàn xiǎo ér bù wéi." (Don't give up doing a good deed just because it is too small.) Supporting public welfare is about whether you have good faith and compassion instead of how much money you contribute. Additionally, in the traditional way of Chinese thinking, what should be praised most is to do good deeds anonymously. Because of this, if a business does charity work or public welfare support work in an overly high-profile way, it will often be questioned by the general public. Obviously, careful planning is needed to let corporate image benefit from this type of activity.

79 Applying for an Exhibition

Key Sentence

Wǒmen gōngsī juédìng cānjiā jīnnián de jiāyòng diànqì zhǎnlǎnhuì.
我们公司决定参加今年的家用电器展览会。
Our company has decided to participate in this year's household appliance exhibition.

Substitution

jìhuà
计划
plan

zhǔnbèi
准备
prepare

shēnqǐng
申请
apply for

bàomíng
报名
sign up

fúzhuāng fúshì
服装服饰
clothing and accessories

nóngchǎnpǐn
农产品
agricultural product

jīdiàn chǎnpǐn
机电产品
mechanical and electrical product

yīliáo qìcái yòngpǐn
医疗器材用品
medical devices & supplies

gāokējì chǎnpǐn
高科技产品
high-tech product

Extension

1. Zhè cì yùjì yǒu guónèi-wài jǐ qiān jiā qǐyè cānzhǎn.
这次预计有国内外几千家企业参展。
By estimation, there will be several thousand enterprises from home and abroad participating in the exhibition this time.

2. Wǒmen bìxū jǐnkuài gǎo yí gè xiángxì de cānzhǎn fāng'àn.
我们必须尽快搞一个详细的参展方案。
We have to make a plan with details about participating in the exhibition as soon as possible.

3. Zhǎnhuì bàomíng de jiézhǐ rìqī shì Wǔyuè dǐ.
展会报名的截止日期是五月底。
The registration deadline for the exhibition is the end of May.

4. Wǒ jiànyì xià xīngqī kāihuì tǎolùn yíxià wǒmen chǎnpǐn zhǎntái de fāng'àn.
我建议下星期开会讨论一下我们产品展台的方案。
I suggest having a meeting next week and discussing the proposal about our products' booth.

Dialogue

A: (Wǒmen) gōngsī juédìng cānjiā jīnnián de jiāyòng diànqì zhǎnlǎnhuì.
(我们)公司决定参加今年的家用电器展览会。
Our company has decided to participate in this year's household appliance exhibition.

B: Wǒ tīngshuō zhè cì yǒu guónèi-wài jǐ qiān jiā qǐyè cānzhǎn.
我听说这次有国内外几千家企业参展。
I hear that there will be several thousand enterprises from home and abroad participating in the exhibition this time.

A: Wǒmen bìxū jǐnkuài gǎo yí gè xiángxì de cānzhǎn fāng'àn.
我们必须尽快搞一个详细的参展方案。
We have to make a plan with details about participating in the exhibition as soon as possible.

B: Shì a, wǒ jìde zhǎnhuì bàomíng de jiézhǐ rìqī shì Sānyuè dǐ.
是啊，我记得展会报名的截止日期是三月底。
Yes, I remember that the registration deadline for the exhibition is the end of March.

A: Nǐ néng shàngwǎng zài chá yíxià cānzhǎn fèiyong ma?
你能上网再查一下参展费用吗?
Could you go online and double-check the cost for participating in the exhibition?

B: Xíng. Wǒ jiànyì xià xīngqī kāihuì tǎolùn yíxià wǒmen zhǎntái de fāng'àn.
行。我建议下星期开会讨论一下我们展台的方案。
Sure. I suggest having a meeting next week and discussing the proposal about our products' booth.

Related Words

1	bólǎnhuì 博览会	exposition; expo	5	zhǎnlǎnguǎn 展览馆	exhibition hall
2	zhǎnxiāohuì 展销会	trade fair	6	huìzhǎn zhōngxīn 会展中心	convention and exhibition center
3	shāngpǐn jiāoyìhuì 商品交易会	commodities fair; trade fair	7	zhǎnqū 展区	exhibition area
4	tóuzī màoyì qiàtánhuì 投资贸易洽谈会	investment and trade fair	8	zhǎnwèi 展位	a site that is used to display items at the exhibition

(Continued)

9	zhǎnshì 展示	to demonstrate; to show; to display	11	zhǎnqī 展期	exhibition period
10	zhǎnpǐn 展品	exhibit; item on display			

Cultural Navigation

Every year, several thousand conventions and exhibitions take place in China. These conventions and exhibitions cover a broad range of fields from traditional agriculture, traditional industries to new advanced technologies. Many of these conventions and exhibitions, such as China Import and Export Fair (Canton Fair), China Beijing International Fair for Trade in Services (Beijing Fair), China International Fair for Investment and Trade (Xiamen) and China High-Tech Fair (Shenzhen), have exerted significant international impact and have attracted many manufacturers and merchants worldwide. After decades of development and accumulation, today the industry of conventions and exhibitions has already become one of the driving forces of China's economy.

80 Products Display and Demonstration

Key Sentence

Zhè shì wǒmen jīnnián shēngchǎn de xīn chǎnpǐn.
这是我们（今年）生产的新产品。
This is the new product that we produced (this year).

Substitution

zhìzào
制造
make

yánfā
研发
invent

shēngjí chǎnpǐn
升级产品
upgraded product

zhuānlì chǎnpǐn
专利产品
patented product

chàngxiāo chǎnpǐn
畅销产品
top-selling product

kāifā
开发
develop

diànqì chǎnpǐn
电器产品
appliances

Extension

1. Gēn qùnián de xínghào xiāngbǐ, xīn chǎnpǐn yǒu nǎxiē bù tóng?
跟去年的型号相比，新产品有哪些不同?
Compared to last year's model, what differences does the new product have?

2. Xīn chǎnpǐn zài gōngnéng hé zhìliàngshang dōu yǒu tígāo.
新产品在功能和质量上都有提高。
The new product has enhanced its function and quality.

3. Zhèxiē shì chǎnpǐn de yǒuguān zīliào.
这些是产品的有关资料。
This is the related information of the product.

4. Wǒmen hái yǒu yí gè chǎnpǐn de shìpín, wǒ xiǎng fànggěi nín kàn yí kàn.
我们还有一个产品的视频，(我)想放给您看一看。
We also have a video of this product that I would like to show you.

Dialogue

A: Qǐng kàn yí kàn, zhè shì wǒmen jīnnián shēngchǎn de xīn chǎnpǐn.
请看一看，这是我们今年生产的新产品。
Please take a look: this is the new product that we've produced this year.

B: Gēn qùnián de xínghào xiāngbǐ, xīn chǎnpǐn yǒu nǎxiē bù tóng?
跟去年的型号相比，新产品有哪些不同?
Compared to last year's model, what differences does the new product have?

A: Xīn chǎnpǐn zài gōngnéng hé zhìliàng shang dōu yǒu tígāo, chǎnpǐn de wàiguān shèjì yě yǒu gǎijìn.
新产品在功能和质量上都有提高，产品的外观设计也有改进。

The new product has enhanced its function and quality, and the product's exterior design has been improved too.

Zhèxiē shì chǎnpǐn de yǒuguān zīliào.
这些是产品的有关资料。

This is the related information of the product.

B: Cóng jiàgé kàn, zhège chǎnpǐn de xìngjiàbǐ díquè búcuò!
从价格看，这个产品的性价比的确不错！

Judging by the price, the performance-price ratio of this product is really not bad!

A: Xièxie! Wǒmen hái yǒu yí gè chǎnpǐn de shìpín, wǒ xiǎng fànggěi nín kàn yí kàn.
谢谢！我们还有一个产品的视频，我想放给您看一看。

Thanks! We also have a video of this product. I would like to play it for you.

Related Words

1	zhǔdǎ chǎnpǐn 主打产品	featured product; main product	4	gāokējì chǎnpǐn 高科技产品	high-tech product
2	héxīn chǎnpǐn 核心产品	core product	5	mínyòng chǎnpǐn 民用产品	product for civilian use
3	jiānduān chǎnpǐn 尖端产品	cutting-edge product	6	jūnyòng chǎnpǐn 军用产品	product for military use

(Continued)

7	réngì 人气 chǎnpǐn 产品	popular product	9	mínyòng diànzǐ 民用电子 chǎnpǐn 产品	civil electronic product
8	fēizhuānlì 非专利 chǎnpǐn 产品	unpatented product	10	huòjiǎng 获奖 chǎnpǐn 产品	award-winning product

Cultural Navigation

This is a story from more than 2,000 years ago. It is called "zìxiāng-máodùn (his spear against his shield or being self-contradictory)." A man was selling his spear and shield at a marketplace. He first held up his shield and said to people, "My shield is the strongest shield and nothing in this world can pierce it through!" Then he picked up his spear and bragged, "My spear is the sharpest spear and it can pierce through anything!" Someone in the crowd asked, "What would happen if your spear is used to pierce your shield?" The man was dumbfounded and couldn't find a word to say in reply. He could only take his spear and shield and walk away. From this story, you can see that Chinese merchants have long understood the importance of advertising and exhibiting one's goods. At the same time, the story gives us a simple lesson: by using exaggerated and unbelievable terms to promote your products, not only may you make a laughable mistake, but you will lose the trust of your customers.

81 After-Sale Services

Key Sentence

Chǎnpǐn shòuchū sānshí tiān zhīnèi, wǒmen tígōng miǎnfèi
产品售出三十天之内，我们提供免费
ānzhuāng hé tiáoshì fúwù.
安装和调试服务。

Within 30 days after the product is sold, we provide free installation and testing services.

Substitution

bǎozhèngqī nèi
保证期内
within warranty period

bǎozhìqī nèi
保质期内
within quality guarantee period

jīnkǎ huìyuán
金卡会员
gold card members

shāngpǐn wánhǎo de qíngkuàng xia
商品完好的情况下
the merchandise in sound condition

wéixiū fúwù
维修服务
maintenance service

24 xiǎoshí de jìshù zhīchí
24小时的技术支持
24 hours technical support

zhōngshēng miǎnfèi fúwù
终 生 免费服务
lifetime free service
tuìhuàn fúwù
退换服务
return and exchange services

Extension

1. Wǒ xiǎng liǎojiě yíxià nǐmen yǒu nǎxiē shòuhòu fúwù.
我想了解一下你们有哪些售后服务。
I would like to know what after-sale services you have.

2. Kèhù kěyǐ yùyuē shàngmén wéixiū fúwù.
客户可以预约上门维修服务。
Clients may make an appointment for an on-site maintenance service.

3. Shòuchū de chǎnpǐn kěyǐ tuìhuàn ma?
售出的产品可以退换吗？
Can a sold product get refunded or exchanged?

4. Zài guīdìng shíjiān nèi hé shāngpǐn wánhǎo de qíngkuàng xia kěyǐ tuìhuàn.
在规定时间内和商品完好的情况下可以退换。
Within the scheduled time and in sound condition, the item can be returned for refund or exchange.

Dialogue

A: Nǐ hǎo. Wǒ xiǎng liǎojiě yíxià nǐmen yǒu nǎxiē shòuhòu fúwù.
你好。我想了解一下你们有哪些售后服务。
Hello. I would like to know what after-sale services you have.

B: Chǎnpǐn shòuchū sānshí tiān zhīnèi, wǒmen tígōng miǎnfèi de ānzhuāng hé tiáoshì fúwù.
产品售出三十天之内，我们提供免费的安装和调试服务。
Within 30 days after the product is sold, we provide free installation and testing services.

Lìngwài, kèhù yě kěyǐ yùyuē shàngmén wéixiū fúwù.
另外，客户也可以预约上门维修服务。
Additionally, the client can also make an appointment for an on-site maintenance service.

A: Nǐmen yǒu sònghuò shàngmén fúwù ma?
你们有送货上门服务吗?
Do you have a home delivery service?

B: Zài wǒmen zhèli gòumǎi de dà jiàn shāngpǐn, wǒmen kěyǐ miǎnfèi sònghuò.
在我们这里购买的大件商品，我们可以免费送货。
For the large item bought from us, we can deliver it for free.

A: Shòuchū de chǎnpǐn kěyǐ tuìhuàn ma?
售出的产品可以退换吗?
Can a sold product get refunded or exchanged?

B: Yìbān shuō, zài guīdìng shíjiān nèi hé shāngpǐn wánhǎo de qíngkuàng xia kěyǐ tuìhuàn.
一般说，在规定时间内和商品完好的情况下可以退换。
Generally speaking, within the scheduled time and in sound condition, the item can be returned for refund or exchange.

Related Words

1	shàngmén 上门 fúwù 服务	door-to-door service	7	shòuhuò 售货 fāpiào 发票	sales invoice; receipt
2	dìngqī 定期 bǎoyǎng 保养	periodic maintenance	8	bāotuì-bāohuàn 包退包换	a guarantee of refund or exchange
3	kèfú gù-kè fúwù 客服/顾客服务	customer service	9	chǎnpǐn 产品 zhèngshū 证书	product certification
4	kèfú 客服 dàibiǎo 代表	customer service representative	10	chǎnpǐn zhìliàng bǎozhèngshū 产品质量保证书/ chǎnpǐn bǎodān 产品保单	quality certificate of the product; product warranty
5	kèfú 客服 rèxiàn 热线	customer service hotline	11	chǎnpǐn 产品 shǒucè 手册	product brochure
6	miǎnfèi shòu-hòu fúwù 免费售后服务	free after-sale service	12	shǐyòng 使用 shuōmíngshū 说明书	user's manual

Cultural Navigation

Some people say that Chinese consumers have become "hard to please." When they choose and purchase a product, they not only pay attention to the product's quality, function, appearance and price, but also pay more attention to after-sale services of the product. More and more Chinese enterprises have realized that after-sale services are an important part of marketing. In today's Chinese market, the after-sale services that manufactures and dealers provide have already covered a series of aspects including product delivery, setting up, testing, maintenance, technical consultation and training, etc. Humanized after-sale services have become a common demand for manufacturers and dealers.

82 Crisis Management

Key Sentence

Zhè cì shìgù sǔnhàile wǒmen gōngsī de shēngyù.
这次事故损害了我们公司的声誉。
This accident has damaged our company's reputation.

Substitution

shìjiàn
事件
incident

zhìliàng wèntí
质量问题
quality problem

wūrǎn wèntí
污染问题
pollution problem

guǎnggào nèiróng
广告内容
advertisement content

cùxiāohuódòng
促销活动
sales promotion

qǐyè
企业
enterprise

pǐnpái
品牌
brand

chǎnpǐn
产品
product

jítuán
集团
group; conglomerate

Jīntiān wǒmen jiēdào shù qǐ xiāofèizhě tóusù.
1. 今天我们接到数起消费者投诉。
We have received several complaints from our consumers today.

Shìchǎngbù zhèngzài jiù shìgù yuányīn jìnxíng diàochá.
2. 市场部正在就事故原因进行调查。
The Marketing Department is conducting an investigation on the cause of the accident.

Wǒmen bìxū lìkè cǎiqǔ xíngdòng yìngduì gōngguān wēijī.
3. 我们必须立刻采取行动应对公关危机。
We must take an immediate action to cope with the public relations crisis.

Wǒ huì dàibiǎo gōngsī gōngkāi dàoqiàn, zhēngqǔ xiāofèizhě de liàngjiě.
4. 我会代表公司公开道歉，争取消费者的谅解。
I'll make an apology to the public on behalf of the company, and make every effort to gain back our consumers' understanding and forgiveness.

Wáng zǒng, jīntiān wǒmen yòu jiēdào shù qǐ xiāofèizhě tóusù.
A: 王总，今天我们又接到数起消费者投诉。
General Manager Wang, we have received several complaints from our consumers again today.

Zhè cì shìgù yǐjīng sǔnhàile wǒmen gōngsī de shēngyù.
B: 这次事故已经损害了我们公司的声誉。

This accident has already damaged our company's reputation.

Shìchǎngbù zhèngzài jiù shìgù yuányīn jìnxíng diàochá.
A: 市场部正在就事故原因进行调查。

The Marketing Department is conducting an investigation on the cause of the accident.

Zhè hái yuǎnyuǎn búgòu. Wǒmen bìxū lìkè cǎiqǔ xíngdòng yìngduì gōngguān wēijī.
B: 这还远远不够。我们必须立刻采取行动应对公关危机。

This is far from enough. We must take an immediate action to cope with the public relations crisis.

Shì, wǒmen zhèngzài nǐdìng quánmiàn jiějué fāng'àn.
A: 是，我们正在拟定全面解决方案。

Yes, we are in the middle of drafting a comprehensive solution.

Yídìng yào zhuājǐn. Jīntiān xiàwǔ gōngsī zhàokāi xīnwén fābùhuì.
B: 一定要抓紧。今天下午公司召开新闻发布会。

You have to speed up. This afternoon the company will hold a news conference.

Wǒ huì dàibiǎo gōngsī gōngkāi dàoqiàn, zhēngqǔ xiāofèizhě de liàngjiě.
我会代表公司公开道歉，争取消费者的谅解。

I'll make an apology to the public on behalf of the company, and make every effort to gain back our consumers' understanding and forgiveness.

Related Words

No.	Term	Meaning	No.	Term	Meaning
1	xìnyù 信誉	credit and reputation	6	péicháng 赔偿	to compensate; compensation
2	tūfā shìjiàn 突发事件	an incident that occurs suddenly	7	bǔjiù cuòshī 补救措施	remedy; remedial measure
3	yìwài 意外	accident; unexpected	8	yìngjí cuòshī 应急措施	emergency measure
4	shànhòu 善后	to deal with the aftermath	9	zérènfāng 责任方	responsible party
5	shòulǐ 受理	to accept and hear a case	10	xiāofèizhě xiéhuì 消费者协会	consumers' association

Cultural Navigation

In Chinese business culture, "chéngxìn jīngshāng (doing business honestly)" has always been considered a virtue. Honesty is the life of an enterprise. How to deal with crises is a test for an enterprise's honesty. Actually, sometimes a bad thing could lead to a good result and a good thing might also draw forth a bad result. This is a concept of "fúhuò-xiāngyī (fortune and misfortune are interrelated)" in ancient Chinese philosophy. The Chinese term "wēijī (crisis)" is a compound word containing "wēixiǎn (danger)" and "jīyù (opportunity)." It precisely reveals the dual characters of a crisis. The ultimate objective of crisis management is to transform a crisis into an opportunity to make progress.

Freight Transport Services

83 Date of Shipment

Key Sentence

Wǒmen yāoqiú zài Shíyuè shíwǔ hào yǐqián (quánbù) jiāohuò zhuāngyùn.
我们要求在十月十五号以前（全部）交货装运。

We request to have (all) the goods ready for shipment before October 15th.

Substitution

zài niándǐ qián
在年底前

before the end of this year

zài liǎng gè yuè zhīnèi
在两个月之内

within 2 months

bù chí yú xià Zhōu'èr
不迟于下周二

no later than next Tuesday

jǐnkuài
尽快

as soon as possible

1. Wǒmen gōngsī yíxiàng yángé ànzhào hétong guīdìng rìqī jiāohuò.
我们公司一向严格按照合同规定日期交货。
Our company always delivers goods strictly in accordance with the contracted date.

2. jiāohuò shíjiān duì wǒmen hěn zhòngyào.
交货时间对我们很重要。
The delivery time is very important to us.

3. Zhèxiē shāngpǐn wǒmen bìxū zài Shíyīyuè zhōngxún tóufàng shìchǎng.
这些商品我们必须在十一月中旬投放市场。
We have to put these merchandises into market by the middle of November.

4. Zhè zhāng dìngdān de shùliàng bǐjiào dà, fēn liǎng cì jiāohuò kěnéng gèng kuài yìxiē.
这张订单的数量比较大，分两次交货可能更快一些。
The quantities on this purchasing list are quite huge. We could handle them faster if we divide them into two shipments.

A: Nín néng bǎozhèng ànshí jiāohuò ma?
您能保证按时交货吗?
Can you guarantee delivery of the goods on time?

B: Zhè yì diǎn nín kěyǐ fàngxīn. Wǒmen gōngsī yíxiàng yángé ànzhào hétong guīdìng rìqī jiāohuò.
这一点您可以放心。我们公司一向严格按照合同规定日期交货。

You can trust us on this. Our company always delivers goods strictly in accordance with the contracted date.

A: Nín zhīdào jiāohuò shíjiān duì wǒmen hěn zhòngyào.
您知道交货时间对我们很重要。

You know that the delivery time is very important to us.

Zhèxiē shāngpǐn wǒmen bìxū zài Shíyīyuè zhōngxún tóufàng shìchǎng.
这些商品我们必须在十一月中旬投放市场。

We have to put these merchandises into market by the middle of November.

B: Zhè yīnggāi méi wèntí. Búguò zhè zhāng dìngdān de shùliàng bǐjiào dà, fēnliǎng cì jiāohuò kěnéng gèng kuài yìxiē.
这应该没问题。不过这张订单的数量比较大，分两次交货可能更快一些。

This shouldn't be a problem. But the quantities on this purchasing list are quite huge. We could handle them faster if we divide them into two shipments.

A: Kěyǐ. Búguò wǒmen yāoqiú zài Shíyuè shíwǔ hào yǐqián quánbù jiāohuò zhuāngyùn.
可以。不过我们要求在十月十五号以前全部交货装运。

That'll be fine. But we request to have all the goods ready for shipment before October 15th.

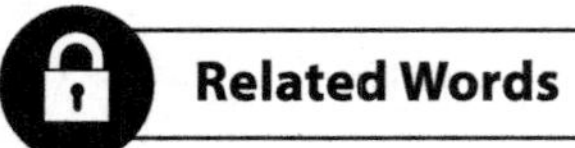

1	tíqián jiāohuò 提前交货	to advance the delivery; to advance the shipment
2	fēnpī jiāohuò 分批交货	delivery spread; delivery by installments; partial delivery

(Continued)

3	yánqī jiāohuò 延期交货	delayed delivery; back order	7	jiāohuò-dān 交货单	delivery order; D/O
4	lìjí zhuāngyùn 立即装运	immediate shipment	8	jiāohuò shíjiānbiǎo 交货时间表	delivery schedule
5	jǐnkuài zhuāngyùn 尽快装运	shipment as soon as possible	9	yùjì jiāohuò shíjiān 预计交货时间	expected time of delivery
6	jíqī zhuāngyùn 即期装运	prompt shipment	10	guīdìng jiāohuò shíjiān 规定交货时间	specified time of delivery

Cultural Navigation

In Chinese, the meanings of "jiāohuò," "jiāohuòqī" and "zhuāngyùnqī" are easily confusing. The original meaning of "jiāohuò" in Chinese is that the seller delivers the goods to the buyer directly. However, in a real business transaction, "jiāohuòqī" is not the date that the buyer will receive the goods, but the date that the seller either loads the goods on a conveyance that will head to the destination (or the port of destination) or hand over the goods to the carrier. In other words, when a Chinese tells you "àn qī jiāohuò (delivery of the goods on time)," it only means to load the goods on the date that the contract requires. Therefore, "jiāohuòqī (the date of delivery)" is also called "zhuāngyùnqī (the date of loading)."

84 Contacting a Forwarder

Key Sentence

Wǒ xiǎng gēn nín jiēqià yíxià yǒuguān dàilǐ chūkǒuhuòyùn de shìyí.
我想跟您接洽一下有关代理出口货运的事宜。

I want to consult with you about the matter of acting as an agent to handle export freight transport.

Substitution

dìngcāng
订舱
booking of shipping space

zūchuán
租船
chartering a ship

kōngyùn
空运
aerial transportation; airlift

bàoguān
报关
customs clearance

shāngjiǎn
商检
commodity inspection

chāixiāng
拆箱
devanning

Extension

1. Wǒmen gōngsī shì běn dìqū zuì dà de yī jí huòdài.
我们公司是本地区最大的一级货代。
Our company is the biggest Class A Forwarder in this region.

2. Wǒmen kěyǐ bāng nín ānpái yǒuguān jìn-chūkǒu huòyùn de yíqiè yèwù.
我们可以帮您安排有关进出口货运的一切业务。
We can help you to arrange all kinds of business related to import and export freight transport.

3. Wǒmen yǒu yì pī huòwù chūkǒu dào Měiguó.
我们有一批货物出口到美国。
We have a batch of goods to be exported to the USA.

4. Wǒmen xiǎng qǐng nǐmen dàiwéi bànlǐ dìngcāng hé bàoguān.
我们想请你们代为办理订舱和报关。
We would like to ask you to handle the booking of shipping space and customs clearance for us.

Dialogue

A: Qǐngwèn shì Tàipíngyáng Huòdài ma?
请问是太平洋货代吗?
Is that Pacific Forwarder?

B: Shìde. Nín shì nǎ wèi?
是的。您是哪位?
Yes. May I ask who is calling?

A: Wǒ shì Shìjì Màoyì de Paul Wilson. Wǒ xiǎng gēn nín jiēqià yíxià yǒuguān dàilǐ chūkǒu huòyùn de shìyí.
我是世纪贸易的Paul Wilson。我想跟您接洽一下有关代理出口货运的事宜。

I'm Paul Wilson from Century Trading (Company). I want to consult with you about the matter of acting as an agent to handle export freight transport.

B: Wǒmen shì běn dìqū zuì dà de yī jí huòdài, kěyǐ bāngzhù nín ānpái yǒuguān jìn-chūkǒu huòyùn de yíqiè yèwù.
我们是本地区最大的一级货代，可以帮助您安排有关进出口货运的一切业务。

We are the biggest Class A Forwarder in this region, and (we) can help you to arrange all kinds of business related to import and export transport.

A: Shì zhèyàng de. Wǒmen yǒu yì pī huòwù chūkǒu dào Měiguó, xiǎng qǐng nǐmen dàilǐ bànlǐ dìngcāng hé bàoguān.
是这样的。我们有一批货物出口到美国，想请你们代理办理订舱和报关。

Here is the situation. We have a batch of goods for exporting to the USA, and would like to ask you to handle the booking of shipping space and customs clearance for us.

B: Xíng, méi wèntí.
行，没问题。

Sure, no problem.

Related Words

1	huòdài 货代/ huòyùn dàilǐ 货运代理	forwarder; freight agency	3	bānlún 班轮	regular cargo ship; liner ship
2	chuándài 船代 / chuánbó dàilǐ 船舶代理	ship agency	4	jiēqià 接洽	to consult with; to arrange sth. with

(Continued)

5	huòzhǔ 货主	owner of cargo	9	dàilǐ 代理	to act as an agent (to handle sth.)
6	gǎngkǒu 港口	port	10	bànlǐ 办理	to handle; to conduct; to transact
7	kōnggǎng 空港	airport	11	jìnkǒu 进口 bàoguān 报关	customs declaration for/of imports
8	cāngkù 仓库	warehouse; storehouse	12	chūkǒu 出口 bàoguān 报关	customs declaration for/of exports

Cultural Navigation

"Lóng (dragon)" is a very special symbol in Chinese traditional culture. But have you ever heard "yìtiáolóng fúwù (one dragon service)?" It refers to a series of services that tightly relate to and interact with each other, just like a long dragon. Normally, "yìtiáolóng fúwù" provided by a forwarder company includes tabulating, chartering ship, booking shipping space, insurance, storing, loading or devanning, customs clearance, commodity inspection, taking delivery of goods and related short haul transports, etc. Freighter agencies in China are divided into Class A, Class B and Class C. Class A freighter agencies provide services of international freight transport, and Class B or C agencies mainly deal with domestic freight transport.

85 Booking Shipping Space

Key Sentence

Zhè pī huòwù xūyào yí gè 20 yīngchǐ de pǔtōng jízhuāngxiāng.
这批货物需要一个20英尺的普通集装箱。
This batch of goods needs a 20' GP (general product) container.

Substitution

nóngchǎnpǐn
农产品
agricultural product

gāngcái
钢材
steel product

huàgōng yuánliào
化工原料
industrial chemical

kuàngchǎnpǐn
矿产品
mineral

chāo gāo jízhuāngxiāng
超高集装箱
HP(higher product) container

gānhuò jízhuāngxiāng
干货集装箱
dry cargo container

kāidǐng jízhuāngxiāng
开顶集装箱
open top container

táijiàshì jízhuāngxiāng
台架式集装箱
platform based container

píngtáishì jízhuāngxiāng
平台式集装箱
platform container

tōngfēng jízhuāngxiāng
通风集装箱
ventilated container

lěngcáng jízhuāngxiāng
冷藏集装箱
reefer container

sǎnhuò jízhuāngxiāng
散货集装箱
bulk container

guànshì jízhuāngxiāng
罐式集装箱
tank container

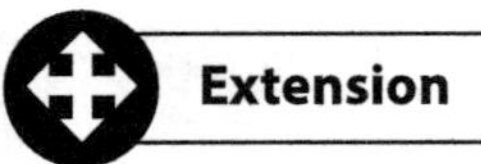

Extension

1. Nín xūyào tuōpán, jízhuāngxiāng háishi pīnxiāng?
您需要托盘、集装箱还是拼箱?
Do you need pallets, containers or LCL cargo?

2. Lìngwài yǒu yì dān huòwù xūyào pīnxiāng.
另外有一单货物需要拼箱。
There is another order of goods that needs LCL cargo.

3. Qǐng nǐ bǎ huòwù shuōmíng hé huòyùn yāoqiú gàosu wǒ.
请你把货物说明和货运要求告诉我。
Would you please give me the description of goods and shipping instructions?

4. Shōudào hòu wǒ huì gěi nín dǎ diànhuà
收到后我会给您打电话。
Once I receive it, I'll call you.

Dialogue

A: Nín zhè cì xūyào yòng tuōpán, jízhuāngxiāng háishi pīnxiāng?
您这次需要用托盘、集装箱还是拼箱?
This time do you need pallets, containers or LCL cargo?

B: Jízhuāngxiāng. Wǒ gūjì zhè pī huòwù xūyào yí gè 20 yīngchǐ de pǔtōng jízhuāngxiāng
集装箱。我估计这批货物需要一个20英尺的普通集装箱。
Containers. I estimate that this batch of goods needs a 20' GP container.

Búguò lìngwài yǒu yì dān huòwù xūyào pīnxiāng.
不过另外有一单货物需要拼箱。
But there is another order that needs LCL cargo.

A: Qǐng nǐ bǎ huòwù shuōmíng hé huòyùn yāoqiú gàosu wǒ.
请你把货物说明和货运要求告诉我。
Would you please give me the description of goods and shipping instructions?

B: Hǎode, Hǎode, wǒ mǎshàng bǎ xiángxì zīliào gěi nín fā guoqu.
好的，好的，我马上把详细资料给您发过去。
Okey-doke, I'll send you details right away.

A: Xíng. Shōudào hòu wǒ huì gěi nín dǎ diànhuà, huòzhě yuē shíjiān jiànmiàn tán.
行。收到后我会给您打电话，或者约时间见面谈。

All right. Once I receive it, I'll call you or arrange a time to meet.

Related Words

1	dìngcāng qīngdān 订舱清单	booking list	7	pīnxiāng 拼箱	Less than Container Load; LCL
2	yuánchǎndì míngchēng 原产地名称	appellation of origin	8	pīnxiāng huòdài 拼箱货代	forwarder
3	yuánchǎndìzhèng 原产地证	certificate of origin	9	xiǎo zōng huòwù 小宗货物	goods of small scale; parcel
4	yùn (huò) dān 运（货）单	shipping ticket; waybill; bill of freight	10	dà zōng huòwù 大宗货物	large quantity of goods; bulk commodities
5	huòwù zhuǎnkǒu 货物转口	cargo transshipment	11	hángkōng xiǎojiàn 航空小件	air express parcel
6	zhěng xiāng 整箱	Full Container Load; FCL	12	guójì huòyùn 国际货运	international freight transport

Cultural Navigation

"Jízhuāngxiāng (container)" is also called "huògui." Of Chinese "professional jargons" in freight transport, there are quite a few expressions associated with "huògui." For instance, a 20' container is called "xiǎogui," and a 40' container is called "dàgui." A loaded container is called "zhònggui," while an empty container is called "jígui." "Tuōgui" means dispatching a trailer towing a container to a factory to load goods, and then delivering them to the port. "Chágui" means that customs conduct a random spot check with containers. "Shuǎigui" means that the container has not been loaded on the ship in time or has been left at a port after it has gone through customs since the port is over-crowded. You may not be able to find these words in your Chinese dictionary, but when you are dealing with your Chinese forwarder, it will be very useful if you know these often used "professional jargons."

86 Packing for Shipment

Key Sentence

Zhèdān huò cǎiyòng biāozhǔn chūkǒu bāozhuāng ma?
这单货采用标准出口包装吗?
Will the goods on this list be packed with the standard export packing?

Substitution

zhè pī huòwù
这批货物
this batch of goods

zhèxiē cáiliào
这些材料
these materials

mùxiāng bāo zhuāng
木箱（包）装
wooden case packing

mùtuōpán zhǐxiāng bāo zhuāng
木托盘纸箱（包）装
carton packing with wooden pallet

chūkǒu hǎiyùn zhǐxiāng bāozhuāng
出口海运纸箱包装
seaworthy carton packing for export

1. Wǒ dānxīn chángtú yùnshū, huòwù huì shòucháo.
   我担心长途运输,货物会受潮。
   I'm worried the goods will be affected by damp during long-distance transport.

2. Huòwù bìxū yòng fángshuǐ zhǐxiāng bāozhuāng.
   货物必须用防水纸箱包装。
   The goods must be packed with waterproof cartons.

3. Xiāng nèi chèn yì céng fángzhèn gécháo pàomò sùliào, xiāng wài zhā sì dào sùliào yāodài.
   箱内衬一层防震隔潮泡沫塑料，箱外扎四道塑料腰带。
   The inside of the case is lined with a single layer of anti-shock waterproof foam, and the case is bound with four plastic belts externally.

4. Qǐng zài xiāng shang biāomíng xiǎoxīn qīngfàng hé zhùyì fángcháo.
   请在箱上标明"小心轻放"和"注意防潮"。
   Please mark the case with "Handle with Care" and "Keep away from Moisture."

A: Zhè dān huò cǎi yòng biāozhǔn chūkǒu bāozhuāng ma?
   这单货（采）用标准出口包装吗?
   Will the goods on this list be packed with the standard export packing?

Xiànzài shì méiyǔ jìjié, wǒ dānxīn chángtú yùnshū, huòwù huì shòucháo.
B: 现在是梅雨季节，我担心长途运输,货物会受潮。

It's the rainy season right now. I'm worried the goods will be affected by damp during long-distance transport.

Nàme, nín duì bāozhuāng yǒu shénme jùtǐ yāoqiú ma?
A: 那么，您对包装有什么具体要求吗?

Well then, do you have any specific requirements for the packing?

Bìxū yòng fángshuǐ zhǐxiāng bāozhuāng, shí zhuāng yì xiāng.
B: 必须用防水纸箱包装，十装一箱。

The goods must be packed in waterproof cartons, and 10 units packed in 1 case.

Xiāng nèi chèn yì céng fángzhèn gécháo pàomò sùliào, xiāng wài zhā sì dào sùliào yāodài.
箱内衬一层防震隔潮泡沫塑料，箱外扎四道塑料腰带。

The inside of the case is lined with a single layer of anti-shock waterproof foam, and the case is bound with four plastic belts externally.

Wǒmen kěyǐ zài xiāng shang biāomíng xiǎoxīn qīngfàng hé zhùyì fángcháo.
A: 我们可以在箱上标明“小心轻放”和“注意防潮”。

We can mark the case with "Handle with Care" and "Keep away from Moisture."

Tài hǎo le.
B: 太好了。

Excellent.

Related Words

1	jízhuāngxiāng 集装箱	container	6	yìrán 易燃 wùpǐn 物品	inflammable goods
2	wǎléng 瓦楞 zhǐxiāng 纸箱	corrugated carton	7	qǐngwù 请勿 dàozhì 倒置	keep upright
3	shuāngcéng 双层 zhǐxiāng 纸箱	2 plies of carton	8	màitóu 唛头	shipping mark
4	bǎntiáoxiāng 板条箱	crate	9	shuāmài 刷唛	marking; to mark
5	yìsuì 易碎 shāngpǐn 商品	fragile commodity	10	zhuāngxiāng 装箱 shuōmíngshū 说明书	packing instruction

Cultural Navigation

Changes in season and the distinctive climate features of different regions are factors that must be considered when goods are shipped. China is a country with a vast territory and a variety of climates. Compared with other regions located at the same latitude, the winter temperature in China is on the low side while the summer temperature is relatively higher. During the winter season, Northern China is often influenced by the Siberian cold currents and has very cold weather with strong winds and heavy snow. Dusty winds are common in the spring season, and sometimes there are even sandstorms. The rains mainly come during July and August in the north. Due to the high temperature in summer, it is quite possible in some cities to have muggy weather that is just like having a "sauna." Winter in Southern China is relatively warmer than in the north, and there is rarely any severe weather with strong winds and heavy snow. The rainy season in the south lasts for a longer period, beginning in May or June in areas south of the Yangtze River. Especially during "huángméiyǔ (yellow plum rains)" period in early summer, it may rain for several weeks continuously, when it is very humid and warm, and it's very easy for articles to go moldy. Therefore, many people call the rains as "mould rains." Summer in the south is normally hotter than in the north. During the summer and autumn seasons, the southeast coast areas of China are often struck by tropical storms—typhoons.

87 Cargo Insurance

Key Sentence

Wǒmen jìhuà wèi zhè dān huòwù tóubǎo hǎiyùnxiǎn.
我们计划为这单货物投保海运险。
We plan to take out marine cargo insurance for the freight listed on this waybill.

Substitution

píng'ānxiǎn
平安险
free from particular average; F.P.A.

shuǐzìxiǎn
水渍险
with particular average; W.P.A.

yíqièxiǎn
一切险
all risks; A.R.

fùjiāxiǎn
附加险
additional risk

yìbān fùjiāxiǎn
一般附加险
general additional risk

tèshū fùjiāxiǎn
特殊附加险
special additional risk

zhànzhēngxiǎn
战争险
war risk

kōngyùnxiǎn
空运险
air risk; air transportation cargo insurance

lùyùnxiǎn
陆运险
land risk; overland transportation insurance

1. Zhè běn shǒucè yǒu wǒmen gōngsī de zhǔyào xiǎnbié, tiáokuǎn hé fèilǜ de jièshào.
这本手册有我们公司的主要险别、条款和费率的介绍。
This brochure has information about our company's primary categories of risk, clauses and rates.

2. Nín kěyǐ tóubǎo píng'ānxiǎn hé shuǐzìxiǎn.
您可以投保平安险和水渍险。
You may want to be insured with F.P.A. and W.P.A.

3. Rúguǒ tóubǎo yíqièxiǎn dehuà, shì bú shì yě bāokuòle zhànzhēngxiǎn ne?
如果投保一切险的话,是不是也包括了战争险呢?
If we are insured with All Risks, does it include War Risk?

4. Zuì zhòngyào de shìyào zhǎo yì jiā xìnyù hǎo de gōngsī tóubǎo.
最重要的是要找一家信誉好的公司投保。
The most important thing is that you are insured with a company that has a good reputation.

A: Wǒ xiǎng zīxún yíxià jìn-chūkǒu huòwù de yùnshū bǎoxiǎn wèntí.
我想咨询一下进出口货物的运输保险问题。

I'd like to consult (you) about cargo insurance of import & export.

B: Zhè běn shǒucè yǒu wǒmen gōngsī de zhǔyào xiǎnbié, tiáokuǎn hé fèilǜ de jièshào.
这本手册有我们公司的主要险别、条款和费率的介绍。

This brochure has information about our company's primary categories of risk, clauses and rates.

A: Wǒmen jìhuà wèi zhè dān huòwù tóubǎo hǎiyùn jīběnxiǎn.
我们计划为这单货物投保海运基本险。

We plan to take out basic marine cargo insurance for the freight listed on this waybill.

Nín yǒu shénme jiànyì ma?
您有什么建议吗?

Do you have any suggestions?

B: Rúguǒ wèile jiéshěng fèiyong, nín kěyǐ tóubǎo píng'ānxiǎn hé shuǐzìxiǎn.
如果为了节省费用，您可以投保平安险和水渍险。

If it's for reducing expense, you may want to be insured with F.P.A. and W.P.A.

A: Hái yǒu yí gè wèntí: rúguǒ tóubǎo yíqièxiǎn dehuà, shì bú shì yě bāokuòle zhànzhēngxiǎn ne?
还有一个问题：如果投保一切险的话，是不是也包括了战争险呢?

Another question: if we are insured with All Risks, does it include War Risk?

B: Bù bāokuò. Zhànzhēngxiǎn shǔyú tèshū fùjiāxiǎn.
不包括。战争险属于特殊附加险。

No, it doesn't. War Risk policy belongs to special additional risk.

A: Èng, nà wǒmen hái yào zài kǎolǜ yíxià.
嗯，那我们还要再考虑一下。
OK, in that case, we need to think it over again.

B: Bùguǎn mǎi nǎ zhǒng bǎoxiǎn, zuì zhòngyào de shì yào zhǎo yì jiā xìnyù hǎo de gōngsī tóubǎo.
不管买哪种保险，最重要的是要找一家信誉好的公司投保。
No matter which policy you are going to take out, the most important thing is that you are insured with a company that has a good reputation.

Related Words

1	tóubǎo shēnqǐngdān 投保申请单	insurance application	7	huòwù bǎoxiǎnfèi 货物保险费	cargo premium
2	huòwù bǎoxiǎnrén 货物保险人	cargo underwriter; cargo insurer	8	huòwù bǎoxiǎn fèilǜ 货物保险费率	cargo insurance rate
3	tóubǎorén 投保人	policyholder	9	bǎoxiǎn jīn'é 保险金额/ bǎo'é 保额	insured amount
4	bǎodān 保单	insurance policy	10	huòwù bǎoxiǎn tiáokuǎn 货物保险条款	cargo clause
5	huòwù bǎoxiǎndān 货物保险单	cargo insurance policy	11	xiéhuì huòwù bǎoxiǎn tiáokuǎn 协会货物保险条款	Institute Cargo Clauses; I.C.C
6	bǎofèi 保费	insurance premium			

Cultural Navigation

China's insurance industry has made great developments in recent decades. In addition to nationwide giant insurance companies, such as PICC (Property and Casualty Company, Ltd.), China life (China Life Insurance Company), Ping An Insurance (Group) Company of China, Ltd., CPIC (China Pacific Insurance Co., Ltd.), China Reinsurance Company, and China Export & Credit Insurance Corporation, a group of joint venture insurance companies with Chinese and foreign investment, such as the AIA Group, Allianz China Life Insurance Co., Ltd., AVIVA-COFCO, have also entered China's market and established their business. However, since every nation has a different market situation and does not have complete unified regulations on import and export management, you should definitely be very clear about specific clauses and related details and avoid having the wrong policy or not being covered when you take out insurance. Additionally, Chinese insurance companies usually accept the request from their clients if they want to take out insurance in accordance with the Institute Cargo Clauses formulated by International Underwriting Association of London (IUA).

88 Cargo Customs Clearance

Key Sentence

Zhè shì huòwù de bàoguāndān hé qítā xiāngguāndānzhèng.
这是货物的报关单和其他相关单证。

These are the goods' customs declaration and other related documents and certificates.

Substitution

jìnkǒu bàoguāndān
进口报关单
import declaration

chūkǒu bàoguāndān
出口报关单
export declaration

jìnkǒu xǔkězhèng
进口许可证
import license

chūkǒu xǔkězhèng
出口许可证
export license

tíhuòdān
提货单
bill of lading

zhuāngxiāngdān
装箱单
packing list

huòyùndān
货运单
shipping list

shāngjiǎn zhèngshū
商检证书
commodity inspection certificate

Extension

1. Zhèxiē shǔyú guójiā guīdìng de jìnkǒu pèi'é shāngpǐn.
   这些属于国家规定的进口配额商品。
   These belong to the goods subject to import quota according to the state regulations.

2. Nín yǒu wàizī qǐyè jìnkǒu pèi'é zhèngmíng ma?
   您有外资企业进口配额证明吗?
   Do you have a certificate of import quota for foreign-funded enterprises?

3. Qǐng nín guòlai pèihé cháyàn yíxià.
   请您过来配合查验一下。
   Would you please come over to cooperate with me for an inspection?

4. Zhè shì nín de shāngjiǎn zhèngshū.
   这是您的商检证书。
   This is your commodity inspection certificate.

Dialogue

A: Nín hǎo! Zhè shì huòwù de bàoguāndān hé qítā xiāngguān dānzhèng.
您好！这是货物的报关单和其他相关单证。
Hello! These are the goods' customs declaration and other related documents and certificates.

B: Nín de zhèxiē huòwù shǔyú guójiā guīdìng de tèdìng jìnkǒu pèi'é shāngpǐn.
您的这些货物属于国家规定的特定进口配额商品。
Your goods here belong to goods subject to import quota according to the state regulations.

Nín yǒu wàizī qǐyè jìnkǒu pèi'é zhèngmíng ma?
您有外资企业进口配额证明吗？

Do you have a certificate of import quota for foreign-funded enterprises?

Zhè shì wǒmen gōngsī de zìdòng jìnkǒu xǔkězhèng.
A: 这是我们公司的自动进口许可证。

This is our company's automatic import license.

Èng, qǐng nín guòlai pèihé cháyàn yíxià.
B: 嗯，请您过来配合查验一下。

OK, would you please come over to cooperate with me for an inspection?

Hǎode.
A: 好的。

Sure.

Zhè shì nín de shāngjiǎn zhèngshū.
B: 这是您的商检证书。

This is your commodity inspection certificate.

Kěyǐ fàngxíng le ma?
A: 可以放行了吗？

Does it have the customs clearance?

Shìde.
B: 是的。

Yes.

Related Words

1	hǎiguān 海关 jiǎnchá 检查	customs inspection	2	hǎiguān 海关 shǒuxù 手续	customs formality

(Continued)

3	tōngguān 通关	to go through customs	8	jiéguān zhèngshū 结关证书	bill of clearance
4	bàoguān 报关	to declare sth. at customs; to apply to customs	9	qīngguān/jiéguān 清关/结关	customs clearance; to clear sth. through customs
5	jìnkǒu pèi'é zhèngmíng 进口配额证明	import quota	10	fàngxíng 放行	to let sb./sth. go or pass
6	zìdòng jìnkǒu xǔkězhèng 自动进口许可证	automatic import license	11	jìnkǒu guānshuì 进口关税	import duty; import tariff
7	huòwù fàngxíngdān 货物放行单	cargo release (form)			

Cultural Navigation

China Customs is a government agency that supervises and manages all arrivals in and departures from the customs territory of the mainland of the People's Republic of China. Under the General Administration of Customs, there are Guangdong Sub-administration and 42 customs districts, which cover all major port cities nationwide, and provide services for all types of import and export business. In order to adapt to the trends of today's e-business, China's General Administration of Customs has also set up China's Customs Online Service Center as well as China's E-Port to provide "one-stop" e-service for customs declaration, tariff payment and logistics information, etc.

89 Notifying Someone of a Shipment

Key Sentence

Guìgōngsī de huòwù yǐjīng zài jīntiān shàngwǔ zhuāngchuán lí gǎng le.
贵公司的货物已经在今天上午装船离港了。

Your company's goods have been loaded onto the ship and left the port this morning.

Substitution

zhuāngjī
装机
loaded onto the plane

zhuāngchē fāhuò
装车发货
loaded on the truck/train and shipped out

ànshí fāhuò
按时发货
shipped out on time

1. Wǒmen yìzhí zài děng nín de fāhuò xiāoxi ne!
我们一直在等您的发货消息呢!
We have been waiting for the shipment news from you!

2. Wǒ huì bǎ tídān hé qítā zhuāngchuán wénjiàn yìqǐ sǎomiáo yǐhòu fāgěi nín.
我会把提单和其他装船文件一起扫描以后发给您。
I'll scan the bill of lading and other shipping documents and send them to you.

3. Huòwù nǎ tiān néng dào gǎng?
货物哪天能到港?
When will the shipment arrive at the port?

4. Wǒmen shōudào tídān hòu huì jǐnkuài bǎ yúkuǎn fùqīng.
我们收到提单后会尽快把余款付清。
Once we receive the bill of lading, we will pay off the balance as soon as possible.

Dialogue

A: Wǒ xiǎng tōngzhī nín yíxià, guì gōngsī de huòwù yǐjīng zài jīntiān shàngwǔ zhuāngchuán lí gǎng le.
我想通知您一下，贵公司的货物已经在今天上午装船离港了。
I would like to notify you that your company's goods have been loaded onto the ship and left the port this morning.

B: Tài hǎo le. Wǒmen yìzhí zài děng nín de fāhuò xiāoxi ne!
太好了。我们一直在等您的发货消息呢!
Great. We have been waiting for the shipment news from you!

A: Wǒ huì bǎ tídān hé qítā zhuāngchuán wénjiàn yìqǐ sǎomiáo yǐhòu fāgěi nín.
我会把提单和其他装船文件一起扫描以后发给您。
I will scan the bill of lading and other shipping documents and send them to you.

B: Nín gūjì huòwù nǎ tiān néng dào gǎng?
您估计货物哪天能到港?
When do you expect that the shipment will arrive at the port?

A: Zhèngcháng dehuà, zài liǎng xīngqī zhīnèi dàodá ba.
正常的话，在两星期之内到达吧。
Normally, it will arrive within 2 weeks.

B: Hǎode. Rúguǒ méiyǒu qítā wèntí, wǒmen shōudào tídān hòu huì jǐnkuài bǎ yúkuǎn fùqīng.
好的。如果没有其他问题，我们收到提单后会尽快把余款付清。
Good. If there are no more questions, we will pay off the balance as soon as possible once we receive the bill of lading.

A: Nà jiù xiān xièxie la. Rúguǒ yǒu shénme qíngkuàng, wǒmen suíshí liánxì!
那就先谢谢啦。如果有什么情况，我们随时联系!
Then I should say thank you in advance. If any situation pops up, we will get in touch immediately!

Related Words

1	fāhuòrén 发货人	consignor; shipper	7	fùběn 副本/ fùyìnjiàn 复印件	duplicated copy
2	shōuhuòrén 收货人	consignee	8	zhuāngchē 装车	to load goods onto a truck
3	zhuāngchuándān 装船单	shipping order	9	zhuāngchuán 装船	to load goods onto a ship
4	zhuāngchuán wénjiàn 装船文件	shipping document	10	yùjì lígǎng shíjiān 预计离港时间	estimated time of departure; ETD
5	zhèngběn 正本 / yuánjiàn 原件	original document	11	yùjì dàodá shíjiān 预计到达时间	estimated time of arrival; expected time of arrival; ETA
6	sǎomiáojiàn 扫描件	scanned document			

Cultural Navigation

China E-Port is a public data center and data interchange platform. It is based on the national public Internet and is networked with Administration for Industry and Commerce, Administration of Taxation, Customs, Administration of Foreign Exchange, Ministry of Foreign Trade, Administration of Quality Supervision, Inspection and Quarantine, banks, import and export enterprises, processing trade enterprises, intermediary companies of foreign trade and consignor companies of foreign trade. It stores the data of import and export management, goods flow and funds flow in a centralized database and allows its users to search and check those data. Meanwhile it provides real-time online services such as customs clearance, settlement of foreign exchange or remittance, export drawback, payment and so on. Companies that have been approved by the administrative departments of industry and commerce as well as tax bureaus and have a valid license can become a user of China E-Port and use related services.

90 Shipment Delayed

Key Sentence

Yīnwèi qiáng táifēng, huòwù de zhuāngyùn bùdébù
因为强台风，货物的装运不得不
tuīchí jǐ tiān.
推迟几天。

Because of a strong typhoon, the shipping of the goods has to be postponed for several days.

Substitution

dìzhèn
地震
earthquake

tiānqì èliè
天气恶劣
bad weather

bānlún qǔxiāo
班轮取消
cancellation of the cargo liner

shēngchǎnxiàn gùzhàng
生产线故障
breakdown of the production line

sān dào wǔ tiān
三到五天
about 3 to 5 days

yì xīngqī zuǒyòu
一星期左右
about a week

dào yuèdǐ
到月底
until the end of this month

Wǒ xiǎng quèrèn yíxià huòwùshì bú shì yǐjīng zhuāngchuán le.
1. 我想确认一下货物是不是已经装船了。
I would like to confirm whether the goods have been loaded on the ship.

Wǒ zhèngyào dǎ diànhuà tōngzhī nǐ zhuāngchuán de qíngkuàng.
2. 我正要打电话通知你装船的情况。
I was just going to call you and notify you of the situation about loading and shipping.

Wǒ dānxīn de jiùshì zhège qíngkuàng!
3. 我担心的就是这个情况！
This is the situation that I am worried about!

Kǒngpà yào děngdào xiàzhōu yùnshū cái néng huīfù zhèngcháng.
4. 恐怕要等到下周运输才能恢复正常。
I'm afraid that the transportation (system) won't go back to normal until next week.

Wéi, Wáng jīnglǐ ma? Wǒ shì Màikè. Wǒ xiǎng quèrèn yíxià huòwùshì bú shì yǐjīng zhuāngchuán le.
A: 喂，王经理吗？我是迈克。我想确认一下货物是不是已经装船了。
Hello, is this Manager Wang? I'm Michael. I would like to confirm whether the goods have been loaded on the ship.

Ò, Màikè a. Wǒ zhèngyào dǎ diànhuà tōngzhī nǐ zhuāngchuán de qíngkuàng.
B: 哦，迈克啊。我正要打电话通知你装船的情况。

Hi, Michael. I was just going to call you and notify you of the situation about loading and shipping.

Yīnwèi qiáng táifēng, huòwù de zhuāngyùn bùdébù tuīchí jǐ tiān.
因为强台风，货物的装运不得不推迟几天。

Because of a strong typhoon, the shipping of the goods has to be postponed for several days.

Zhēn zāogāo! Wǒ dānxīn de jiùshì zhège qíngkuàng!
A: 真糟糕！我担心的就是这个（情况）！

That's really bad! This is the situation that I am worried about!

Nà nǐ gūjì zuì zǎo jǐ hào kěyǐ zhuāngchuán fāhuò ne?
那你估计最早几号可以装船发货呢？

Well then, when is the earliest possible date that you expect to make shipment?

Hěn nánshuō. Kǒngpà yào děngdào xiàzhōu yùnshū cái néng huīfù zhèngcháng ba.
B: 很难说。恐怕要等到下周运输才能恢复正常吧。

It is hard to say. I'm afraid that the transportation (system) won't go back to normal until next week.

Related Words

1	bèipò 被迫	forced; compelled	5	yìwài qíngkuàng 意外情况	unexpected situation; unforeseen situation
2	zhìliú 滞留	held up; detained			
3	jǐnkuài 尽快	as soon as possible	6	tèshū yuányīn 特殊原因	exceptional cause
4	yōuxiān 优先	to have priority			

(Continued)

7	tiānzāi-rénhuò 天灾人祸	natural and man-made calamities	9	zhìqīfèi 滞期费	demurrage
8	bǔjiù cuòshī 补救措施	corrective measure; remedy	10	yúqī jiāohuò 逾期交货	delayed in delivery

Cultural Navigation

Chinese consider "shǒushí (being on time)" as a good personal habit. "Shǒushí" also means "shǒuxìn (keeping promises)." Therefore, "shǒushí" not only shows your respect to others, but also is one of the factors that make you gain trust from others. In various business activities, "being on time" is especially important. People often say "time is money." All these matters, including keeping an appointment punctually, making a payment on time and delivering goods on time, test one's attitude or a company's attitude toward "punctuality" and "integrity."

91 Cargo Delivery Notice

Key Sentence

Qǐng píng tíhuòdān zài yì xīngqī nèi tíhuò.
请 凭提货单在一星期内提货。
Please take the delivery of goods by providing the bill of lading within one week.

Substitution

tíhuò tōngzhī
提货通知
cargo delivery notice

huòwù fàngxíngdān
货物放行单
cargo release form

xiāngguān dānjù
相关单据
relevant documents

yuèdǐ qián
月底前
before the end of the month

Liùyuè jiǔ hào zhīqián
六月九号之前
before June 9th

Guì gōngsī de huògui yǐjīng dàogǎng.
1. 贵公司的货柜已经到港。

Your company's container has arrived at the port.

Wǒ yǐjīng shōudàole tíhuò tōngzhī.
2. 我已经收到了提货通知。

I have received the cargo delivery notice.

Yúqī wèi tí bìxū jiāonà zhìgǎngfèi.
3. 逾期未提必须交纳滞港费。

A demurrage charge must be paid for overdue pickup of goods.

Wǒmen huì jǐnkuài ānpái tíhuò.
4. 我们会尽快安排提货。

We will make arrangements for taking the goods as soon as possible.

Chángchéng kējì gōngsī ma? Guì gōngsī de huògui yǐjīng dàogǎng le.
A: 长城科技公司吗？贵公司的货柜已经到港了。

Is this Great Wall Technology Company? Your company's container has arrived at the port.

Xièxie! Wǒmen yǐjīng shōudào tíhuò tōngzhī le.
B: 谢谢！我们已经收到提货通知了。

Thanks! We have received the cargo delivery notice.

Qǐng nín píng tíhuòdān zài yí gè xīngqī nèi tíhuò.
A: 请您凭提货单在一个星期内提货。

Please take the delivery of goods by providing the bill of lading within one week.

B: Wǒxiǎng qǐngwèn yíxià, wǒmen kěyǐ yánchí yí gè xīngqī tíhuò ma?
我想请问一下，我们可以延迟一个星期提货吗？
May I ask if it is possible for us to postpone taking the delivery of goods for one week?

A: Yúqī wèi tí bìxū jiāonà zhìgǎngfèi.
逾期未提必须交纳滞港费。
A demurrage charge must be paid for overdue pickup of goods.

B: Hǎoba, wǒmen huì jǐnkuài ānpái tíhuò.
好吧，我们会尽快安排提货。
Well then, we will make arrangements for taking the goods as soon as possible.

Related Words

1	shōuhuòrén 收货人	consignee	5	diànfàng tídān 电放（提单）	telex release; TLX
2	yùndān 运单/ huòyùndān 货运单	waybill	6	hǎiyùn tídān 海运提单	ocean bill of lading; marine bill of lading
3	tí (huò) dān 提（货）单	bill of lading; B/L	7	huòguì tídān 货柜提单	container bill of lading
4	jiāohuò dān 交货单/ huàndān xiǎo tídān 换单/小提单	delivery order; D/O	8	píng dān jiāohuò 凭单交货	delivery against B/L; surrender of B/L

(Continued)

9	zhuāng xiāngdān （装）箱单	packing list	11	zhìgǎng-fèi 滞港费	demurrage charge
10	xièhuò 卸货	to unload goods			

Cultural Navigation

When you are going to pick up delivered goods at a port, you must have every document needed in hand. There are different requirements of customs supervision for different types of commodities. Generally, the packing list, the receipt and the bill of lading are the most essential documents needed for taking the delivery of goods. Certain commodities may need a certificate of origin, a certificate of inspection and a certificate of import license, etc. when you take delivery of them. Additionally, you cannot take the delivery of goods until customs clearance has been completed.

92 Rejection of Goods

Key Sentence

Yīnwèi huòwù pòsǔn, wǒfāng wúfǎ qiānshōu tíhuò.
因为货物破损，我方无法签收提货。

Due to damage to the goods, we can't sign for acceptance and take the delivery.

Substitution

duǎn zhòng
短重
short weight

shòucháo zhìsǔn
受潮致损
damaged by damp

míngchēng bù fú
名称不符
inconformity

yǒu zhìliàng wèntí
有质量问题
quality problem

Extension

1. Wǒ xiǎng tōngzhī nín yíxià yǒuguān 103 hào dìngdān huòwù de yànshōu qíngkuàng.
我想通知您一下有关103号订单货物的验收情况。

I want to notify you about the inspection result of the goods of Order 103.

Huòwù zài jiāofù huòdài gōngsī de shíhou shì jīngguò jiǎnyàn de.
2. 货物在交付货代公司的时候是经过检验的。

When the goods were delivered to the forwarder company, they went through inspection.

Wǒmen yǐjīng liánxìle fùzé yùnshū de huòdài gōngsī.
3. 我们已经联系了负责运输的货代公司。

We have already contacted the forwarder who was in charge of transportation.

Wǒmen xīwàng néng jǐnkuài chámíng yuányīn, fēnqīng zérèn.
4. 我们希望能尽快查明原因，分清责任。

We hope that we will be able to ascertain the cause and determine who is responsible as soon as possible.

Dialogue

Wǒ xiǎng tōngzhī nín yíxià yǒuguān 103 hào dìngdān huòwù de yànshōu qíngkuàng.
A: 我想通知您一下有关103号订单货物的验收情况。

I want to notify you of the inspection result of the goods of Order 103.

Huòwù yǒu shénme wèntí ma?
B: 货物有什么问题吗?

Is there a problem with the goods?

Shì zhèyàng de, yīnwèi bùfen huòwù pòsǔn, wǒ fāng bù néng qiānshōu tíhuò.
A: 是这样的，因为部分货物破损，我方不能签收提货。

This is the situation: because of damage to some of the goods, we can't sign for acceptance and take the delivery.

Wǒxiǎng wèntí kěnéngshìchūzàiyùnshū guòchéng zhōng.
B: 我想问题可能是出在运输过程中。
I think that the problem probably happened during transportation.

Huòwù zài jiāofù huòdài gōngsī de shíhou shì jīngguò jiǎnyànde.
货物在交付货代公司的时候是经过检验的。
When the goods were delivered to the forwarder company, they went through inspection.

Wǒmen yǐjīng liánxìle fùzé yùnshū de huòdài gōngsī.
A: 我们已经联系了负责运输的货代公司。
We have already contacted the forwarder who was in charge of transportation.

Wǒmen xīwàng néng jǐnkuài chámíng yuányīn, fēnqīngzérèn.
我们希望能尽快查明原因，分清责任。
We hope that we will be able to ascertain the cause and determine who is responsible as soon as possible.

Wǒ fāngyídìng huì jìnlì pèihé diàochá.
B: 我方一定会尽力配合调查。
We will definitely do our best to cooperate with the investigation.

Related Words

1	suǒpéi 索赔	to claim damage	3	tuìhuò 退货	to return merchandise; to return the shipment
2	tuìkuǎn 退款	refund; to refund			

(Continued)

4	shuǐzì 水渍	water damage	8	duǎn liàng 短量	shortage; loss of quantity
5	fāméi 发霉	to become moldy; to mold	9	huòwù yì-duǎndān 货物溢短单	over-landed and short-landed cargo list
6	biànzhì 变质	to go bad; to deteriorate; deterioration	10	lǐpéi 理赔	to settle a claim; settlement of a claim
7	pèngsuì pòsǔn 碰碎破损	clashing & breakage			

Cultural Navigation

"Bú pà yīwàn, jiù pà wànyī." (Don't be afraid of "what"; be afraid of "what if.") This is what Chinese often say when they are dealing with uncertain circumstances. The purpose of taking out an insurance policy is to reduce the loss as much as possible when an accident happens. If the consignee has found shortage or damage of his insured goods when he takes the delivery, he should contact the forwarder immediately and inform them of the specific details. At the same time, the consignee must request an inspection from a claim settling agent appointed by the insurance company as soon as possible and determine the percentage of the loss, and get a damage certificate or a shortage certificate in order to file a claim with the forwarder or related responsible parties. The claim should be submitted within the valid time period of the insurance policy. Otherwise, the insurance company may reject the claim.

Investigation and Investment

93 Introducing a Project

Key Sentence

Wǒmen zhè cì dàiláile yí gè tàiyángnéng xiàngmù.
我们这次带来了一个太阳能项目。
We have brought a solar power project this time.

Substitution

yídòng tōngxìn
移动通信
mobile communication

nóngyè jìshù
农业技术
agricultural technology

wūshuǐ chǔlǐ
污水处理
sewage disposal

qīngjié néngyuán
清洁能源
clean energy

1. Tīngshuō guìgōngsī zhèng dàlì fāzhǎn xīnnéngyuán xiàngmù.
听说贵公司正大力发展新能源项目。
We have heard that your company is making great efforts toward developing new energy projects.

2. Gōngsī zhèngzài jījí xúnzhǎo hézuò huǒbàn.
公司正在积极寻找合作伙伴。
The company is seeking partners actively.

3. Zhège xiàngmù hěn yǒu xīyǐnlì.
这个项目很有吸引力。
This project is very attractive.

4. Zhè shì mùqián zuì xiānjìn de dì-sān dài jìshù.
这是目前最先进的第三代技术。
This is the most advanced third-generation technology currently available.

Dialogue

A: Wǒmen tīngshuō guì gōngsī zhèng dàlì fāzhǎn xīnnéngyuán xiàngmù.
我们听说贵公司正大力发展新能源项目。
We have heard that your company is making great efforts toward developing new energy projects.

B: Shìde. Gōngsī zhèngzài jījí xúnzhǎo hézuò huǒbàn.
是的。公司正在积极寻找合作伙伴。
Yes. The company is seeking partners actively.

A: Wǒmen zhè cì dàiláile yí gè tàiyángnéng xiàngmù. Wǒ xiǎng nín kěnéng huì yǒu xìngqù.
我们这次带来了一个太阳能项目。我想您可能会有兴趣。
We have brought a solar power project this time. I think that you might be interested.

B: Èng, cóng zhè fèn jièshào cáiliào shang kàn, zhège xiàngmù hěn yǒu xīyǐnlì.
嗯，从这份介绍材料上看，这个项目很有吸引力。
Yes, based on this introductory brochure, this project is very attractive.

A: Méi cuò. Zhè shì mùqián zuì xiānjìn de dì-sān dài jìshù.
没错。这是目前最先进的第三代技术。

You are right. This is the most advanced third-generation technology currently available.

B: Hǎo. Ràng wǒmen ānpái yí gè shíjiān, shēnrù tàntǎo yíxià hézuò de kěnéngxìng.
好。让我们安排一个时间，深入探讨一下合作的可能性。

Good. Let's arrange a time so that we can further explore the possibility of partnership.

Related Words

1	zhāoshāng 招商	to attract business; to invite outside investment	7	gāokējì 高科技	high-technology
2	yǐnjìn 引进	to bring in; to introduce from elsewhere	8	jìshù luòhòu 技术落后	to lag in technology
3	wàizī 外资	foreign capital; foreign investment	9	zhīchí 支持	to support
4	xiānjìn 先进	advanced	10	gǔlì 鼓励	to encourage; encouragement
5	jiānduān 尖端	cutting-edge	11	jíxū 急需	badly in need of; urgent need
6	xīn yí dài 新一代	new generation	12	yōuhuì zhèngcè 优惠政策	preferential policy

Cultural Navigation

Currently, China has established six special economic zones (SEZs). Shenzhen SEZ, Zhuhai SEZ, Shantou SEZ in Guangdong Province and Xiamen SEZ in Fujian Province were established in the early 1980s when China began to implement the Reform and Opening-up policy. In 1988, the entire province of Hainan was designated as the biggest SEZ in China. In 2010, Kashgar in Xinjiang Uygur Autonomous Region became the newest SEZ in China. The government of China gives SEZs special economic policies and flexible government measures, including a more free market economy orientated system, special tax incentives and more independent international trade activities. These advantages make SEZs more attractive to foreign investors.

94 Expressing Intentions

Key Sentence

Kànle yǎnshì yǐhòu, wǒmen duì zhège xiàngmù hěngǎn xìngqù.
看了演示以后，我们对这个项目很感兴趣。
After watching the presentation, we are very interested in this project.

Substitution

tīngle jièshào
听了介绍
have listened to the introduction

tīngle shuōmíng
听了说明
have listened to the explanation

kànle jìhuàshū
看了计划书
have read the proposal

kànle yǒuguān cáiliào
看了有关材料
have read the related materials

zhèxiàng jìhuà
这项计划
this plan

zhèxiàng zhāobiāo
这项招标
this bid

nín de tíyì
您的提议
your proposal

nín de bàojià
您的报价
your offer/quoted price

1. Gāngcái shì guānyú zhège xiàngmù de shìpín yǎnshì.
   刚才是关于这个项目的视频演示。
   That was a video presentation about this project just now.

2. Qǐngwèn nín yǒu shénme jùtǐ wèntí ma?
   请问您有什么具体问题吗？
   May I ask if you have any specific questions?

3. Nín kěyǐ wèi wǒmen ānpái yí cì shídì kǎochá ma?
   您可以为我们安排一次实地考察吗？
   Could you arrange an on-site trip for us?

4. Rúguǒ nín xiànzài yǒu shíjiān dehuà, wǒmen kěyǐ mǎshàng ānpái.
   如果您现在有时间的话，我们可以马上安排。
   If you have time now, we can make an arrangement right away.

A: Gāngcái shì guānyú zhège xiàngmù de shìpín yǎnshì. Huānyíng gèwèi tíwèn.
刚才是关于这个项目的视频演示。欢迎各位提问。
That was a video presentation about this project just now. You are welcome to ask questions.

B: Kànle yǎnshì yǐhòu, wǒmen duì zhège xiàngmù hěn gǎnxìngqù.
看了演示以后，我们对这个项目很感兴趣。
After watching the presentation, we are very interested in this project.

A: Nà tài hǎo le. Qǐngwèn nín yǒu shénme jùtǐ wèntí ma?
那太好了。请问您有什么具体问题吗?
That is great. May I ask if you have any specific questions?

B: Nín kěyǐ wèi wǒmen ānpái yí cì shídì kǎochá ma?
您可以(为我们)安排一次实地考察吗?
Could you arrange an on-site trip for us?

A: Dāngrán! Rúguǒ nín xiànzài yǒu shíjiān dehuà, wǒmen kěyǐ mǎshàng ānpái.
当然!如果您现在有时间的话,我们可以马上安排。
Of course! If you have time now, we can make an arrangement right away.

Related Words

1	qīngxiàng 倾向	inclined to; to prefer; tendency	6	qiánjǐng 前景	prospect; future
2	xuǎnzé 选择	to choose; choice	7	yìyuàn 意愿	wish; desire
3	huáiyí 怀疑	to doubt; to suspect; doubt	8	tóuzī yìyuàn 投资意愿	willingness to invest
4	yǒu zhēngyì 有争议	in dispute; controversial	9	xiāngxìn 相信	to believe
5	yǒu qiánlì 有潜力	to have potential	10	xìnxīn 信心	confidence

Cultural Navigation

In addition to Special Economic Zones (SEZs), China has also established more than 100 National High-Tech Industrial Development Zones, or "NHIDZ" for short, nationwide so far. NHIDZ are unique industrial parks designated as knowledge-intensive and technology-intensive. The high-tech enterprises located in NHIDZ will enjoy a series of preferential policies, for instance, tax preference, tariff preference, subsidy or fund support and many other convenient services provided by local government departments. In order to further promote economic reform, the first free trade zone within China's borders, China (Shanghai) Pilot Free Trade Zone, was established with the approval from the Chinese government in August of 2013. The China (Shanghai) Pilot Free Trade Zone will be given much greater freedom in trade and enjoy more convenience in banking and investment, with the latter one including loosened regulation of interest rates and free convertibility of China's currency, the RMB.

95 On-Site Investigation

Key Sentence

Jīchǔ shèshī jiànshè dōu yǐjīng wánchéng le ma?
基础设施建设都已经完成了吗?
Has infrastructure construction been completed?

Substitution

tōngxìn shèshī
通信设施
communication facility

jiāotōng shèshī
交通设施
traffic facility

gōnggòng shèshī
公共设施
public utility

pèitào shèshī
配套设施
auxiliary/supporting facility

Extension

1. Huānyíng gèwèi guānglín wǒmen gōngyè yuánqū.
欢迎各位光临我们(工业)园区。
Welcome to our (industrial) park!

2. Zhège gōngyè yuánqū shèlìle duō jiǔ le?
这个工业园区设立了多久了?
How long has this industrial park been established?

3. Xiànzài yǐjīng yǒu duō jiā qǐyè qiānyuē rùzhù le.
现在已经有多家企业签约入驻了。
Now several enterprises have signed contracts and moved in already.

4. Dāngdì zhèngfǔ jiāng zài tǔdì zūlìn hé shuìshōu fāngmiàn tígōng yōuhuì dàiyù.
当地政府将在土地租赁和税收方面提供优惠待遇。
The local government will offer preferential terms in the lease of land and taxation.

Dialogue

A: Huānyíng gèwèi guānglín!
欢迎各位光临!
Welcome, everyone!

B: Qǐngwèn zhège gōngyè yuánqū shèlì duō jiǔ le?
请问这个工业园区设立多久了?
May I ask how long this industrial park has been established?

A: Zhè shì qùnián gānggāng kāifā de xīn yuánqū.
这是去年刚刚开发的新园区。
This is a new (industrial) park that was started last year.

B: Jīchǔ shèshī jiànshè dōu yǐjīng wánchéng le ma?
基础设施建设都已经完成了吗?
Has infrastructure construction been completed?

A: Shìde. Xiànzài yǐjīng yǒu duō jiā qǐyè qiānyuē rùzhù le.
是的。现在已经有多家企业签约入驻了。
Yes. Now several enterprises have signed contracts and moved in already.

Qǐngwèn rùzhù yuánqū de qǐyè kěyǐ xiǎngyǒu nǎxiē yōuhuì zhèngcè?
B: 请问入驻园区的企业可以享有哪些优惠政策?

May I ask what preferential policies can be expected when an enterprise moves into the park?

Dāngdì zhèngfǔ jiāng zài tǔdì zūlìn hé shuìshōu fāngmiàn tígōng yōuhuì dàiyù.
A: 当地政府将在土地租赁和税收方面提供优惠待遇。

The local government will offer preferential terms in the lease of land and taxation.

Related Words

1	tóuzī huánjìng 投资环境	investment environment	7	jiāotōng yùnshū 交通运输	communication and transportation
2	tóuzī chéngběn 投资成本	investment cost	8	shìzhèng shèshī 市政设施	municipal facility
3	dāngdì zhèngfǔ 当地政府	local government	9	shèqū fúwù 社区服务	community service
4	jīchǔ shèshī 基础设施	infrastructure	10	chāiqiān 拆迁	to demolish old buildings and relocate the inhabitants
5	tǔdì gōngyìng 土地供应	supply of land	11	xiūjiàn 修建	to construct; to build
6	rénlì zīyuán 人力资源	human resources	12	chóngjiàn 重建	to rebuild; to reconstruct

Cultural Navigation

Making a new investment is a challenge for any enterprise. Before the decision is made, many Chinese companies usually send off their business delegations to carry out some on-site investigations. The activities of this kind of investigation normally include field study, observing the business management situation of the other party, as well as trying to establish the preliminary understanding and trust between the two sides. Chinese often say, "Ěr tīng wéi xū, yǎn jiàn wéi shí" (What you hear may be false and what you see through your eyes is true); "Bǎi wén bùrú yíjiàn" (It is better to see once than to hear a hundred times). You have to admit that even today these old sayings which have been floating around for a very long time still make sense.

96 Risk Assessment

Key Sentence

Zhège xiàngmù de fēngxiǎn kěnéng bǐjiào gāo.
这个项目的风险可能比较高。
The risk of this project will possibly be relatively high.

Substitution

bǐjiào xiǎo
比较小
relatively small

hěn nán yùgū
很难预估
very difficult to predict

bìxū kǎolǜ
必须考虑
must reconsider

xūyào chóngxīn pínggū
需要重新评估
need to reevaluate

Extension

1. Duìfāng xīwàng wǒmen jiù xiàngmù hézuò wèntí jǐnkuài zuòchū juédìng.
对方希望我们就项目合作问题尽快做出决定。
The other side wants us to make a decision on the cooperative project as soon as possible.

2. Wǒmen de kěxíngxìng bàogào zhège xīngqī jiù kěyǐ chūlai le.
我们的可行性报告这个星期就可以出来了。
Our feasibility study report will be coming out this week.

3. Wǒmen huì zài bàogào li tígōng fēngxiǎn yīnsù hé huíbàolǜ de bǐjiào hé pínggū.
我们会在报告里提供风险因素和回报率的比较和评估。
We will provide the comparison and estimation on risk factors and the rate of return in our report.

4. Zài fēngxiǎn pínggū wánchéng yǐqián, wǒmen bù kěnéng zuòchū rènhé chéngnuò.
在风险评估完成以前，我们不可能做出任何承诺。
We cannot make any promises before the risk assessment has been completed.

A: Duìfāng xīwàng wǒmen jiù xiàngmù hézuò wèntí jǐnkuài zuòchū juédìng.
对方希望我们就项目合作问题尽快做出决定。
The other side wants us to make a decision on the cooperative project as soon as possible.

B: Kěshì wǒmen duì zhège dìqū de tóuzī huánjìng hái bú tài liǎojiě.
可是我们对这个地区的投资环境还不太了解。
But we still do not know the investment environment in this area well.

A: Wǒmen de kěxíngxìng bàogào zhège xīngqī jiù kěyǐ chūlai le.
我们的可行性报告这个星期就可以出来了。
Our feasibility study report will be coming out this week.

B: Wǒ gèrén juéde zhège xiàngmù de fēngxiǎn kěnéng bǐjiào gāo.
我个人觉得这个项目的风险可能比较高。
I personally feel that the risk of this project will possibly be relatively high.

A: Wǒmen huì zài bàogào li tígōng fēngxiǎn yīnsù hé huíbàolǜ de bǐjiào hé pínggū.
我们会在报告里提供风险因素和回报率的比较和评估。

We will provide the comparison and estimation on risk factors and the rate of return in our report.

B: Zǒngzhī, zài fēngxiǎn pínggū wánchéng yǐqián, wǒmen bù kěnéng zuòchū rènhé chéngnuò.
总之，在风险评估完成以前，我们不可能做出任何承诺。

In short, we cannot make any promises before the risk assessment has been completed.

Related Words

1	tóuzī fēngxiǎn 投资风险	investment risk	8	jīnróng wēijī 金融危机	financial crisis
2	fēngxiǎn tóuzī 风险投资	venture capital	9	jīngjì guòrè 经济过热	economic overheating
3	shìchǎng xūqiú 市场需求	market demand	10	pàomò jīngjì 泡沫经济	bubble economy
4	xūqiú wàng shèng 需求旺盛	thriving demand; demand is strong	11	shāngyè tóujī 商业投机	business speculation
5	xūqiú píruǎn 需求疲软	weak demand; demand is soft	12	(jīngjì) yìngzhuólù (经济)硬着陆	hard landing (of economy)
6	jīngjì xiāotiáo 经济萧条	economic depression	13	(jīngjì) ruǎnzhuólù (经济)软着陆	soft landing (of economy)
7	jīngjì wēijī 经济危机	economic crisis			

Cultural Navigation

Due to cultural differences, many foreign companies once had some experiences of suffering when they first started their businesses in China. Chinese would make a joke about this as "shuǐtǔ-bùfú (to fail to acclimate oneself in a new natural environment)." Today, the localization strategy of multinationals has been proved as an effective way to enter the overseas market and utilize local resources. There is a well-known Chinese idiom and it says, "rùxiāng-suísú (when in a different country, do as the natives do)." Whether you work in China or do business in China, you always should remember this idiom.

97 Investment Methods

Key Sentence

Wǒmen qīngxiàngyú cǎiyòng dúzī de fāngshì.
我们倾向于采用独资的方式。
We prefer to choose the method of single proprietorship.

Substitution

kǎolǜ 考虑 consider	jìhuà 计划 plan
dǎsuàn 打算 plan	xīwàng 希望 hope
hézī 合资 joint venture	dàijiāgōng 代加工 OEM

hézuò jīngyíng
合作经营
cooperative business operation

jìshù zhuǎnràng
技术转让
technology transfer

tèxǔ jīngyíng
特许经营
franchising

Extension

1. Zhège xiàngmù de tí'àn yǐjīng tōngguò le ma?
这个项目的提案已经通过了吗?
Has the proposal of this project been approved?

2. Dǒngshìhuì rènwéi zhège xiàngmù hěn yǒu qiánlì.
董事会认为这个项目很有潜力。
The board of directors believes that this project has great potential.

3. Rúguǒ dúzī dehuà, wǒmen yào tóurù de zījīn bù shǎo a.
如果独资的话，我们要投入的资金不少（啊）。
If it's single proprietorship, we will need large funds to put into it.

4. Gōngsī yě zài quánhéng qítā de xuǎnzé.
公司也在权衡其他的选择。
The company is also weighing up other options.

Dialogue

A: Zhège xiàngmù de tí'àn yǐjīng tōngguò le ma?
这个项目的提案已经通过了吗?
Has the proposal of this project been approved?

B: Shìde. Dǒngshìhuì rènwéi zhège xiàngmù hěn yǒu qiánlì.
是的。董事会认为这个项目很有潜力。
Yes. The board of directors believes that this project has great potential.

A: Nàme, tóuzī fāngshì juédìngle méiyǒu?
那么，投资方式决定了没有?
In that case, has the investment approach been decided yet?

Hái méiyǒu.Zǒng de lái shuō, wǒmen qīngxiàngyú cǎiyòng dúzī de fāngshì.
B: 还没有。总的来说，我们倾向于采用独资的方式。

Not yet. Overall, we prefer to choose the method of single proprietorship.

Rúguǒ dúzī dehuà, wǒmen yào tóurù de zījīn bù shǎo a.
A: 如果独资的话，我们要投入的资金不少啊。

If it's single proprietorship, we will need large funds to put into it.

Shì a. Gōngsī yě zài quánhéng qítā de xuǎnzé.
B: 是啊。公司也在权衡其他的选择。

It's true. The company is also weighing up other options.

Related Words

1	zūlìn 租赁	to lease; to rent	7	wěituōjiāgōng 委托加工	consigned processing
2	jiānbìng 兼并	merger; to merger	8	dìngdān jiāgōng 订单加工	processing on order
3	bìnggòu 并购	to merger and acquire; acquisition	9	jiāgōng chūkǒu 加工出口	export processing
			10	tiē pái dài jiāgōng 贴牌/代加工	original equipment manufacturer; OEM
4	wàibāo 外包	outsourcing	11	gǔfèn yǒuxiàn gōngsī 股份有限公司	join-stock company; limited company
5	hézuò kāifā 合作开发	joint exploitation	12	yǒuxiàn zérèn gōngsī 有限责任公司	limited liability company; LLC.
6	bǔcháng màoyì 补偿贸易	compensatory trade			

Cultural Navigation

There are a few investment options in China for a foreign investor to choose. Among them, three major means are Sino-foreign joint ventures, cooperative businesses and exclusively foreign-owned enterprises, which are also called "sānzī qǐyè (three types of foreign-invested enterprises)." Sino-foreign joint ventures are also known as equity joint ventures. They are founded in China with joint investments by foreign companies or enterprises and Chinese companies or enterprises. Their main feature is that the joint parties invest together, operate together, and take risks according to the ratio of their capitals, as well as share losses and profits. Cooperative businesses are also called contractual joint ventures. To establish a cooperative business, the foreign party usually supplies all or most of the capital while the Chinese party supplies land, factory buildings and usable facilities, and some supply a certain amount of capital, too. The rights and obligations of different parties are embedded in the contract. Exclusively foreign-owned enterprises are totally invested by the foreign party in accordance with *Law of the People's Republic of China on Foreign Capital Enterprises*. The foreign-owned enterprises often take the form of limited liability.

98 Loans and Financing

Key Sentence

Wǒmen zhǔnbèi lìyòng xiàngmù dàikuǎn lái jiějué zījīn bùzú de wèntí.
我们准备利用项目贷款来解决资金不足的问题。

We plan to utilize a project loan to solve the problem of money shortage.

Substitution

xiàngmù róngzī
项目融资
project financing

qǐyè dàikuǎn
企业贷款
enterprise loan

fēngxiǎn tóuzī
风险投资
venture capital

sī mù zījīn
私募资金
private financing

Extension

1. Zhège xiàngmù de zījīn chóucuò wǒmen jìnxíng de zěnmeyàng le?
这个项目的资金筹措我们进行得怎么样了？
How are we doing in the financing of this project?

2. Chūbù gūsuàn wǒmen kěyǐ tóurù de zījīn dàgài shì wǔbǎi wàn Měiyuán zuǒyòu.
初步估算我们可以投入的资金大概是五百万美元左右。
By preliminary estimation, the money that we can put in is about five million US dollars.

3. Zhège xiàngmù de zǒng tóuzī xūyào liǎngqiān wàn Měiyuán.
这个项目的总投资需要两千万美元。
This project requires a total investment of twenty million US dollars.

4. Xiànzài yíngēn hěn jǐn, dà'é dàikuǎn kǒngpà bú tài róngyì.
现在银根很紧，大额贷款恐怕不太容易。
Now the money market is tight, so a large sum of loan might not be easy (to get).

Dialogue

A: Zhège xiàngmù de zījīn chóucuò wǒmen jìnxíng de zěnmeyàng le?
这个项目的资金筹措我们进行得怎么样了?
How are we doing in the financing of this project?

B: Chūbù gūsuàn wǒmen kěyǐ tóurù de zījīn dàgài shì wǔbǎi wàn Měiyuán zuǒyòu.
初步估算我们可以投入的资金大概是五百万美元左右。
By preliminary estimation, the money that we can put in is about five million US dollars.

A: Kěshì zhège xiàngmù de zǒng tóuzī xūyào liǎngqiān wàn Měiyuán.
可是这个项目的总投资需要两千万美元。
But this project requires a total investment of twenty million US dollars.

B: Shìde. Wǒmen zhǔnbèi lìyòng xiàngmù dàikuǎn lái jiějué zījīn bùzú de wèntí.
是的。我们准备利用项目贷款来解决资金不足的问题。

It's true. We plan to utilize a project loan to solve the problem of money shortage.

A: Xiànzài yíngēn hěn jǐn, dà'é dàikuǎn kǒngpà bú tài róngyì.
现在银根很紧，大额贷款恐怕不太容易。

Now the money market is tight, so a large sum of loan might be not easy (to get).

B: Wǒmen duō jiēqià jǐ jiā tóuhángba.
我们多接洽几家投行吧。

Let's contact a few more investment banks.

Related Words

1	tóuzī yínháng / tóuháng 投资银行/投行	investment bank	6	lìxī 利息	interest (of a loan)
2	fēngtóu 风投	venture capital	7	gǔfèn 股份	share (of stock)
3	gèrén róngzī 个人融资	private financing	8	fènqī fùkuǎn 分期付款	payment by installments
4	fāxíng zhàiquàn 发行债券	issuing bonds	9	zījīn zhōuzhuǎn 资金周转	turnover of capital; circulation of funds
5	dàikuǎn 贷款	loan	10	zījīn bùzú 资金不足	lack of capital

(Continued)

11	zī bù dǐ zhài 资不抵债	one's possessions are insufficient to cover his debts	12	qǐyè 企业 fǎrén 法人	business legal person/entity

Cultural Navigation

Chinese stocks are divided into five categories, which are based on where the stocks are listed and what investors that the stocks target. They are A-shares, B-shares, H-shares, N-shares and S-shares. A-shares are RMB common stocks which are issued by public companies registered in the mainland of China. A-shares are traded at Shanghai Stock Exchange and Shenzhen Stock Exchange in RMB only. B-shares are RMB Special Stocks which are issued by public companies registered in the mainland of China. Although RMB are still used as the denomination for B-shares, B-shares can only be traded in foreign currency at Shanghai and Shenzhen Stock Exchanges. H-shares are issued by companies registered in the mainland of China but the stocks are listed and traded at the Hong

Kong Exchanges. The shareholders of these kinds of public companies are mainly the Chinese government and local governments. Therefore, H-shares are also called "state-owned enterprises stocks." N-shares are issued by companies registered in the mainland of China with their stocks listed in the New York Stock Exchange. S-shares are issued by companies that mainly conduct their business in China, but the companies have registered in Singapore or elsewhere and their stocks are listed in the Singapore Exchange.

99 Open Tender

Key Sentence

Wǒmen yǒu xìnxīn zhòngbiāo.
我们有信心中标。
We have confidence in winning the bid.

Substitution

tóubiāo chénggōng
投标成功
bid successfully

jībài jìngzhēng duìshǒu
击败竞争对手
beat competitors

zuìhòu shèngchū
最后胜出
be a winner at the end

náxia zhège xiàngmù
拿下这个项目
get this project

Extension

Zhège xiàngmù, wǒmen juédìng cǎiqǔ gōngkāi zhāobiāo.
1. 这个项目，我们决定采取公开招标。
We have decided to have an open bidding for this project.

2. Wǒmen duìzhè cì zhāobiāo hěn gǎnxìngqù.
我们对这次招标很感兴趣。
We are interested in this bidding.

3. Jùtǐ yāoqiú dōu liè zài zhāobiāo shuōmíngshū li le.
具体要求都列在招标说明书里了。
All the specific requirements are listed in the bid specification.

4. Tóubiāoshū qǐng wùbì zài Qīyuè yī hào qián sòngdá.
投标书请务必在七月一号前送达。
The tender must be delivered by July 1st.

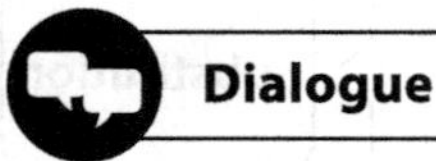

Dialogue

A: Zhège xiàngmù, wǒmen juédìng cǎiqǔ gōngkāi zhāobiāo.
这个项目，我们决定采取公开招标。
We have decided to have an open bidding for this project.

B: Wǒmen duì zhè cì zhāobiāo hěn gǎn xìngqù. Qǐngwèn yǒu nǎxiē jùtǐ yāoqiú?
我们对这次招标很感兴趣。请问有哪些具体要求?
We are interested in this bidding. May I ask what the specific requirements are?

A: Jùtǐ yāoqiú dōu liè zài zhāobiāo shuōmíngshū li le.
具体要求都列在招标说明书里了。
All the specific requirements are listed in the bid specification.

B: Tóubiāo de jiézhǐ rìqī shì nǎ tiān?
投标的截止日期是哪天?
When is the deadline for the bidding?

A: Tóubiāoshū qǐng wùbì zài Qīyuè yī hào qián sòngdá.
投标书请务必在七月一号前送达。
The tender must be delivered by July 1st.

B: Méi wèntí. Wǒmen yǒu xìnxīn zhòngbiāo!
没问题。我们有信心中标！
No problem. We have confidence in winning this bid!

Related Words

1	zhāobiāo 招标	to invite tenders/ bids	7	tóubiāorén 投标人	bidder; tenderer
2	yāoqǐng zhāobiāo 邀请招标	selective bidding; restricted bidding; invitational tender	8	tóubiāo hétong 投标合同	bidding contract
3	tóubiāo 投标	to enter a bid	9	zhāobiāo/tóubiāo shuōmíngshū 招标/投标说明书	bid specification
4	jìngbiāo 竞标	to compete in bidding	10	tóubiāo bǎozhèngshū 投标保证书	tender guarantee
5	tóubiāo jiàgé 投标价格	tender price	11	liúbiāo 流标	a bid-invitation or auction that fails due to lack of response
6	tóubiāojīn 投标金	bid bond			

Cultural Navigation

In China, "bidding" can be traced back to the early years of the last century. For instance, bidding was adopted for the design and construction of the renowned Sun Yat-sen's Mausoleum in Nanjing. However, bidding was not widely used until China's economic reforms began. During the mid-1980s, some construction projects began to use bidding as a way of choosing contractors and signing contracts. In the year of 2000, *Law of the People's Republic of China on Tenders and Bids* was officially put into effect. This law divides bidding into two categories, i.e., "Public Invitation to Bid" and "Invitation to Bid by Request," and has also standardized the bidding procedure in China for the first time. In addition, the State Council has passed *Regulation on the Implementation of the Law of the People's Republic of China on Tenders and Bids* in November of 2011, which has made further explanations and detailed regulations toward each specific segment of bidding. Currently in China, bidding is mainly used for large projects and government purchases, etc.

100 Signing a Contract

Key Sentence

Rúguǒ guì gōngsī rènkě dehuà, hétong jiù zhèyàng dìng le.
如果贵公司认可的话，合同就这样定了。
If your company has approved it, the contract will be settled just like this.

Substitution

nín méiyǒu wèntí
您没有问题
you have no questions about

nín tóngyì
您同意
you have agreed with

guì gōngsī jiēshòu
贵公司接受
your company has accepted

bù xūyào zài zuò xiūgǎi
不需要再做修改
no needs to make further changes

Extension

1. Zhè shì xiàngmù de Zhōng-Yīngwén hétong.
这是项目的中英文合同。
This is the project's contract in Chinese and English.

2. Qǐng nín zài kàn yí biàn yǒu méiyǒu shénme wèntí.
请（您）再看一遍有没有什么问题。
Please take one more look and see if there are any questions.

3. Wǒ juéde zhè fèn hétong zuò de fēicháng zǐxì.
我觉得这份合同做得非常仔细。
I think that this contract was drawn up very carefully.

4. Měi xiàng tiáokuǎn dōu xiě de fēicháng qīngchu.
每项条款都写得非常清楚。
Every single article is stated very clearly.

Dialogue

A: Lǐ xiānsheng, zhè shì xiàngmù de Zhōng-Yīngwén hétong. Qǐng nín zài kàn yí biàn yǒuméiyǒu shénme wèntí.
李先生，这是项目的中英文合同。请（您）再看一遍有没有什么问题。
Mr. Li, this is the project's contract in Chinese and English. Please take one more look and see if there are any questions.

B: Èng, wǒ juéde zhè fèn hétong zuò de fēicháng zǐxì. Měi xiàng tiáokuǎn dōu xiě de fēicháng qīngchu.
嗯，我觉得这份合同做得非常仔细。每项条款都写得非常清楚。
Yes, I think that this contract was drawn up very carefully. Every single article is stated very clearly.

A: Nín guòjiǎng le. Rúguǒ guì gōngsī rènkě dehuà, hétong jiù zhèyàng dìng le.
您过奖了。如果贵公司认可的话，合同就这样定了。
You have over-praised me. If your company has approved it, the contract will be settled just like this.

B: Méiwèntí. Wǒmen xiànzài jiù kěyǐ qiānyuē!
没问题。我们现在就可以签约！
No problem. We can sign the contract right now!

Related Words

1	qiānmíng 签名/ qiānzì 签字	to sign (one's name); signature	7	xìmù 细目	specific item; detail; detailed catalogue
2	qiāndìng 签订	to conclude and sign (a contract, a treaty, etc.)	8	fùběn 副本	duplicate; transcript; copy
3	qiānyuē 签约	to sign a contract	9	cǎoqiān 草签	to initial (a contract, a treaty, etc.)
4	hétong 合同/ héyuē 合约	contract; agreement	10	yìxiàngshū 意向书	letter of intent
5	tiáokuǎn 条款	clause; article; provision	11	xiéyìshū 协议书	agreement
6	tiáojiàn 条件	condition; term; prerequisite	12	bèiwànglù 备忘录	memorandum

Cultural Navigation

When a company or a store sets up its business in China, there will be certain celebrative activities. For instance, setting off firecrackers, cutting a ribbon, having a reception and so on. The invited guests, friends and people of the same trade will take the opportunity to present gifts and express their congratulations. The traditional presents for this kind of event include gaily decorated baskets, silk banners or inscribed boards with congratulations written or carved on it. When giving a present, please be careful about the colors of the gift. In the Chinese view, red color represents joy and good luck, and golden and yellow colors symbolize wealth. Those colors are particularly welcomed at this kind of occasions.

101 Investigation and Investment

Key Sentence

Wǒ gāng shōudàole wàizī qǐyè pīzhǔn zhèngshū.
我刚收到了外资企业批准证书。
I have just received the foreign enterprise approval certificate.

Substitution

qǐyè míngchēng hézhǔn zhèngshū
企业名称核准证书
enterprise name approval certificate

qǐyè dàimǎzhèng
企业代码证
certificate of organization code

zhèngshì pīfù
正式批复
official written reply

yíngyè zhízhào
营业执照
business license

Extension

1. Wǒ xiǎng gàosu nǐ yí gè hǎoxiāoxi.
我想告诉你一个好消息。
I want to tell you a piece of good news.

Wǒmen kěyǐ shēnlǐng yíngyè zhízhào le.
2. 我们可以申领营业执照了。
We can apply for the business license now.

Ànzhào wàizī qǐyè zhùcè zhǐnán, hái yǒu hěn duō shǒuxù yào bàn.
3. 按照外资企业注册指南，还有很多手续要办。
According to the Guide for Foreign Enterprises Registration, there are still many procedures to go through.

Wǒmen hái xūyào bànlǐ qǐyè dàimǎ, yínháng kāihù hé shuìwù dēngjì děng shǒuxù.
4. 我们还需要办理企业代码、银行开户和税务登记等手续。
We still need to get an organization code, open a bank account, handle the tax registration, etc.

Dialogue

Wáng jīnglǐ! Gàosu nǐ yí gè hǎo xiāoxi. Wǒ gāng shōudàole wàizī qǐyè pīzhǔn zhèngshū.
A: 王经理！告诉你一个好消息。我刚收到了外资企业批准证书。
Manager Wang! I want to tell you a piece of good news. I have just received the foreign enterprise approval certificate.

Gōngxǐ, gōngxǐ! Xià yí bù wǒmen kěyǐ shēnlǐng yíngyè zhízhào le.
B: 恭喜、恭喜！下一步我们可以申领营业执照了。
Congratulations! For the next step we can apply for the business license.

Búguò ànzhào wàizī qǐyè zhùcè zhǐnán, hái yǒu hěn duō shǒuxù yào bàn.
A: 不过按照外资企业注册指南，还有很多手续要办。
But according to the Guide for Foreign Enterprises Registration, there are still many procedures to go through.

Shì de. Wǒmen hái xūyào bànlǐ qǐyè dàimǎ, yínháng kāihù hé shuìwù dēngjì děng shǒuxù.
B: 是的。我们还需要办理企业代码、银行开户和税务登记等手续。

Yes. We still need to get an organization code, open a bank account, handle the tax registration, etc.

Tiān a! Wǒ de tóu dōu yào dà le! Wǒ xiǎng zhèxiē dōu děi máfan nǐ bàn le.
A: 天啊！我的头都要大了！我想这些都得麻烦你办了。

Oh, my god! I'm overwhelmed! I guess that I will have to trouble you to handle all of these.

Related Words

1	shēnqǐng 申请/ shēnlǐng 申领	to apply for	7	zhùcè zhèngshū 注册证书	registration certificate
2	shòuquán 授权	to authorize	8	gōngsī zhùcèdì 公司注册地	place of incorporation
3	wěituō 委托	to entrust	9	gōngsī fǎdìng dàibiǎorén 公司法定代表人	a legal person/ representative for the company
4	yànzī 验资	registered capital verification	10	Duìwài Jīngjì Màoyì Wěiyuánhuì 对外经济贸易委员会	Foreign Economic & Trade Commission
5	zhànghù 账户	bank account	11	Duìwài Màoyì Jīngjì Hézuòjú 对外贸易经济合作局	Bureau of Foreign Trade and Economic Cooperation
6	zhùcè gōngsī 注册公司	registered company	12	Zhōnghuá Rénmín Gònghéguó Gōngsī Fǎ 《中华人民共和国公司法》	*Company Law of the People's Republic of China*

Cultural Navigation

Handling various kinds of procedures is always a big headache. There is no exception in China either. Take registering a company as an example. The process of setting up a foreign-funded enterprise may contain a dozen of different procedures. For instance, having the enterprise's name registered, getting an official approval certificate, applying for a business license and the certificate of organization code, processing statistics registration, customs registration, foreign exchange registration, tax registration, receiving the permit of opening a bank account as well as setting up the account, and having the registered capital verification. All of these procedures normally take two months to be completed. The best way to handle these is to hire an agent from local registration service firms. Of course, there is no free lunch in the world. You have to pay for the services that you are getting.

附　录 Appendixes

紧急情况用句

Sentences Used under Emergency Circumstances

1. 卫生间在哪儿?	Where is the rest room?
2. 我现在遇到大麻烦了。	I'm in big trouble now.
3. 我该怎么办呢?	What should I do?
4. 小心!	Watch out!
5. ——你要干什么?	What do you want?
6. ——好的，别伤害我。	Okay. Don't hurt me.
7. ——你是谁?	Who are you?
8. 别碰我!	Don't touch me!
9. 离我远点儿!	Leave me alone!
10. 我叫警察啦!	I'll call the police!
11. 救命呀!	Help!
12. 来人呀!	Somebody!
13. 警察!	Police!
14. 你能帮我叫警察吗?	Can you call the police for me?
15. 抓住他!	Get him!
16. 着火啦!	Fire!
17. 开门!	Open the door!
18. 站住！小偷!	Stop! Thief!
19. 我的护照丢了。	I lost my passport.
20. 您能马上注销我的信用卡吗?	Will you cancel my credit card immediately?
21. 我的行李找不到了。	I can't find my baggage.
22. 警察局在哪儿?	Where is the police station?
23. 我遇到交通事故了。	I am in a car accident.
24. 请叫救护车!	Please call an ambulance!
25. 我什么也不知道。	I don't know anything about it.
26. 我是受害者。	I'm the victim.
27. 这是哪儿呀?	Where am I?
28. 我迷路了。	I'm lost.
29. 我找不到我的朋友了。	I can't find my friend.
30. 我的汽车坏了。	My car broke down.
31. 请叫医生来。	Please call a doctor.

个人简历模板 **Resume Template**

个人简历
Resume

姓名Full name:____
性别Gender:____
出生年月Date of birth:__________________________________
婚姻状况Marital status:__________________________________
国籍Nationality:______________________________________
身份证/护照号码 ID/Passport #:____________________________
家庭地址Residential address:______________________________
通信地址Mailing address:________________________________
联系电话Contact phone:__________________________________
电子邮件Email address:__________________________________

教育背景Educational background:
______年(Y)____月(M) – ______年(Y)____月(M)________________
______年(Y)____月(M) – ______年(Y)____月(M)________________
______年(Y)____月(M) – ______年(Y)____月(M)________________

工作经历 Work experiences:
______年(Y)____月(M) – ______年(Y)____月(M)________________
______年(Y)____月(M) – ______年(Y)____月(M)________________
______年(Y)____月(M) – ______年(Y)____月(M)________________

技能与专长 Skills & Specialties:

____

____

获奖与荣誉 Awards & Honors:

____

____

30家重要中国公司名录

30 China's Notable Corporations

1. 中国石油化工股份有限公司
   China Petroleum & Chemical Corporation
2. 中国石油天然气股份有限公司
   PetroChina Company Limited
3. 中国建筑股份有限公司
   China State Construction Engineering Corporation Limited
4. 中国移动有限公司
   China Mobile Limited
5. 中国工商银行股份有限公司
   Industrial and Commercial Bank of China Limited
6. 中国铁建股份有限公司
   China Railway Construction Corporation Limited
7. 中国中铁股份有限公司
   China Railway Group Limited
8. 上海汽车集团股份有限公司
   SAIC Motor Corporation Limited
9. 中国建设银行股份有限公司
   China Construction Bank Limited
10. 中国农业银行股份有限公司
    Agricultural Bank of China Limited
11. 中国人寿保险股份有限公司
    China Life Insurance Company Limited
12. 中国银行股份有限公司
    Bank of China Limited
13. 中国平安保险(集团)股份有限公司
    Ping An Insurance (Group) Company of China, Ltd.
14. 中国交通建设股份有限公司
    China Communications Construction Company Limited
15. 中国电信股份有限公司
    China Telecom Corporation Limited
16. 中国人民保险集团股份有限公司
    The People's Insurance Company (Group) of China Limited

17. 中国联合网络通信股份有限公司
    China United Network Communications Limited
18. 中国神华能源股份有限公司
    China Shenhua Energy Company Limited
19. 中国海洋石油有限公司
    CNOOC Limited
20. 中国冶金科工股份有限公司
    Metallurgical Corporation of China Limited
21. 联想集团有限公司
    Lenovo Group Limited
22. 宝山钢铁股份有限公司
    Baoshan Iron & Steel Co.,Ltd.
23. 中国太平洋保险（集团）股份有限公司
    China Pacific Insurance (Group) Co., Ltd.
24. 中国人民财产保险股份有限公司
    PICC Property and Casualty Company Limited
25. 江西铜业股份有限公司
    Jiangxi Copper Company Limited
26. 中国铝业股份有限公司
    Aluminum Corporation of China Limited
27. 五矿发展股份有限公司
    Minmetals Development Co.,Ltd.
28. 交通银行股份有限公司
    Bank of Communications Co.,Ltd.
29. 国药控股股份有限公司
    Sinopharm Group Co. Ltd.
30. 华能国际电力股份有限公司
    Huaneng Power International,Inc.